IN-YOUR-FACE POLITICS

IN-YOUR-FACE POLITICS

THE CONSEQUENCES OF UNCIVIL MEDIA

DIANA C. MUTZ

PRINCETON UNIVERSITY PRESS
PRINCETON AND OXFORD

Copyright © 2015 by Princeton University Press
Published by Princeton University Press, 41 William Street, Princeton,
New Jersey 08540
In the United Kingdom: Princeton University Press, 6 Oxford Street,
Woodstock, Oxfordshire OX20 1TW
press.princeton.edu
   Author photo courtesy of the Annenberg School for Communication
All Rights Reserved
ISBN 978-0-691-16511-0
   Library of Congress Control Number: 2014956135
British Library Cataloging-in-Publication Data is available
This book has been composed in Folio Std & Sabon Next LT Pro
Printed on acid-free paper ∞
Printed in the United States of America
1 3 5 7 9 10 8 6 4 2

DEDICATION

To BS,
and
the era
of chaos

CONTENTS

ILLUSTRATIONS

TABLES

ACKNOWLEDGMENTS

This project has occupied my attention intermittently over a long period of time, starting out when I was on sabbatical at the Center for Advanced Study in the Behavioral Sciences. With the luxury of additional time on my hands, I decided to pursue a much more ambitious plan for developing stimuli for a new series of experiments. Instead of using existing media content and the relatively poorly controlled stimuli it would create, I produced my own political talk show in order to obtain high levels of control over the experimental stimuli, the show's content, and its presentation. Doing so led me back to my undergraduate days as a radio, television, and film major at Northwestern University, where I learned how to edit film (with scissors and tape!), how to direct a multicamera shoot, and how to cut from one shot to another. Although the technology was different, the principles remained the same.

For encouragement and expertise when first embarking on this project, I thank Byron Reeves of Stanford University. Byron's research served as the inspiration for many of these studies, and he was instrumental in getting the ball rolling, as well as helping with the production of stimuli, which occurred in a professional television studio in the basement of McClatchy Hall. Although the candidates were paid professional actors hired for this occasion, my old friend and mentor Don Roberts served as unpaid talent for this production by playing a Phil Donahue look-alike who moderated the candidate exchanges. Neil Smelser, Bob Scott, and Gardner Lindzey from the Center for Advanced Study served as inspirations for the two fictitious candidates used in the original experiments (Neil Scott and Bob Lindzey).

I have many graduate and undergraduate students at several locations to thank for their help with running experimental subjects, managing my lab, and analyzing data. At Ohio State University, Brandon Bartels, Andrew Holbrook, and Justin Taylor served as research assistants on the earliest experiments. At the University of Pennsylvania, Andrew Daniller, Susanna Dilliplane, Danielle Dougherty, Seth Goldman, Shiloh Krieger, Kelli Lammie, Elaine Miller, Jason Miller, Laura Silver, and Lori Young each contributed to some portion of this project. Without their time, their commitment to detail, and their delightful companionship, this project would never have succeeded.

At Penn I have benefitted from the support of too many colleagues to mention individually, in both the Department of Political Science and the Annenberg School for Communication. Nonetheless, I particularly want to thank Sharon Black, Kyle Cassidy, and Joe Diorio for their willingness to provide many kinds of support throughout this project. For funding support, I thank the National Science Foundation and the Center for Advanced Study in the Behavioral Sciences, as well as the Institute for the Study of Citizens and Politics at the Annenberg Public Policy Center. Finally, I also thank Eric Crahan and his team at Princeton University Press for making production of this book as quick and painless as humanly possible.

Some of the ideas in this book have appeared elsewhere in their early stages. For example, in "How the Mass Media Divide Us," an essay I wrote for the Brookings Institution volume titled *Red and Blue Nation?* (edited by David Brady and Pietro Nivola), I suggested the potential for media to produce a more divided public. I informally described these effects in an essay titled "Television and Uncivil Political Discourse" in *Can We Talk? The Rise of Rude, Nasty, Stubborn Politics* (edited by Daniel M. Shea and Morris P. Fiorina). Some of the empirical findings were also published as articles in the *American Political Science Review*.

But most of the studies in this book have been slowly accumulating over the years, with my ideas on in-your-face politics evolving as the media environment has experienced a period of extremely rapid change. The tension between the need for larger audiences for political media content and the need for productive political discourse make this a formidable problem that is not likely to disappear anytime soon.

Finally, to my family, Robin, Walden, Maria, Simi, and the critters too many to mention by name, I thank you all for the many distractions that make everything worthwhile.

Diana C. Mutz
Philadelphia

IN-YOUR-FACE POLITICS

CHAPTER 1

WHAT IS "IN-YOUR-FACE" POLITICS?

It was March 2003 and my mother-in-law was visiting from Berkeley. I was watching George W. Bush speak to the nation about the impending war with Iraq. As she walked into the room, she turned her head away from the television in disgust. "Aach!" she exclaimed, "I can't *bear* to have that man in my face. It makes me sick to my stomach!" Of course, the president was not actually in her face, he was speaking to us from Washington, D.C. But as I watched, the images to a significant extent bore out her impression. For the next twenty minutes, I viewed George Bush from a far more intimate, close-up visual perspective than I had viewed my own family across the dinner table. His face often filled the entire television frame, so much so that the top of his head was cut off. To obtain the same visual perspective in person, my mother-in-law would need to be either his lover or his dentist. Given her politics, the mere thought of being that close probably did make her sick to her stomach. While I initially had considered her statement a display of political histrionics, when viewed from this perspective it seemed far more plausible that she might have such a visceral reaction.

Television gives us a unique visual perspective on other human beings, one that is far more intimate than we are accustomed to having with strangers in everyday life. But I had not previously thought about the consequences this might have for how we react to politicians and politics. As a film student in college, I learned to use the close-up camera shot to create a sense of emotional intensity in films; but do we really want that kind of intimacy with our politicians? In face-to-face social contexts, there are strong social norms guiding the distance we put between ourselves and other people, particularly people with whom we disagree. Do televised interactions follow these same rules? Apparently not. Instead, televised political interactions often violate face-to-face social norms for social distance by producing the appearance of being close to viewers. Television simulates a lack of physical distance between us and them and thus violates some deeply ingrained social norms involving spatial distance.

The fact that viewers' visual perspective on politicians is now commonly "in your face," in the sense of the spatial closeness that television conveys to viewers, is only part of the story. Television is also "in your face" in a second respect. Political discourse on television regularly violates norms for polite conversation. Complaints about uncivil political discourse on television are by now so widespread that incivility goes almost unquestioned. It is obvious to most Americans that televised expressions of differences of political opinion do not follow the usual face-to-face social norms of American culture. As young viewer Caitie Casey of Alma, Michigan, wrote in a letter to *The O'Reilly Factor*, "Mr. O'Reilly, I am 13 and have noticed that some people are very mean to you. You laugh it off, but my feelings would be hurt if that happened to me."

Ms. Casey is correct that much of what transpires on political talk shows these days would be highly unlikely to happen in the face-to-face "real" world. And most of us would, indeed, have hurt feelings if someone talked to us how Bill O'Reilly does to his guests and vice versa. To be sure, there will always be a few people who jump up and down and get screaming mad when talking about politics with others. But when it comes to expressing political views in face-to-face settings, most people are polite most of the time. If they don't agree, they either keep this information to themselves, or they downplay their differences of opinion by shifting the conversation toward commonalities. With political television, in contrast, there is considerable (if not incessant) political disagreement, and the opinion holders that we see and hear are often chosen specifically as exemplars of extremely divergent, highly polarized positions.

By "in-your-face politics," I refer to these two characteristics of political television both individually and in combination. It is well established that violating norms for interpersonal distance or norms for polite conversation can have important consequences in real life. This book addresses whether these same norm violations have consequences when they occur via television. Overwhelmingly, Americans experience politics and politicians through television. In this chapter I begin by providing background on what I mean by incivility in political discourse and what is known about the importance of spatial distance in how people react to one another. In the remainder of the book I provide a series of original studies exploring the consequences of in-your-faceness for American politics.

UNCIVIL POLITICAL DISCOURSE

In a keynote address in 1996, Judith Rodin argued that "across America and increasingly around the world, from campuses to the halls of Congress, to talk radio and network TV, social and political life seem dominated today by incivility, . . . an unwillingness to compromise and an intolerance for opposition. . . . No one seems to question the premise that political debate has become too extreme, too confrontational, too coarse." Likewise, law professor Stephen Carter argued in his 1999 volume titled *Civility*, "Sadly, we are losing the skill for respectful debate—if, indeed, we ever truly had it." Academics were far from the first to recognize incivility in political discourse as prevalent in America. Indeed, many historians date this problem to the country's birth, noting that harsh invective has always been part and parcel of American politics.[1]

Whether this is a new or age-old problem, calls for greater civility in political discourse are now commonplace.[2] To suggest that political discourse in America is uncivil is by now a banal observation. Although there are certainly those who would dispute whether it is more uncivil now than at some point in the past, I know of no one who views this designation as inappropriate today. It is simply widely accepted that incivility pervades political discourse, and television is the major means by which citizens are exposed to that incivility, although the Internet may be fast on its heels.

Radio talk shows were the first to attract public attention for impolite discourse, though television was not far behind.[3] According to radio and television critic Lawrence Laurent, who wrote for the *Washington Post* in the early days of broadcasting,[4] television journalists of the earlier era had etiquette guides from the networks that instructed them how to treat their guests politely, what to ask and not, and how to maintain a friendly rapport. By contrast, today's no-holds-barred interview style throws Emily Post and Miss Manners out the window; there is typically no effort to maintain etiquette-book levels of politeness. Instead, both interviewers and their political guests commonly adopt highly confrontational interview styles, particularly on television talk shows.

Examples of incivility in political discourse are by now too numerous to recount. For those who nonetheless desire additional examples, I include links to videos of a few of my personal favorites.[5] To describe just a few illustrative examples, in a 2005 incident television contributor Robert Novak stormed off the set of CNN's *Inside Politics* midprogram after growing frustrated in a conversation with liberal political analyst James Carville. In a 2004 interview during coverage of the 2004 Republican Convention, *Hardball* host Chris Matthews ripped into Democratic Senator Zell Miller, creating such a fiery exchange that Miller ended up yelling back at Matthews, "I wish I could challenge you to a duel!" In so doing, Miller incidentally made an excellent point: it is worth remembering that many of our most admired Founding Fathers sometimes resolved their differences of political opinion through the use of force. More commonly today, participants in television talk shows simply yell over one another, interrupt frequently, and even derogate the legitimacy of their opponents' views.

Other highly publicized incidents of uncivil discourse have occurred beyond the context of political talk shows, further contributing to public awareness of uncivil political discourse. For example, Congressman Joe Wilson breached decorum by yelling "You lie!" at President Barack Obama during a 2009 presidential address to a joint session of Congress outlining Obama's proposal for reforming health care. Still more recently, it was noted in a headline in the *Huffington Post* that "John Boehner's F-Bomb at Harry Reid Plunges D.C. Civility to New Low."[6]

Journalists and academics regularly decry incivility in political discourse, and public opinion polls suggest that average Americans share a similar disdain. In a recent national poll, over 95 percent of Americans concurred that civility in politics was important.[7] Foundations and civic groups likewise fund initiatives to call attention to this problem and publicly admonish both media and politicians, while clamoring for change in the civility of discourse. Even politicians themselves express concerns about uncivil discourse and its potential consequences. Nonetheless, this nearly universal condemnation does not appear to have affected the prevalence of political incivility.

As I discuss extensively later in the book, I am not convinced that the political advocates of today are necessarily any more uncivil than politicians of previous centuries. It is certainly possible, but I have yet to see convincing evidence to this effect over a substantial historical period. Nonetheless, I am convinced that the way the American public experiences these uncivil exchanges has changed in important ways. When Aaron Burr famously dueled with Alexander Hamilton, there was no audience. Not a single firsthand observer could recount precisely what happened during the duel itself, although Hamilton died from his wounds the following day. People learned of the event via newspapers or word of mouth.

If an event involving dueling politicians were held today, we would surely have "on the scene" video. If no video of the event itself were available, we would still have tearful interviews with family members or with eyewitnesses, perhaps video of the body being taken away, and probably televised reenactments of the event as well. When politicians rip into each other today, we see them do so because they are in front of a camera rather than behind closed doors. As we shall see in Chapter 7, it is one thing to read about an act of incivility in a newspaper, and quite another to witness it "firsthand" via television.

To be clear, what I refer to in this book as "incivility" refers to the style rather than the substance of political discourse. Indeed, as subsequent chapters will make clear, I am interested in the impact of incivility *independent of* political substance, and thus go to great lengths methodologically to separate the two. In part because complaints about incivility are so widespread, the term has been applied to the substance of discourse purely because it is partisan, inaccurate, negative, or polarized in the issue positions that are held by discussants. I do not consider these characteristics either necessary or sufficient.[8] Thus uncivil discourse should not be confused with polarized issue positions or with negative political appeals. Instead, I am referring to violations of norms for interpersonal interaction, the type of behavior that would be considered impolite in face-to-face contexts. Differences of opinion both small and large can be expressed civilly or in an uncivil fashion.[9] Because political discourse on television typically involves human interaction, it would be surprising if the style of disagreement were inconsequential given that it has well-documented consequences in the real world.

It is likewise important to distinguish incivility from the extent of conflict or extremity of opinion in the political environment. Although conflict is an essential part of the democratic process, Americans tend not to react favorably to conflict.[10] Serious concerns have been voiced about elite polarization and the role of partisan media, but the extent of substantive political differences is conceptually separable from the style of discourse used to discuss those conflicts.

For my research purposes, I define "uncivil discourse" as communication that violates the norms of politeness for a given culture. A wealth of empirical studies substantiates the importance of adhering to social norms of politeness in the course of everyday interactions. Although uncivil discourse has been deemed difficult to define by many who have examined political discourse,[11] fortunately the field of linguistics has done an admirable job of defining "politeness."[12] According to this definition, politeness is the expression of a speaker's intention to mitigate face threats carried by acts toward another.[13] In other words, consistent with linguistic definitions of politeness that Grice and Lakoff provided, civil interaction allows both participants to save face.[14]

An expression of politeness/impoliteness can take both verbal and nonverbal forms. It can be a matter of tone and inflection rather than the actual words spoken. In what I define as a polite or civil interaction, participants cooperate to maintain each other's positive public self-images. In an uncivil interaction, they do not. There may be varying degrees of civility/incivility, but it is a characteristic of the style of interaction rather than of any given individual's opinions per se. For example, ignoring another person can be highly impolite and uncivil, even though it requires no words.

It is noteworthy that, according to this definition, incivility is not the same thing as negativity, though the two are often conflated in everyday discourse about politics. It is possible to make positive statements that are impolite (such as excessive bragging about one's accomplishments in order to cause another to lose face), just as it is possible to make negative statements in a civil fashion.[15] Contrary to some previous examinations of incivility, I make no distinctions between positive and negative claims, whether statements are made about issues or personal traits, and so forth. Instead, civility is defined strictly in terms of whether participants adhere to cultural norms for polite face-to-face conversation. A claim that is positive in the sense typically meant by those who study political advertising tone could be expressed in either a civil or uncivil fashion; likewise, a negative claim need not be uncivil.[16]

Civil discourse by this definition requires politeness in social interaction, and politeness is widely established to have important consequences. Brown and Levinson's theory of politeness argues that it "makes possible communication between potentially aggressive parties," and promotes the "maintenance of social equilibrium" by promoting comity.[17] In the political world, as well as in social interaction more generally, politeness and civility are not arbitrary norms of etiquette akin to using the correct fork; they are rules that allow people of diverse views to smooth over differences and promote social harmony. Following the rules of civility/politeness is thus a means of demonstrating mutual respect.[18]

In the book I document several consequences of *televised* political incivility and find that they closely parallel claims about the role of politeness in face-to-face interaction. My findings suggest that civility is particularly important for purposes of facilitating respect for oppositional political viewpoints. Furthermore, civility influences citizens' levels of trust in politicians and the political process more generally.

Incivility also has indirect consequences that flow from the fact that it is physiologically arousing. Arousal in this case means simply that a person becomes psychologically and physiologically prepared to respond to stimuli of some kind. The mind and body are on alert, preparing to respond if necessary. Arousal goes hand in hand with the experience of emotions, but it is nonspecific with respect to the kind of emotion that is being experienced. Both positive and negative emotions can occur with high or low levels of arousal.

My purpose in this book is not to advance a particular theoretical perspective on emotion so much as to apply what we already know about emotional arousal to explain in-your-face politics. For these purposes, it matters little which specific emotions people are experiencing, so appraisal-based theories, which ask people to self-identify emotions, are unnecessary.[19] My focus on arousal does not negate the utility of studying more nuanced emotions for other purposes, but these distinctions are unnecessary for purposes of understanding in-your-face politics. Simpler, more parsimonious explanations are preferable in this particular case.

Although not all political conflict rises to the level of making our hearts race, uncivil discourse is particularly likely to increase levels of emotional arousal in television viewers because it openly violates social norms. Even if a viewer is not particularly interested in the issues at stake in the discussion, she knows when someone is out of line with respect to norms for social interaction. This heightened tension is symptomatic of arousal.

Interestingly, even when we ourselves are not personally involved in a disagreement, and are mere third-party observers of others' conflict, it is still tense and uncomfortable to watch. Anyone who has been at a dinner party where a couple is quarreling has experienced the discomfort of merely watching others engage in disagreement. Conflict affects observers as well as participants; we can't help but notice it. This discomfort generally manifests itself in heightened physiological arousal among both participants and observers. Evolutionary psychology suggests that people become aroused, alert, and ready to respond to conflicts in their environment because these responses are important to their survival.[20] We pay attention and prepare to take action if necessary.

But what about conflict on television? When watching television, there is obviously no need to react in any immediate sense to a conflict that is presented. To ignore what is happening on a television screen—even when it is quite violent—does not put a person at risk. So do people react similarly to televised conflicts of political opinion when they violate norms for politeness? This is one of two central questions addressed by this book.

PERCEIVED SPATIAL DISTANCE

A second key question addressed by this book is whether the mere *appearance* of physical closeness produced by television matters. In addition to less civil exchanges of opinion, the television world provides a uniquely intimate perspective on politicians, one that regularly violates people's perceptions of appropriate social distance. The study of proxemics, that is, how physical space affects communication, suggests that different cultures maintain different standards for how much personal space is appropriate to an interaction with a family member, acquaintance, or stranger.[21] However, violating someone's personal space has similar consequences across cultures. Interestingly, the distance deemed appropriate for face-to-face interactions with public figures in American culture is beyond twelve feet.[22] Yet most citizens' exposure to politicians via television has the appearance of being far closer—sometimes just a few inches.

As discussed further in Chapter 3, there is something particularly unnatural and disturbing about being in close proximity to someone we dislike a great deal, at least in real life. In the face-to-face world, people tend to automatically back away from others they dislike, putting greater physical distance between themselves and those with whom they disagree. This reaction occurs without conscious thought or deliberation. At a cocktail party, for example, if two people discover a political difference of opinion, they will normally back away from one another, even if the conversation continues. To lean in or come closer during a disagreement could seem aggressive, so we naturally allow one another some space, both literally and figuratively, in order to preserve social harmony.

It is easy to underestimate the importance of spatial distance precisely because it is so primitive. Spatial relations are among the earliest concepts acquired by infants,[23] perhaps because all of the relevant information is easily available to the senses. Moreover, physical distance cues have evolutionary significance because they are tied to the notion of safety from threat,[24] so it makes sense that proximity plays an important role in how humans process information. Cognitive neuroscience demonstrates that the human brain is designed to be sensitive to information about physical distance.[25] Furthermore, Williams and Bargh argue that humans' early primitive understanding of physical distance serves as the basis for later understanding of psychological distance.[26] To the extent that we "conceptualize the mental world by analogy to the physical world,"[27] spatial distance and affective reactions to others are closely linked.[28]

Extending this same logic to the appearance of physical distance as conveyed by television, one important thing television has changed about the way citizens experience political discourse is the proximity of their perspective on political advocates. Filmmakers have long recognized the potential for facial close-ups to intensify emotional reactions. As Russian film director Sergei Eisenstein described it, "A cockroach filmed in close-up seems on the screen a hundred times more terrible than a hundred elephants captured in long shot."[29] The close-up creates a sense of spatial intimacy that violates individuals' boundaries for personal space, particularly when close contact with the target on the screen is undesirable, as with cockroaches or disliked politicians.

When people do not agree, the tendency is to allow more even more space between them.[30] In contrast, as televised political conflicts intensify, the camera generally does not back away, and may even dolly or zoom in for tighter and tighter perspectives on the people involved. This norm violation may create a highly unnatural experience for viewers, one in which they view confrontation—something they would normally back away from—from an extremely intimate perspective, one that would be highly unlikely to occur in the real world, where we seek distance from things we dislike.

Thus televised political dialogue is often doubly norm violating; it violates norms for polite discourse as well as for appropriate social distance between people with conflicting views. To suggest that others are "in your face" may mean they are inappropriately aggressive and confrontational. But it can also mean that they appear to be "in your face" in the quite literal sense of the appearance of close physical proximity.

Of course, whether any of these norm violations matter depends on the extent to which research findings based on face-to-face social interaction can be extrapolated to how viewers process social interaction on television. Emerging research on human-media interaction suggests that the findings are remarkably similar. Surprisingly, people expect technology to follow many of the same social rules that people use in face-to-face interaction. For example, in an experimental study, both men and women were more influenced by praise from a male-voiced computer than from an identical female-voiced computer.[31] Consistent with human gender stereotypes, the female-voiced computer was judged as a better teacher about love and relationships, and as a worse teacher about computers than an identical male-voiced computer.

Likewise, the appearance of movement on a television screen is responded to in the same way that motion is in real life; people orient toward motion and pay greater attention. In the real world, objects moving toward a person demand a quick response. Televised objects that appear to come toward us by virtue of growing in size on the television screen obviously do not require a response; nonetheless, our perceptual systems appear to be hardwired to respond in much the same way. People attend to increased spatial proximity automatically.

In yet another example of face-to-face rules applied to media, the social rule that leads people to be systematically more positive in their evaluations of people to their faces as opposed to behind their backs also gets unwittingly applied to technology. For example, experimental subjects are more likely to evaluate a computer positively to its "face" than they are when evaluating that same machine using another computer.[32]

Many recent findings in this vein make the proposed consequences of in-your-face politics all the more plausible. To the extent that viewers unconsciously respond to televised images of other human beings as they do real ones, violations of face-to-face norms on television should matter. Uncivil political discourse should be especially threatening when viewed from the perspective of a close-up, and the processing of information should be affected by both incivility and perceived spatial distance.

A MULTIMETHOD APPROACH

To ensure the ability to make strong causal inferences while also taking into account the broader political context, I draw on a wealth of resources to examine my research questions. They include a series of seven different laboratory experiments, some incorporating psychophysiological measures, a population-based survey experiment using a representative national sample, a representative national survey of political television viewership, a visual as well as verbal content analysis of the most popular political programs currently on television, and, finally, an over-time analysis of the verbal and visual content of television news from the advent of television news through the present. This wealth of information allows me to document change over time in political television, as well as to draw strong inferences about the effects these changes have had on the public. The end result is a more complex understanding of both why uncivil political discourse remains alive and well and the consequences thereof.

I begin with a series of experiments focused on similar research goals; they include understanding the impact of incivility in political discourse independent of political substance, and examining how these effects are exacerbated by the perception of close physical distance. I describe one experimental design at length in Chapter 2. For the sake of efficiency, in describing subsequent experiments I mention only how and why they deviate from the original design. For reference, Appendix A summarizes all of the experimental designs and provides details on when and where they were conducted. All of the laboratory experiments incorporated adults who were not college students.[33] These participants were recruited in many different ways. Some came from temporary employment agencies and were paid their regular hourly temp rate to take part. Others were recruited as part of online meet-up groups or organizations to which they belonged, and participation was used as a group fund-raiser. As indicated in Appendix A, the experiments occurred in three different cities over a period of many years. Different recruitment methods produced different demographic profiles, and participants included people from a variety of occupations, including lawyers, a Catholic priest, the unemployed, part-timers, retirees, and stay-at-home parents.

Experiments force exposure to specific kinds of content on all subjects and therefore raise issues of generalizability. To address these issues, I incorporate into this research a representative national survey experiment and survey data from the National Annenberg Election Panel Study (NAES) from 2008. The 2008 NAES provided an extensive array of information about the viewership of specific political programs. When combined with the experimental data, these studies allowed me to examine whether those who watch various political television programs on a daily basis are also those likely to be affected by them.

The 2008 NAES provided three advantages for purposes of exploring the generalizability of in-your-face politics. First, despite widespread skepticism about media exposure measures in general, the method of assessing exposure used in this survey has been empirically validated to a much greater extent than any other contemporary media measures.[34] In addition, this approach to measurement provided information on which individual programs respondents watched regularly, not just how much political media exposure they experienced overall. Scholars studying political television in the 1970s might have cared about simply how much total television news people viewed, but today scholars are interested also in what kind of programs people watch because not all political programming is cut of the same cloth. This remains doubly true for how "in your face" these programs are. Third, program viewership measures make it possible to match program exposure measures to characteristics of individual viewers.

Because many of the results in this book are from experimental studies, findings are presented in simple graphic form whenever possible. Experimental designs are free of the need for complex statistical analyses in order to establish causation, so experimental results can be presented in terms of the raw means broken down by experimental

condition. Random assignment to experimental conditions elimi-
nates the need for control variables to protect against potentially
spurious relationships, and researcher control over the independent
variable makes the direction of causation clear. To ensure the widest
possible audience, observational data are also presented in graphic
form whenever possible. In some cases, those interested in technical details are referred to other publications; otherwise, I include all
relevant information in an appendix.

ORGANIZATION OF THE BOOK

My goal in Part I is to document the specific kinds of effects—both
positive and negative—that flow from in-your-face politics. Because
of the experimental method's superior ability to establish cause and
effect, laboratory experiments serve as the basis for initiating an understanding of how in-your-face politics affects viewers. Chapter 2
uses highly controlled laboratory experiments to evaluate the consequences of close-ups and incivility for viewers' levels of emotional
arousal and their memory of political television content. Chapter 3
uses additional experiments to investigate effects of these same independent variables on viewers' perceptions of the legitimacy of the
candidates and issue positions they like least. Chapter 4 examines the
consequences of perceived distance and incivility on levels of political trust.

In Part II, I address the generalizability of these effects. In Chapter 5, I do so by varying characteristics of the experimental treatments
that are used to manipulate incivility, and by expanding the kinds
of people used in the experiments. These studies allow me to say
more about the kinds of people most likely to be affected by in-your-
face politics. In Chapter 6, I use survey data to address the issue of
whether those who watch in-your-face politics in the real world are
also those likely to be affected by it. By combining content analyses
of forty different contemporary political programs with viewership
data, I gain some purchase on who watches political programs that
include this kind of content as opposed to less in-your-face political
programming.

Finally, in Part III I address the historical implications of in-your-face politics. In Chapter 7, I report on additional experiments designed to answer the question of whether these effects are specific to television or are reactions to incivility more generally, regardless of medium. In Chapter 8, I report on a content analysis evaluating the ways in which the visual content of television has changed since the inception of television news. By analyzing news programs that have aired continuously since the 1960s, I demonstrate that even within mainstream legacy media such as network news broadcasts, in-your-face politics is increasingly prominent. Finally, Chapter 9 outlines the problem facing contemporary political television, regardless of whether it is experienced through networks news or cable talk shows, or through a traditional television set in real time, a time-delayed recording, or as digital video over the Internet.

Ultimately, I argue that television poses unique problems as a political medium because, more so than other media, people respond to it in fundamentally social ways. In other words, watching political figures heatedly debate political issues through the audiovisual medium of television is all too much like experiencing an argument face-to-face. People do, in fact, respond to mediated representations of other people in ways that are rooted in expectations drawn from the world of face-to-face interaction. While I won't venture to say my mother-in-law was right, it turns out that we respond to having politicians in our faces in much the way we would to any other person with whom we disagree.

Although people fully understand that the world depicted on television is not a simple window on reality, they nonetheless are guided by the same set of norms that they use in everyday interactions in how they respond to it. The story I tell is about how and why that matters. As I discover, the consequences of in-your-face politics are neither uniformly beneficial, nor completely malevolent. Despite the widespread cry for more civil political discourse in the United States, there are some very good reasons that political television looks the way it does.

When I began this research agenda I had the working hypothesis that television's norms for portraying conflict would produce negative reactions from viewers because they violate the norms people are accustomed to in the face-to-face world. As will become clear from the chapters that follow, I was correct about this in many respects. But the ways in which in-your-face politics affects viewers are more complex than I had initially assumed. Although the findings did not ultimately change my mind about the potential problems inherent to this kind of political television, they convinced me that the many calls for more civil political dialogue were overly simplistic in their understanding of the mass audience. In the final chapter, I wrestle with this dilemma by proposing potential approaches to incorporating the beneficial effects of in-your-face politics without the negative externalities that it also creates.

PART I

WHAT DIFFERENCE DOES IT MAKE?

THE EFFECTS OF IN-YOUR-FACE POLITICAL TELEVISION

CHAPTER 2

THE CONSEQUENCES OF IN-YOUR-FACE POLITICS FOR AROUSAL AND MEMORY

In Chapter 1, I defined in-your-face politics as when political actors are in our faces in two different respects. First, they appear to be in closer physical proximity to us than is appropriate for face-to-face interactions with strangers. And second, they are far more uncivil than in typical unmediated interpersonal interactions. These two characteristics, now common in political television, have several important consequences.

In this chapter I address their implications for levels of viewers' emotional arousal. Emotional arousal is a common component of everyday experience. When we feel happy, sad, angry, curious, or disgusted, we experience arousal. Arousal can be positive and/or negative, and it can vary greatly in its intensity. Importantly, arousal is a state of excitation that involves activation of the autonomic nervous system and heightened activity in both mind and body.[1] We enter a state of enhanced attention when arousal increases because we are preparing to take action. In cases of extreme arousal, we can even sense our hearts pounding and our palms sweating, although most day-to-day arousal does not rise to this level. Our bodies are energized and prepared for action, including anything from running away from a negative trigger to running toward an extremely positive one.

Visual and auditory stimuli are probably the most common triggers for arousal. Not surprisingly, television has been viewed as particularly capable of prompting emotional arousal relative to print.

This attribution is due in part to the fact that television tells many stories with emotional components to large audiences. But as anyone who has read a good novel knows, the printed page can produce tremendous emotional arousal as well. The reason television generates more concern about emotional reactions than print is probably because of its superior ability to mimic the real world in both sight and sound. We can read what politicians said in the newspaper, but watching them on the screen and hearing them say things themselves produce a much closer approximation of the stimuli we process in the nonmediated world.

Because arousal has physiological manifestations, it is relatively easy to measure, and much is already known about its causes. Television is clearly one of them. Studies of media effects have focused primarily on the effects of television on arousal in the form of fear and aggression in response to violent media. But even political television—which is not generally known for its heart-pounding drama—has the capacity to produce emotional arousal in its viewers. Moreover, as I explain throughout this chapter, in-your-face political television is particularly likely to create strong emotional reactions in its viewers.

When considering the potential implications of in-your-face politics, there are two ways one might view the aggressively uncivil conflicts of opinion that are often portrayed. One is that most people know and understand that all politics is theater in the contemporary television age. Sure, politicians may scream and yell at one another, but we viewers know it is all for show. Campaigns are made-for-TV affairs these days, so the kinds of social norm violations that we commonly see may not be particularly consequential for how we process information or think about political actors. After all, these are the "norms" for the contemporary televised political world, so why should they give us pause?

A second possibility, however, emerges from the field of human-media interaction where scholars have explored the capacity for audiovisual media to produce reactions from viewers that are similar to how they react to unmediated objects and people. In other words, they are responding to audiovisual media not as if they were a portrayal of the real world, but as if the people or objects were immediately present in their environments.[2]

I have seen this most directly when observing my pets watch television. Indeed, there is an entire genre on YouTube these days consisting of dogs intently watching television, and sometimes attacking it or barking at people or animals on the screen. Likewise, one of my cats was quite enthusiastic about a video titled "Video Catnip," portraying squirrels and birds flitting about captured by a backyard video camera. For humans watching, it is extremely dull; but watching a cat watch it can be extremely entertaining. The first thing mine did was bat at the screen. When this was unsuccessful in generating a catch, he would look behind the television set to see if he could find the birds and squirrels there. It was clearly a puzzling experience for him, and it turns out he is not alone in that regard. Two biologists discovered that jumping spiders were similarly confused. When they showed these spiders video images of prey, predators, or members of the opposite sex, they stalked the prey, ran from the predators, and tried to court potential mates.[3]

But surely we, as highly sophisticated human beings, can override what we know to be such irrational behavior? Very young human children report believing that the people in the television can see them as they watch from the other side of the screen,[4] but adult viewers obviously don't believe that the people and places on the screen are right there in their living rooms.

Instead, what this research suggests is that people's brains to some extent respond to the portrayal of people and events *as if* they were responding to the presence of the same things in real life. This assertion is much less far-fetched. After all, a picture of chocolate cake can make us salivate just as the presence of a real one does. At a conscious level we know that television is just a bunch of small colored dots that form a quick succession of pictures. Nonetheless, a number of studies have demonstrated that people respond to familiar patterns of stimuli just as they would to the same stimuli from an unmediated event. The human brain responds in certain primitive ways that do not change just because the stimulus is television.

For example, people naturally respond to loud noises, movement, and other novel stimuli via what is known as an orienting response; blood vessels dilate, skin conductance and cortical brain waves change, and all of this occurs in support of turning visual attention to the new stimuli.[5] When a train appears to come toward us on the screen, without thinking we pull back from the television. Even though cognitively we know there is no way for it to hit us, we instinctively recoil. Movement in particular evokes attention on television just as it does in the real world. When a technique called subjective camera movement is used to produce the impression of movement for viewers by putting a camera on a moving object such as a sled or roller coaster, the video produces enhanced excitement, physiological arousal, and a sense of physical movement (and sometimes nausea), as if one were actually riding a sled or a roller coaster.[6]

In *The Media Equation*, Reeves and Nass make a more general argument that people—regardless of technological expertise—treat media in fundamentally social ways, even when it makes no sense to do so.[7] The usual explanation for this relies on the idea that at this point in human history our brains simply have not evolved enough to differentiate real and representational images: "At some level, what is part of nonmediated reality and what is pictorial representation must be treated as equivalent because the cost of confusing a real threat with a symbolic representation of a real threat is too great."[8]

Whether or not one buys the argument that it is preferable that our brains over-respond to innocuous representational images, rather than accidentally under-respond to real threats, most would concur that television increasingly simulates the sights and sounds of unmediated experience with great fidelity. We know that it is only television, but the sights and sounds in front of us suggest otherwise, and our brains have not adapted to this distinction.

Although these many assorted findings converge in suggesting that the mediated/unmediated divide is highly porous in terms of how our brains react, far less research has been done on the interpersonal aspect of mediated versus unmediated experience. After all, most of what we see on television involves other people. To what extent do reactions to mediated social interaction operate according to the same rules as when we witness real-world social interaction?

Assuming, for the moment, that the mediated human beings we see on television are processed as if they were real people, I outline what the implications would be for how people would respond to in-your-face politics. I start by describing research on real-world spatial proximity, and then describe the limited research on the mediated appearance of proximity. Next I outline what previous research tells us about the impact of incivility in face-to-face discourse, and then its mediated analogue, televised uncivil discourse.

SPATIAL PROXIMITY

Do people react to the mediated appearance of interpersonal distance in the same way they do to actual interpersonal distance? The importance of distance in unmediated settings is widely accepted based on extensive research. The physical distance separating two people in the real world is rife with implications. Whether people are consciously aware of it or not, distance communicates information about how people feel about each other. What specific distances communicate may vary by culture, but spatial proximity communicates important information in all cultures and in most species as well.

Among humans, invading someone's personal space causes increased levels of arousal. The classic study illustrating this phenomenon is as memorable for its research design as its findings. To test the hypothesis that proximity would produce higher levels of arousal, Middlemist, Knowles, and Matter wanted to measure arousal using a nonreactive measure.[9] They knew (as I did not before reading) that men's restrooms offer an opportunity to observe a concrete indicator of arousal. It turns out that emotional arousal in any form delays the onset of micturation, known more colloquially as peeing. Arousal also shortens the duration of micturition once begun. In other words, the higher the level of arousal, the longer the delay between when men would like to begin urinating and when urination actually occurs, and the lower total volume of urine as well.

Armed with this knowledge, they set up an infamous field experiment in university urinals. Without any awareness that they were taking part in a study, sixty lavatory subjects were randomly assigned to one of three interpersonal distance conditions: (1) a confederate standing directly adjacent to the subject, (2) a confederate standing one urinal removed from the subject, or (3) a confederate who was absent from the lavatory altogether. In order to record both time delay and volume, an accomplice remained in a private toilet stall using a periscope placed over its wall to inconspicuously observe the men who came in to urinate.

If one can get past wondering what kind of drugs the human subjects committee was on when they approved this study,[10] the findings are unequivocal; closer physical distance causes increased arousal, whether measured as delay before onset or total volume of urination. When people come toward us, we not only orient toward them because of the movement, we also experience increased physical arousal from the sheer fact that they are invading our personal space. The literature on proxemics now details the many implications of physical distance expectations and their violations. Scholars have interpreted these findings from the framework of an evolutionarily adaptive reaction; when others come closer, our bodies prepare to react in some way, whether they be friend or foe, through increased arousal. These results are automatic and not consciously controlled.

In reality, arousal in and of itself is seldom the outcome of interest to researchers; instead, they focus on the process by which arousal influences other outcomes.[11] In this chapter I examine its impact on memory in particular. By heightening arousal, spatial proximity can focus attention more acutely on the target; people are more attentive and thus may tend to remember more. If extremely high levels of arousal occur, patterns of recall may become curvilinear; when people are emotionally overwhelmed, such as when a serious accident occurs, arousal can become so high that it interferes with the encoding of information in memory.[12] However, barring assassinations or coups, most political media never rises to a level where such high arousal levels come into play.

As a result, in-your-face politics may have consequences not only for arousal levels, but also for what people learn and remember from political television. Although previous findings from the world of face-to-face experience are suggestive of how the appearance of physical distance might affect us, this research does not directly address whether the mediated appearance of distance also matters. I turn next to the mediated analogues of spatial proximity.

THE CLOSE-UP CAMERA PERSPECTIVE

Televised political discourse has long been claimed to create a sense of intimacy with viewers, but typically this is interpreted to mean *psychological* intimacy, not the appearance of actual physical closeness.[13] When scholars discuss the impact of "the candidate in the living room," they do not generally mean that people react as if the candidate were actually there. Nonetheless, from the perspective of the human visual field, it is worth noting that few people will ever appear as physically close as do the public figures shown in televised political discourse. Such perspectives heighten our sense of being up close and in their faces because the field of vision approximates this perspective; if a person fills our entire visual field, we can be certain he or she is physically close to us.

In the early days of television, the cameras were so large and heavy that they were entirely stationary, at times with a fixed focal length. However, as illustrated in Figure 2.1, in the head shots that now characterize much of televised political discourse, and many still photographs as well, the cameras are zoomed in so close that even portions of the speaker's head are routinely cut off and out of frame.

Does the mere appearance of physical closeness to a person who is on a TV screen produce the same kinds of consequences for arousal as real physical distance? Because of the many similarities between nonmediated experience and the audiovisual experience of television, this hypothesis seems plausible. Television and film editing purposely seeks to re-create familiar perceptual phenomena. Many editing devices "acquire . . . meaning by approximating some feature of real world experience. In the case of shot tightness being used as an intensifier, the aspect of experience being replicated is surely the greater involvement that comes with increased proximity to people and objects."[14]

As an undergraduate majoring in film, I was implicitly taught these same ideas as a means of communicating with audiences. To make

Figure 2.1. Close-up camera perspectives in contemporary media. From *left*: Vladimir Putin, Sarah Palin and George W. Bush

people look big and tough, shoot them from a low camera angle; to create the appearance of small stature and weakness, shoot them from a high angle. In fact, a study using photos taken from differing camera angles as manipulations found precisely these predicted differences in perceptions of characters.[15]

If the conventions used in television and film are based on analogues to real-world experiences, it should not be surprising that people react similarly to them. This general assumption has been around in film theory for many years, but there have been only a few empirical investigations to date. Interestingly, in Iranian cinema, a close-up of a female looking into the camera was long assumed to be far *too* arousing for male audiences and was thus forbidden; when women were allowed to appear in films at all, they were shown exclusively in long and medium shots, ostensibly to avoid having the audience feel too physically close.[16] The unstated assumption here was that close-ups were experienced by viewers as if they were actually (inappropriately) spatially close to the women on the screen.

To date, however, only a few studies have empirically documented that close-ups have the capacity to enhance levels of emotional arousal, just as real physical proximity does. Distance cues can come in more than one form. Reeves and Nass suggest that the key to how our brains interpret distance is the extent to which any image fills our visual field, that is, the space one can see all at once.[17] When a human face takes up a person's entire visual field, the brain logically concludes that it is very close. How else could a face fill our entire visual field? On the other hand, a face on television is also framed by the edges of the television screen, so the entire visual field might be considered to extend beyond it.

Thus far, researchers have looked at distance in three different ways, including viewer distance from the screen, shot length (close-up versus more distant camera), and screen size. In one study, a person appearing on a large-screen television (not necessarily in a close-up, but having the appearance of being larger and closer to the viewer) was found to be more likely to invoke a violation of the viewer's sense of personal space than one on a smaller screen, but viewing distance did not matter.[18] A more elaborate examination of the effects of apparent spatial distance was accomplished by showing subjects videotaped talking faces while simultaneously varying all three of these dimensions: viewer distance, close-up versus distant camera perspectives, and small and large screen sizes.[19] In all of the variously simulated close conditions, levels of attention and memory for content were enhanced.

Although research on this topic has been limited, these two studies provide some credible evidence that real physical proximity and the symbolic appearance of proximity may affect people in similar ways. As Reeves and Nass summarize, "Human responses to media are social even though media supposedly offer only symbolic representations of people in the real world."[20] When applied to televised politics, this research suggests that the content of political discourse may be processed quite differently depending upon the way political advocates are framed when they express these views on television. For example, outcomes such as memory for the content may be affected when norms for personal space are violated. Next I consider implications of the social norm of politeness for these same outcomes, arousal and memory.

INCIVILITY IN FACE-TO-FACE AND MEDIATED CONTEXTS

Unlike the mediated appearance of distance, there has been quite a bit of research on reactions to mediated incivility. While there has been no direct evidence to date that political incivility heightens levels of viewer arousal, this hypothesis is easily inferred from the voluminous literature on reactions to televised violence. It is by now well established that violence in films and on television increases levels of physiological arousal.[21] Violent video games also produce temporarily increased levels of physiological arousal.[22] Arousal is thought to be one the main mechanisms by which TV violence promotes aggressive behavior. A high state of arousal prompts stronger emotional reactions to what might otherwise be seen as minor annoyances.

With political media, few in the United States have gone so far as to suggest that uncivil political discourse produces actual violence. In one recent exception, the shooting of Representative Gabrielle Giffords, the incivility of conservative political discourse was blamed because her congressional seat had been "targeted" for defeat on a website featuring crosshairs. Violent metaphors are common in political discourse, but the fact that the Clinton campaign had a "War Room" during the campaign was not used as grounds for claiming they intended violence in support of their candidate. For the most part, such claims have been appropriately dropped as more has become known. Within the United States, few today claim that uncivil discourse is causing political violence, although that claim is considerably more tenable in countries where talk radio has been used as a purposeful strategy for inciting people to arms.[23]

Regardless of the potential effects of televised violence on actual behavior, there is a strong consensus that it causes heightened levels of arousal among viewers. Incivility in political discourse obviously pales in level of intensity to physical violence. But its implications should be the same, even if at a smaller magnitude. Much of the political discourse that transpires on television is highly uncivil in tone. As Wilson notes, "Once the media talked to us; now they shout at us."[24]

The social norms for politeness in face-to-face settings are routinely violated on television. On political talk shows, in particular, people clearly do not obey the same set of social rules that ordinary citizens do in everyday life. Most people in real life are polite to others when disagreeing. The norms for politeness are very strong, thus one might expect that violating these norms—even on television—should not go unnoticed. Indeed, people may back off or avoid political discussion altogether if they fear that highly charged disagreements may erupt.[25]

On political talk shows, in contrast, violating conversational norms seems to be commonplace. Production values and intense market competition put a premium on conflict and drama. As a result, the political advocates who represent various viewpoints on TV may come across as nasty, boorish sorts who scream and yell at one another regularly.[26]

Those involved in the production of political television argue that lively and passionate debate is a necessary ingredient for a successful political television program. Anything less is too boring to attract television audiences.[27] As Bill O'Reilly, host of *The O'Reilly Factor*, claims, "If a producer can find someone who eggs on conservative listeners to spout off and prods liberals into shouting back, he's got a hit show. The best host is the guy or gal who can get the most listeners extremely annoyed over and over and over again."[28]

It is not conflict per se that concerns many observers—after all, politics has always involved conflict—but rather the incivility with which political elites disagree. Uslaner, for example, has suggested that members of Congress are increasingly likely to violate norms of politeness in their discourse, and Tannen characterizes the contemporary United States as "a culture of argument" that encourages "a pervasive warlike atmosphere."[29] Even journalists concur that in American politics, "hyperbole and venomous invective are common talk." Viewers' sense that politicians are engaged in pointless bickering is fed by media coverage emphasizing the intensity of conflict whenever possible.[30] To the casual observer, politicians seem to be perpetually involved in bitter conflict.[31]

Because incivility—just as invading personal space—involves violating social norms from the face-to-face world, I predicted that incivility in the expression of political differences of opinion would heighten levels of arousal, just as spatial proximity is expected to do. Underlying any political exchange in which norms for polite interaction are violated is the possibility that people might come to blows. If incivility with its insinuation of the potential for violence appears on television, arousal levels should go up, even if the discussion remains centered on common differences of political opinion.

THE EXPERIMENTS

This book presents results from many different experiments, but most follow a predictable format. For this reason, I describe the first study in some detail, and then note only deviations from that pattern in subsequent chapters. Appendix A summarizes each of the experimental designs, while Appendix B summarizes the dependent variables used in these experiments.

Based on the evidence described above, in-your-face politics should be an especially arousing form of political television. Granted, political television starts from a low bar when it comes to arousal. Political television shows do not garner large audiences, nor are they known for generating great excitement among viewers. But relative to the same program without incivility and/or close-up camera perspectives, in-your-face politics should heighten viewer arousal.

Thus the first experiment was directed toward answering two simple questions. First, are viewer arousal levels higher when politicians engage in uncivil as opposed to civil discourse? Second, are levels of arousal greater when people are exposed to politicians using close-ups as opposed to more distant camera perspectives?

As simple and straightforward as these hypotheses may seem, testing them in a highly controlled way was not easy. For example, even if one were to use two different episodes of the same political talk show, one a civil discussion and another uncivil, it would still be very difficult to claim that civility alone was causing any observed difference in viewer reactions. After all, the content of the two programs would also be very different, including the issues discussed, the views expressed, the complexity of the issues, and possibly even the people involved, their attractiveness, and so on. To simultaneously manipulate whether the program used close-ups or more distant camera angles, along with varied levels of civility, combined with the need for comparability on other dimensions posed a seemingly insurmountable task.

I toyed with the idea of sampling from many different civil and uncivil political discussions on the air, but ultimately decided to start with the purest possible test, one in which the political advocates were the same, the issues were the same, and even the viewpoints expressed were the same. The only way to hold all other aspects of the program constant in this fashion was to produce a political program myself. It seemed at least plausible that with an undergraduate background in film and television I could produce a program that was of the quality of a local political broadcast.

The pretext was an actual program called *Indiana Week in Review*, a weekly talk show program in the state of Indiana billed as where "Hoosiers 'in the know' are getting their answers." As their promotional materials suggest, "You may watch for the news, but you'll stay for the no-holds-barred debate and discussion. A look at issues facing Indiana from differing viewpoints makes for an entertaining, lively and informative half-hour." The introductory credits from the actual program were used to enhance the realism of the experimental episodes. In reality, the set used was the talk show studio used for *Uncommon Knowledge*, a professional talk show taped weekly on a set in California that happened not to be used on weekends.

Two professional actors were hired to portray congressional candidates vying for an open seat in the state of Indiana. One of the actors was also, in reality, a failed candidate from a congressional district in California. Both were white males between the ages of thirty-five and forty-five. Pretest subjects rated them as equally attractive based on still photographs.

In order to maintain tight control over content, the program was scripted in advance using differences of opinion across seven different issues. These included funding for additional space exploration through NASA, insurance coverage of mental health benefits, free trade, restrictions on tobacco advertising, the repeal of the Glass-Steagall Act affecting financial industries, taxes on Internet purchases, and whether previous public-sector experience is beneficial for a potential congressperson or taints the candidate as a Washington insider. The arguments and terms of debate were lifted directly from websites and campaign materials of actual congressional candidates.

Notably, these were not exactly hot-button, emotional issues. Some were complex and technical (e.g., Glass-Steagall), while others were relative easy to follow (allowing tobacco companies to advertise at sporting events, or covering mental health needs under insurance plans). But whether simple or complex, they were not highly emotional issues for the most part; one might wax poetic about space exploration, but it rarely brings people to blows. For this reason, the civil and uncivil exchanges in the experiment were not extremes of incivility at the level one might find in an exchange over abortion or immigration. Moreover, to ensure that results did not hinge on any one particular issue segment, a different subset of four of the seven issue discussions was used in each experiment (see Appendix A).

The filming was done as a four-camera shoot, meaning that four separate professional television cameras were used to cover the same event simultaneously. This way I was able to devote two cameras to each candidate, one remaining on a tight facial close-up, the second at a medium to long perspective incorporating the speaker's upper body. The cameras maintained these shots through two complete takes of the program, the civil and uncivil tapings. The tapes were later edited by a professional editor, using the same conventions as for a typical talk show. After an initial long shot established the set and the location of the candidates and moderator, the subsequent shots were almost exclusively tight close-ups in the close-up version. In the medium version, the same event was shown from the perspective of cameras that had backed away in their framing of the participants, and no tight close-ups of the candidates were included.

The exchange was not a formal debate but an informal political discussion as is most common on talk shows. A moderator intervened at times predetermined by the script and directed questions to the two candidates and occasionally forced a change of topic, but he purposely said very little. Because the purpose of the program was to highlight differences of opinion between the two candidates for potential voters, it was not surprising that they held opposing views on each of the issues raised. In order to present the same political content in the civil and uncivil versions of the debate, the actors stuck closely to a script with the aid of teleprompters. The discussion of all seven issues lasted forty minutes, but each experiment used at most four issues in order to keep the programs at the length appropriate for a thirty-minute program, and the total experimental time under an hour.

The candidates expressed exactly the same issue positions in both the civil and uncivil versions of this program and offered identical arguments in support of their positions. But in the civil version the candidates went to extremes to be polite to the opposition, inserting phrases such as "I'm really glad Bob raised the issue of . . ." and "I don't disagree with all of your points, Bob, but . . ." before calmly making their own positions clear. Both candidates fully observed the interpersonal norms for civility in expressing their viewpoints, not only in their own speech, but also by waiting patiently while the other person answered and by paying attention to the opponent while he was speaking.

In the uncivil version of these exchanges, the candidates said basically the same things, but they inserted gratuitous phrases devoid of explicit political content. Sample statements include comments such as "You're really missing the point here Neil" and "What Bob is *completely* overlooking is. . . ." The candidates also raised their voices and never apologized for interrupting one another. Nonverbal cues such as rolling of the eyes and rueful shaking of the head from side to side further suggested a lack of respect for what the opponent was saying. Voices were raised when conflict intensified, in contrast to the persistently calm voices of the candidates in the civil version.

These were not exaggerated renditions of a real-world talk show; indeed, they were relatively muted. Unlike what has occurred in the recent past on many popular programs, no one compared their opponent to Hitler, threw a chair, or stomped off the set in anger.[32] To ensure that these subtle differences adequately manipulated civility, subjects were asked to rate the candidates on scales ranging from quarrelsome to cooperative, hostile to friendly, agitated to calm, and rude to polite. As shown in Figure 2.2, the uncivil versions of the issue exchanges were consistently perceived as significantly less polite, more quarrelsome, and less friendly. Respondents in all of the experiments described in Appendix A were asked to rate the candidates on these same scales.[33] Even though each experiment used a different combination of discussion segments, the manipulation check

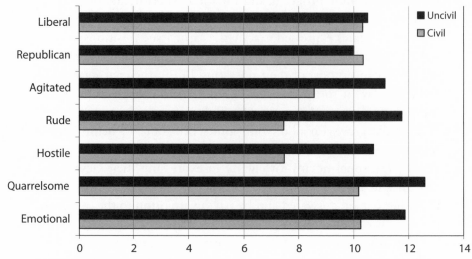

Figure 2.2. Effects of experimental treatments on viewer perceptions of candidate civility and partisanship

Note: Bars represent the mean level from summed judgments for each of the two candidates on each dimension. All mean differences are significantly different except for the extent to which the candidates were judged as liberal-conservative or Republican-Democrat.

items confirmed in all cases that both candidates were perceived to be significantly more hostile and rude in the uncivil conditions than in the civil ones.

Because the goal of these studies was to manipulate the civility of interaction *without* manipulating the partisanship, political substance or extremity of views represented by the two candidates, it was equally important that the civility treatments not influence perceptions of the candidates' strength of party identification or ideology. Fortunately, as also shown in Figure 2.2, the civility manipulations successfully induced differences in the perceived civility/incivility of both candidates, without changing viewer perceptions of the partisanship or ideology of the candidates. Because the chosen issues were not hard-core partisan issues in which the partisanship of the candidate would necessarily be inferred from his stand on a given issue, it was possible to assign party identifications to the candidates in some versions of the experiment, but not others, simply by adding an "R" or a "D" after each candidate's name on the graphic superimposed when he was speaking.

The civil and uncivil tapings of the same debate, combined with the four-camera shoot, made it possible to produce four different versions of the same political exchange that were either civil or uncivil in tone, and that created the impression of either moderate physical distance between the viewer and candidates or a close-up "in-your-face" experience of the same conflict. Moreover, with all four versions produced and edited for eight different issue discussions, there was ample material to ensure that results did not hinge on one particular exchange.

Procedures were roughly the same for all experiments. Participants were recruited through temporary employment agencies and community groups and either the group treasury or the individual participants were compensated for their time. Subjects sat alone on a couch in a room with a coffee table and in front of a thirty-two-inch television screen. All sat the same distance from the television screen. After obtaining consent and filling out a pretest questionnaire, subjects viewed twenty minutes of the televised political program, then filled out posttest questionnaires. Subjects were debriefed after all experiments.

This basic procedure was modified slightly for individual experiments based on the goal of the study. For the first experiment, I wanted to determine whether camera perspective and televised incivility produce physiological reactions similar to what physical distance and disagreement produce when experienced in person. Toward that end, arousal was measured using skin conductance levels assessed by attaching two electrodes to the palm of each subject's non-dominant hand while he or she watched the videotapes. Skin conductance is one indicator of sympathetic activation,[34] and has been widely used in studies investigating emotional responses to media.[35] Data collection began at the start of each presentation, with a ten-second period of baseline data recorded while the screen was blank prior to the start of each segment. Skin conductance was sampled from subjects every ten milliseconds, and then averaged over the length of the issue segment within each experimental condition. Because these measures may be affected by ambient room temperature and the volume on the television set, these were also standardized within each study.

In addition to employing skin conductance measures, Experiment I utilized a powerful Latin-square design and a small sample of sixteen subjects, each of whom experienced all four possible conditions formed by crossing incivility/civility and close/medium camera perspective. By using four different video segments, each focused on discussion of a different issue controversy, it was possible for each respondent to view all four possible treatment combinations, without viewing the same content in more than one condition.

The assignment of issue controversies to conditions was random for each respondent, as was the order of their presentation. The Latin-square design is particularly advantageous for studying arousal because individual differences in arousability tend to be quite large, thus making the within-group variance extensive. The Latin-square design allows comparisons of each subject to his or her own mean level of arousal across the four conditions, and thus enables greater statistical power in examining whether viewers' levels of arousal varied systematically due to close-ups and incivility. Given that four different video segments were used, the results are also unlikely to depend on the peculiarities of any individual presentation.

To what extent do incivility and the appearance of distance matter to viewers' levels of emotional arousal? Figure 2.3 shows the average skin conductance level for each of the four experimental conditions in the Latin-square design. Consistent with expectations, there were clear differences between conditions for both experimental factors. Most obviously, uncivil public discourse was significantly more arousing than civil versions of the same discussions ($t = 14.38$, $df = 1,299$, $p < .001$). The analysis of camera perspectives likewise confirmed that close-ups of the exact same events were significantly more arousing to viewers than medium shots ($t = 28.90$, $df = 1,299$, $p < .001$). The two main effects combined to make uncivil exchanges of political views featuring tight close-ups the most arousing of all, while highly civil exchanges shown through medium shots were least arousing.

Politics is not a highly arousing topic for most people, so these differences may well explain why audiences are willing to watch so-called shout shows on television. Given that they elicit high levels of

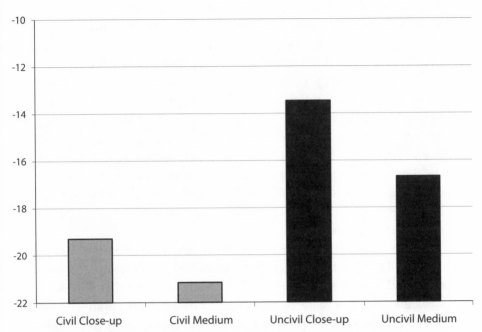

Figure 2.3. Average levels of arousal by civility and camera perspective

Note: The dependent variable was measured using skin conductance. A repeated-measures analysis of variance indicated that uncivil discourse was significantly more arousing to viewers than a civil version of the same political discussion ($t = 14.38$, $df = 1,299$, $p < .001$). The close-up camera perspective was significantly more arousing to viewers than the same event shown using a medium camera perspective ($t = 28.90$, $df = 1,299$, $p < .001$).

arousal, attention levels to such programs are naturally quite high, whether viewers like them or not. But it remains to be seen whether these differential levels of arousal have implications for the processing of televised political discourse.

EXPERIMENT II: RECALL OF PROGRAM CONTENT

Arousal is widely accepted as an indicator of attention, but by itself it reveals nothing about what people learn from content. For these purposes, a second experiment was required, one in which some people experienced all of the content under conditions of low arousal, and others viewed the same content under conditions of high arousal.

To accomplish this, I used a between-subjects design in which both civility and camera perspective were treatment factors, as before, but this time each person experienced all four issue exchanges in only one of the four combinations of civility and camera perspectives. Given that respondents in Experiment I went from one condition to another throughout the experiment, and rotated through different video clips for each, it was impossible to compare recall of material from a discussion of one issue to recall from a totally different discussion that included entirely different content. Although the Latin-square design rotated people through all condition-issue combinations, subject recall could be affected by the issue as well as by their experimental condition, and the sample was too small to partial out such effects.

In Experiment II, the goal of the between-subjects design was to evaluate how recall was affected by incivility and close-ups. Studies of arousal suggest that people should retain more of what they have viewed when in a state of increased arousal because high arousal levels prompt them to pay close attention. Barring overwhelmingly high levels of arousal, memory and learning should be enhanced.

Experiment II drew on a large sample of 155 participants who were exposed to only one of the four possible experimental conditions formed by crossing civility/incivility with close-up versus medium camera perspective. Three kinds of recall were assessed in the posttests administered after viewing the program. One version asked for simple recall of the candidate's positions on each of the four issues that were discussed. This measure turned out to be too easy for a laboratory setting; fully 88 percent of subjects across all conditions successfully recalled all candidate issue positions, thus producing too little variation to be useful as a variable.

A second form of recall was tapped by an indicator of recognition recall. For each issue exchange included in the program, respondents were presented with a series of ten statements and asked if one of the candidates had said them. For example, "Which of these statements are things that [candidate name] said? For each statement below please circle **Yes** if it is something he said and **No** if it is not something he said. It does not matter if it is exactly word-for-word what [candidate name] said. Still circle **Yes** if he made that same general statement or argument." After one series, a second series of ten items was presented for the other candidate and respondents were again asked to indicate yes or no as to whether the candidate had said each of them. Thus respondents could register knowledge of one or both of the candidates' statements on each issue, offering many opportunities to demonstrate recognition recall. Order of issues and candidates was randomized, and correct responses were summed to produce a summary measure of recognition recall.

As a third indicator of recall, I utilized open-ended items that asked subjects to recall the arguments made by the two candidates, including those made on both sides of an issue controversy. After issuing their own opinions on a given controversy, respondents were asked to write down as many of the arguments as they could possibly think of in response to a question: "What are some of the reasons [candidate name] gave in support of his opinion on the talk show? Please write as many as you can think of in the box below." After completing that question, respondents were next asked, "Are there other reasons that were not mentioned that you think [candidate name] might have for holding this opinion? Please describe them in the box below." The same sequence was repeated for each candidate.

This approach allowed an assessment of the totality of respondents' awareness of arguments on each side of the issue controversy under discussion. As with the recognition recall series, respondents were asked a separate set of open-ended recall questions for each of the issue controversies. Responses were coded by two independent coders, producing a reliability of .90 for the number of unique arguments generated.

Did the arousal of in-your-face political discourse enhance recall as predicted? The answer to this question depends upon which form of recall is considered. As described above, candidate position recall was too invariant in the context of an hour-long laboratory experiment to demonstrate any effects on a simple 0 to 4 scale. Recognition recall was more extensive, but it generated null findings across experiments in all but one case. Thus there was no consistent support for enhancement of recognition memory due to high arousal conditions.

However, the open-ended recall measures generated highly consistent results throughout the entire series of experiments. Figure 2.4 illustrates the main effect of camera perspective on the left, and the main effect of incivility on the right. Both differences were

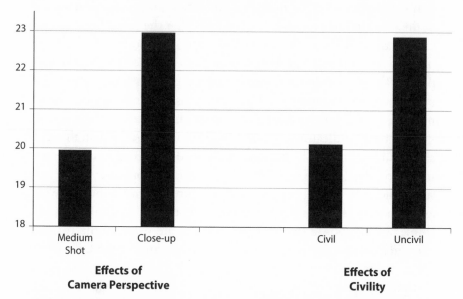

Figure 2.4. Effects of camera perspective and civility on recall of issue arguments
Note: The main effects of camera perspective ($F = 3.54, p < .05$) were significant as were the main effects of incivility ($F = 2.87, p < .05$). Total $n = 155$.

statistically significant and in the expected directions. As in the analysis of arousal, there was no interactive effect of these two factors; incivility coupled with close-up camera shots combined to additively enhance the total amount of open-ended recall people had from watching the programs.

This same pattern of recall findings occurred in Experiments II, III, and V, that is, all of the experiments in which issue content was held constant between the civil and uncivil conditions, so it was possible to compare recall from substantively identical versions of the programs. These were also all experiments in which the more highly arousing close-up conditions were included. Overall, these results suggest a very logical connection between arousal and memory. Violations of social norms enhance arousal, and produce enhanced attention to the content, and thus greater recall.

Why might these effects occur so predictably for open-ended recall but not for the other types of recall? Lack of variance in the knowledge of candidate issue positions was probably due to the short time frame between viewing and answering questions; in this case the null finding seems unlikely to bear on phenomena of importance in the real world.

But the fact that recall recognition did not generate a consistent pattern of results, whereas open-ended recall did, may suggest something of note. What's the difference between recognizing a statement one has heard before, and the ability to recall it spontaneously on one's own? In the latter case, the information must be more accessible than in the former. One needs to encode the information, store it at least temporarily, and then also be able to retrieve it when prompted. Open-ended recall also would seem to involve greater depth of understanding and retention; one needs to be able to articulate an actual argument rather than simply recognize familiar words and phrases. The higher level of attention required for this more difficult type of recall appears to be facilitated by in-your-face politics.

Is one of these forms of recall more important than the other in the context of politics? Arguably both are important, but given the limited forms of political tasks in which Americans engage—forming issue opinions, possibly voting on issue referendums, and regular voting on candidates—open-ended recall seems the most important. When people enter a voting booth or are asked for an issue opinion, they may be limited to drawing on what they can recall at the time.

On the other hand, to the extent that people are online versus memory-based processors of new political information,[36] they may be constantly "updating" their candidate assessments in line with the online processing model, and thus do not need to actually recall information in order to be affected by it. Realistically, however, based on what is known about people's susceptibility to short-term influences based on what is accessible at the time, information that is easily retrieved from memory is also likely to have greater influence.

THE LURE OF IN-YOUR-FACE POLITICS

The results thus far in this chapter suggest that people are more likely to remember content that is viewed during a highly arousing program than a less arousing one. But the advantages of high arousal television are unlikely to end with enhanced memory. Highly arousing political television is also more likely to attract the viewer's attention to begin with. At the end of Experiment II, and in all of the experiments described in this book, study participants were asked a series of questions about their level of interest in and enjoyment of the program. This measure of the popularity of the program asked viewers if the show was good at keeping their attention, if it was entertaining for a political talk show, and if it was dull and boring even by the standards of political talk shows (see Appendix B for details on scale). These questions formed a highly reliable index. Because entertainment value is obviously not the only reason people watch political television—some genuinely want to be well informed—we simultaneously asked about how informative they found the programs to be.

As shown in Figure 2.5, and as replicated in other experiments, the uncivil versions of the program were consistently perceived as more entertaining by a significant margin. As producers of uncivil content have long suspected, incivility is entertaining and draws interest. Doesn't this contradict all of the complaints in Chapter 1 about how much people dislike the endless political bickering on television? Not really. Remember that no one viewing the uncivil programs knew that others were viewing a civil version of the same broadcast, nor did anyone know the point of the study was to see how people reacted differently based on levels of civility. I'm fairly certain that if they were confronted with both versions of the program, and could compare them self-consciously, side by side, respondents would claim the uncivil one was worse. But the arousal brought on by incivility caught their attention and thus made the program more enjoyable to watch than a calm, dry version. Some level of arousal is absolutely necessary in order to hold viewers' attention to material that they would not necessarily find all that exciting.

This phenomenon is similar to rubbernecking, slowing down and gawking at accidents or other, predominantly negative, events.[37] People slow down and stare at accidents because they are hardwired to look at important things. Even though we may be appalled by what we see, it is clear to the most basic parts of our brains that matters of life and death deserve our attention. Likewise, violence and incivility

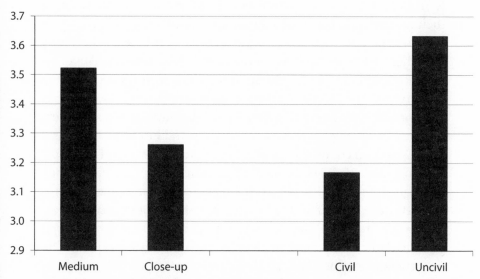

Figure 2.5. Popularity of program by civility and camera perspective
Note: The main effects of civility ($F = 11.30, p < .001$) were significant; the effects of camera perspective approached statistical significance ($F = 3.76, p < .10$), and there was no interaction.

solicit our attention because they connote something extraordinary, particularly as they get spatially close to us. That uncivil programs were more entertaining to watch was seen repeatedly throughout the studies in this book; close-ups, on the other hand, did not consistently correspond with greater or lesser entertainment value across experiments. Measures of the programs' perceived informativeness likewise showed no differences by civility or camera perspective.

WHY IN-YOUR-FACE POLITICS IS GOOD FOR DEMOCRATIC POLITICS

Critics of shout-show politics abound, and journalists and the public alike regularly scorn "infotainment," that is, news that attempts to entertain as well as inform. But there is one important fact that critics of in-your-face politics typically do not address: political television cannot educate the public unless people watch it. Calm, rational exchanges of the kind one might see on a PBS program are not sufficiently arousing to attract viewers to begin with, nor to hold their attention. Those involved in the production of political television routinely argue that lively and passionate debate is a necessary ingredient for a successful political television program. Anything less is too boring to attract the attention of television audiences.[38]

Sharing what one has learned with other friends and associates also appears to be boosted by high states of arousal. In an experimental study in which people were shown high and low arousal videos,[39] the low arousal conditions (in which people felt either sad or simply content) made people less likely to tell others about the videos than the high arousal conditions (in which people felt amusement or anxiety). It didn't matter so much what specific emotion people were feeling; so long as the emotion was intense and produced high levels of arousal, they were more likely to want to share a subsequent neutral article with others due to their aroused state.

Importantly, even when the arousal is not due to the nature of the information that is being shared, it still causes people to be more likely to retransmit its content. For example, when arousal was induced by having people jog in place as opposed to sitting, they were more likely to email an online news article to others in what they were told was a second, unrelated study directly afterward.

This mechanism is likely to account for the retransmission of highly arousing video on television and especially via the Internet. It is difficult to imagine a calm exchange of political ideas going viral. When it comes to uncivil outbursts, however, they are emailed, posted, and rebroadcast with commentary elsewhere. Even the networks that originate the uncivil outbursts appear happy to have attention focused on them. In one recent example of this well-known pattern, CNBC reporter Rick Santelli ranted against President Obama on air to an audience of only a few hundred thousand who were watching *Squawk Box* that Thursday. But then CNBC immediately posted the clip on their website for further viewing, promoting its retransmission.[40] By that Sunday it had been viewed 1.7 million times and had been featured as the lead story on several other television programs. It was no coincidence that this particular segment was selected for uploading, and it probably surprises no one that it was picked up by other television programs as well as by private individuals for retransmission.

Physiological arousal drives virality online.[41] Thus as more people get their news online, the arousal associated with political messages will be increasingly important to reaching large audiences. Arousal is necessary in order to produce attention to the content of political discourse. In-your-face political discourse heightens levels of physiological arousal, and thus enhances attention to content as well as the desire to share, both online and offline. Confirming a long-standing suspicion, empirical evidence shows that controversy increases the likelihood that something will be discussed with others.[42]

To summarize, there appear to be three advantages to political discourse that involves incivility. First, outside of experimental contexts, highly arousing political television is more likely to attract viewers' attention to begin with. Second, its content is more likely to be remembered by viewers. And third, stories that generate high levels of arousal are more likely to be retransmitted, whether interpersonally, via the Internet, or from being picked up and rebroadcast by other television programs.

CHAPTER 3

EFFECTS ON PUBLIC PERCEPTIONS OF THE LEGITIMACY OF THE OPPOSITION

In many respects, Chapter 2 was quite reassuring. Despite all the hand-wringing reviewed in Chapter 1, in-your-face politics turns out to be a relatively harmless gimmick that encourages the public to pay more attention to political television. They are significantly more likely to remember what they have seen when it is presented in such a highly arousing fashion. Moreover, the political content that is broadcast is more likely to be talked about and retransmitted as a result. All of this is welcome news for those who fear that uncivil political discourse will bring about an unraveling of democracy.

But this is not the whole story. In this chapter, I outline the darker side of in-your-face politics. On the one hand, conflict is central to the democratic process, and it is altogether appropriate that media highlight differences of political opinion. The legitimacy of democratic outcomes requires that political options be contested, and the in-your-face style could be just another way to present conflicting ideas to the public. Unfortunately, it has some detrimental side effects.

The results in Chapter 2 suggested that televised political discourse plays an important role in familiarizing viewers with issue arguments related to matters of public controversy. If television did so for rationales for *oppositional* political perspectives in particular, then it could be extremely valuable in discouraging polarization and encouraging perceptions of a legitimate opposition. Given that few people speak directly to political advocates of opposing political views, it is unclear how else, if not through media, Americans could come to perceive that reasonable people may disagree on any given political controversy.

I began this research with the optimistic hope that political television might play a beneficial role in educating people about the opposition. My earlier work on face-to-face political communication had convinced me that too few people speak directly to those with opposing political views for face-to-face communication to accomplish this on a large scale.[1] The limited potential for accomplishing this end in the realm of face-to-face discourse has led many to suggest that for most people, most of the time, exposure to opposing political perspectives happens via mass media.[2]

Conversely, when much of this exposure occurs without the trappings of civility and the mutual respect that it implies, political television could easily backfire, and do more harm than good when it encourages exposure, but discourages respect for oppositional views. The central purpose of this chapter is to examine whether in-your-face politics enhances the extent to which oppositional views are perceived to be legitimate or, alternatively, contributes to disdain for the opposition. Here I shift my focus from mere awareness of issue arguments, to attitudes toward the opposition.

I begin with a brief discussion of what I mean by perceiving legitimacy in oppositional views. Next I look at in-your-face television's advantages and disadvantages as a medium for promoting perceptions of a legitimate opposition. In order to assess the impact of in-your-face politics on attitudes toward the opposition, I develop several empirical measures that tap whether people are aware of and believe in a legitimate opposition when it comes to their own political views. Finally, I describe some highly consistent, though normatively disappointing, findings about the impact of in-your-face politics on these indicators.

FOSTERING PERCEPTIONS OF A LEGITIMATE OPPOSITION

The legitimacy of democratic outcomes requires that political options be contested. And yet it also rests on the premise that each side in any given controversy perceives the opposition as having some reasonable foundation for its positions. Few question that the quality of public discourse on matters of political controversy is important toward that end. But the typical reasons for concern generally involve the extent to which the public develops well-informed opinions as a result of exposure to public discourse.

In what is widely perceived to be today's highly polarized political environment, it is arguably equally if not more important that they develop some understanding of the "other side," that is, the candidate or policy position that is not their preferred option. Although this outcome is far less studied, it is important to the stability of a political system. Without the acquiescence of those on the losing side, democratic government could not continue peaceably. And without some degree of respect for oppositional views, it is doubtful that the losers in any given contest would tolerate the winners for long. Although some might argue that it is respect for the process, not for oppositional perspectives, that compels those on the losing side to continue, a process that produces outcomes that seem totally without justification is unlikely to persist.

Normative political theory has long been convinced of the importance of respect for oppositional views. For example, deliberation is so strongly advocated in part because it requires that reason giving occur among those of diverse views, with the ultimate goal that individuals come to respect and appreciate those with views unlike their own.[3] Public deliberation is assumed to promote greater awareness of both oppositional views and their justifications.[4] By making public the rationales behind opposing sides of a controversy, the losers in a given controversy come to know the reasons or arguments the winners judged to be stronger: "Hence discussion rather than private deliberation would be necessary to 'put on the table' the various reasons and arguments that different individuals had in mind, and thus to ensure that no one could see the end result as arbitrary rather than reasonable and justifiable, even if not what he or she happened to see as most justifiable."[5]

Some studies of electoral behavior suggest that being on the losing side in any given contest has consequences for the way citizens feel about their political system. In research on what they term "losers' consent," Anderson and colleagues demonstrate that beyond the understandable initial disappointment suffered by losers, there are also effects on system-level attitudes that persist and accumulate over long periods of time, leading to diminished support for democratic principles, and to greater support for institutional change.[6] To maintain democratic stability, it is therefore important to understand not only who wins and why people support a given candidate, but also why those on the losing side accept the decision to the point that they are willing to be governed by this person or policy.

Increasing concern about polarization within the American electorate has made the perceived legitimacy of the opposition an even greater concern. At present, there is far more consensus on the existence of political polarization among elites than among the mass public.[7] Scholars looking for greater extremity in the issue preferences of the mass public have not produced consistent conclusions. Nonetheless, more attention has been focused on how much citizens despise the opposition, as well as how much they like their own candidate or party. Some have suggested that it is partisan affect that has intensified rather than issue preferences.[8] For example, the gap between Republican and Democratic citizens' approval of the president has become wider.[9] Feeling thermometer ratings also show a pattern of increased differences between individuals' feelings toward conservatives and liberals.[10] Based on open-ended questions, Hetherington likewise reports that more Americans now have positive things to say about one party and negative things to say about the other.[11] Findings of this kind suggest an increasing lack of respect for oppositional political groups.

In short, it is critical that political systems incorporate a means by which partisans can develop some degree of respect for the other side. If citizens remain unaware of any legitimate opposition, then political conflict itself seems petty and unnecessary, a view already held by many Americans.[12] Moreover, if the losing side in any given controversy perceives no legitimate basis for the positions of the winning side, then the losers are unlikely to cooperate in maintaining and perpetuating the rules of the game.[13] When citizens end up on the losing side, ideally they should perceive the opposition as having *some* basis for its positions, however mistaken, shortsighted, or benighted that perspective might seem. The democratic process rests on the premise that each side in any given controversy perceives the opposition as having some reasonable foundation for its positions.

ADVANTAGES AND DISADVANTAGES OF TELEVISION

Television has both advantages and disadvantages as a means of exposing people to oppositional political perspectives. On the one hand, television is less subject to the constraints of parochialism that plague face-to-face interactions. Because people tend to live among those like themselves, their interactions are often limited in their ability to expose them to oppositional perspectives. Broadcast media have always reached much larger and more heterogeneous audiences than newspapers.[14] Moreover, television transcends time and space in a way that makes less insular perspectives more widely available.[15] In addition, television's propensity to present controversial material in a point-counterpoint fashion ensures that at least some opposing perspectives are heard.

On the other hand, it is probably naïve to expect exposure to oppositional views through television to easily convince partisans that the opposition is worthy. Watching others discuss opposing perspectives on television is qualitatively different from participation in face-to-face discussion, and the evidence on face-to-face deliberation is already mixed in regard to producing such beneficial outcomes. Moreover, many such presentations on television are not discussions at all, but rather successive airings of opposing positions, sometimes from people in different physical locations.

The fact that viewers do not need to participate in an exchange personally in order to be exposed to oppositional views has both advantages and disadvantages. When citizens are simply third-party observers of others' conflicting viewpoints, they may be able to observe more impartially and listen better than when they are in the thick of their own political discussion, possibly mentally preparing their next response to their adversary rather than truly listening to what the opposition has to say. Studies of what is known as the "extended contact effect" likewise suggest that face-to-face encounters may increase anxiety and suppress the potential positive effects of intergroup contact.[16] At the same time, the personal setting of face-to-face exchanges is often assumed to have a superior ability to make people pay attention to others' views and to seriously consider alternatives. To date this has been more of an assumption in deliberative theories than an empirical finding, however.

Of course, mere exposure to alternative perspectives is only a first step along the road to attributing legitimacy to opposing views. After viewing the typical point-counterpoint format of so much televised political discourse, do citizens remember the rationales for opposing issue arguments? Do they come away with a sense that the opposition has a legitimate basis for its views, or do viewers become still more convinced that the opposition is ill motivated and/or unjustifiable? Next I attempt to answer this question in the context of in-your-face political television.

IN-YOUR-FACE POLITICAL TELEVISION

To be sure, not all televised political conflict is cut of the same cloth. So what are the implications of the in-your-face style for television's ability to encourage perceptions of a legitimate opposition? Even in the widely idealized face-to-face context, disagreements tend to be tense situations that do not always result in acknowledgment of the legitimacy of others' positions. Granting legitimacy to those with whom one has significant differences of opinion is a complex and cognitively difficult task. To comprehend the logic and motivation behind views that are not one's own is an effortful, multistep process.[17] Incivility and close-ups may make this potential benefit less likely.

But surely such exposure can't hurt? As demonstrated in Chapter 2, the incivility and close-ups that characterize in-your-face political discourse heighten arousal and strengthen open-ended recall. But do viewers also come away with an enhanced appreciation for the merits of the other side as a result of their viewing? Unfortunately, if television is anything like the real world, then previous research points precisely in the opposite direction when it comes to in-your-face-style political discussions. The reason for this is, at root, the same

Figure 3.1. The push for less physical distance between Republicans and Democrats in State of the Union seating

reason that in-your-face politics is beneficial for attention and recall: the importance of distance in how people react to one another.

In certain respects, it is obvious that we draw inferences about people from their physical closeness to one another. Take, for example, the new pattern of seating at State of the Union speeches, initiated in the wake of the shooting of Representative Giffords. Traditionally Republicans and Democrats had sat on opposite sides of the aisle for the speech, close to their like-minded partisans. As shown in Figure 3.1, beginning in 2011, they started what has become known as "date night," in which most lawmakers purposely sit in mixed company for the speech. As Senator Lisa Murkowski explained it, "This is an opportunity for us, as lawmakers, to demonstrate that we can be civil with one another."

It is both fascinating and noteworthy that political disagreement brings with it the assumption that two people could not possibly sit right next to one another. Close physical proximity simply does not jibe with the idea of intense partisan differences. Although some of the earlier enthusiasm for the bipartisan State of the Union seating arrangement has flagged, and it is widely acknowledged to be merely a symbolic gesture, it is nonetheless telling that spatial proximity communicates information about people's relationships to one another. Of course, as the cartoon in Figure 3.2 demonstrates, many made fun of the effort as well. Sitting next to one another for a couple of hours on a single day once a year is nowhere near as difficult as building genuine respect for oppositional views.

Nonetheless, research on face-to-face interaction confirms that the distance between two people has important consequences for how people react to one another. For example, in one study bogus questionnaire results were used to convince an experimental subject that a confederate he was about to meet held political views that were either quite similar to or dissimilar from his own views.[18] In addition to being randomly assigned a like-minded or non-like-minded confederate, when the confederate came into the room, he was also randomly assigned to sit either right next to or across the table from the subject. Not surprisingly, subjects reported liking the confederate they thought to be similar to themselves more than the one thought to hold differing views, despite the fact that politics was not discussed. More important for purposes of my research, when the

"IT'S ENCOURAGING TO SEE THAT MEMBERS OF BOTH PARTIES HAVE CROSSED THE AISLE TO SIT WITH ONE ANOTHER TONIGHT..."

Figure 3.2. The push back: limits of bipartisan seatmates
Illustration by R. J. Matson, © St. Louis Post-Dispatch

confederate sat unusually close to the subject, violating the norms for personal space, physical distance interacted with perceived political agreement so that a politically similar person who sat close was even better liked, and a dissimilar person who sat close was even more strongly disliked.[19]

The process of influence responsible for this effect appears to be one in which increased arousal results from the close proximity of another human being, and other external cues are relied upon for the cognitive interpretation of that arousal.[20] For example, if a subject is positively predisposed toward a person who moves closer to her, she will experience even stronger positive feelings as a result of the arousal. If she is negatively predisposed toward the person, then arousal will result in stronger negative feelings.

Dissimilarity breeds dislike, and closeness generally intensifies whatever kind of reaction—positive or negative—a person has to another person or object. This intensification of affect is produced by the greater arousal that physical closeness produces.[21] Higher arousal levels signal a greater intensity of emotional reaction, and the valence of the person or object—whether liked or disliked—produces the valence that is assigned to that intensification.

By now, this pattern has been well documented in the realm of face-to-face interactions. When people disagree with someone in real life, the tendency is to back off and put greater distance between the self and the person of opposing views. In contrast, as political conflicts intensify on television, the cameras do not necessarily back off. This creates a highly unnatural experience for the viewers because they are forced to view the televised person from a very intimate perspective, one that would be highly unlikely to occur with a person they dislike in any real-world scenario.

If this same logic extends to television, it suggests that physical distance—even when manipulated as the mere appearance of distance—will intensify people's positive or negative reactions to the political actors they see on television. Although this specific hypothesis has not yet been examined, in a related study of the effects of apparent spatial distance as manipulated through media, results pointed in that same general direction. In an experiment showing subjects videotaped talking faces in which perceived viewer distance was varied, attitudes toward the simulated close faces were more intense than attitudes toward the same faces in the distant conditions, and this was especially true when distance was manipulated via close-up versus distant camera shots.[22]

What does political television's tendency to violate everyday norms of civility and personal space imply about its ability to serve as a source of exposure to a legitimate opposition? To the extent that political advocates of the opposing side create the impression of being uncomfortably close when featured in televised discourse, and/or unusually impolite, viewers should experience higher levels of emotional arousal, which should enhance attention to content and promote greater awareness of oppositional perspectives. At the same time, heightened arousal should intensify whatever affect a viewer holds, thus producing greater dislike for an already disliked political advocate.

From a more positive, constructive angle, this theoretical framework also specifies the conditions under which televised discourse might improve perceptions of the perceived legitimacy of the opposition. To the extent that televised political discourse is able to draw viewer attention, without intensifying opponents' already negative views toward one another, greater oppositional legitimacy should result. So under what conditions should exposure to televised political discourse have positive versus negative or neutral consequences for perceptions of the legitimacy of the opposition? I describe these expectations in terms of hypotheses about recall, attitudes toward the oppositional candidate, and the perceived legitimacy of oppositional issue arguments.

In addition to hypotheses about the impact of civil as opposed to uncivil discourse, and close-up versus medium camera perspectives, in this chapter I also offer predictions about the effects of exposure relative to no exposure at all, that is, compared to a control group's level of knowledge of these issues and awareness of rationales for their own as well as oppositional political positions. The participants randomly assigned to the control group watched a nonpolitical program (on improving basketball free throw shooting) for the same amount of time that the treatment groups watched the candidates debate. A control group is important for purposes of situating these effects in a real-world context. If in-your-face politics does, in fact, create some of the negative externalities that I have predicted, it is important to know whether people are better or worse off relative to not watching any political television at all. The control group makes such conclusions possible.

PROPOSED EFFECTS

Relative to not watching at all, I expected televised exposure to oppositional perspectives to enhance the extent to which viewers were aware of oppositional arguments, regardless of the way in which these views were presented. The logic of this expectation is straightforward: no matter how arguments are presented, exposure to political discourse cannot reduce the level of awareness people have of arguments promoted by disliked candidates or about the rationales for what seem to them disagreeable policy positions. So viewers are likely to become more aware of oppositional perspectives from viewing. In addition, heightened arousal should increase levels of recall. Thus the same independent variables that increase arousal—incivility and close-up camera perspectives—also should enhance awareness of oppositional rationales that are heard via television.

At the same time, the increased arousal from in-your-face discourse also should intensify the negative affect viewers have for disliked people and issue positions. So, when political advocates promote viewpoints with which a viewer disagrees, and do so in an in-your-face manner (i.e., uncivil discourse viewed from an intimate camera perspective), such presentations should detract from the legitimacy that viewers accord those oppositional perspectives. Just as in the face-to-face psychology experiment where lack of distance intensified people's reactions to the confederate, non-like-minded people and policies should be even less well liked when viewers are forced to experience disagreeable views from a highly intimate, in-your-face perspective. Likewise, well-liked people and their perspectives should be even more positively regarded as a result of the up-close and personal perspective.

Finally, I also predicted that close-up camera perspectives would interact with levels of civility. Relative to not watching at all, or to a medium camera perspective, close-up camera perspectives should intensify viewers' reactions to opposing political arguments and candidates. When political conflict is presented in civil fashion, viewers will see those arguments in favor of the opposition as even more legitimate, whereas viewers who witness an uncivil exchange will perceive the opposition as having even less of a legitimate rationale for their views than they would have otherwise. The combination of incivility and close spatial proximity should be especially powerful in its double violation of social norms.

MEASURING EXPOSURE TO AND RESPECT FOR THE OPPOSITION

Three indicators related to the political opposition were analyzed in this experiment. First, I measured *affect toward the least liked candidate*. In the posttest, respondents were asked for which of the two candidates they would vote if they were voting in this congressional district. The candidate who was not chosen became their least liked candidate. The value attached to this measure was based on subjects' feeling thermometer rating of the candidate for whom they said they would be least likely to vote. For the sake of comparison, *affect toward the most liked candidate* was also examined by experimental condition in order to evaluate whether those in the civil/close-up condition enjoyed an additional boost in positivity as a result of the arousal produced by this treatment.

For a political process to create legitimacy, it must foster preferences for one candidate without demonizing the opposition. When people retain a degree of respect for the opposing candidate, they support the notion of a legitimate opposition. The attitudes people hold toward their nonoptimal candidates matter because some portion of the time they can expect their government leaders to be other than their preferred candidates.[23] Given that people react negatively to those with whom they disagree, and given that closeness intensifies this reaction, I predicted that respondents would react particularly negatively to the least liked candidate when that person violated norms for civility and distance.

In addition, *awareness of rationales for oppositional positions* was measured using open-ended recall measures from the posttests, which asked respondents to write down all arguments they could remember the candidates having made in support of, or in opposition to, a given issue position. Respondents were asked, "What are some of the reasons people are in support of [stated position]? Please write as many reasons as you can think of in the box below." Unlike the candidate feeling thermometers utilized above, these measures existed for treatment conditions and for the control group that viewed a nonpolitical video. Because these were actual public issues in the news at the time, subjects had opinions on the controversies, so the control group was used to establish rationales people would have been able to generate without watching any political television.

For all respondents, separate measures were created corresponding to arguments on the side they opposed or favored in the posttest, in other words, the number of legitimate arguments respondents could generate for the "other" side, as well as their own side.[24] Although simple knowledge of oppositional arguments is not the same thing as granting legitimacy to oppositional views, having some awareness of arguments on the other side is an important prerequisite to granting them legitimacy.

A third measure, *perceptions of the legitimacy of the opposition*, involved a series of closed-ended questions more directly assessing respondents' perceptions of the legitimacy of the two candidates' arguments. After completing the open-ended portion of the questionnaire, participants were asked to judge the general strengths and weaknesses of a list of arguments, *regardless of the respondents' own personal views on the issue*. For each of the four issue segments they viewed, the closed-ended items listed six of the arguments that were featured in the program (three made by each candidate). Subjects were then asked to label each argument as a "very strong argument, a somewhat strong argument, a somewhat weak argument, or a very weak argument."

People naturally rated the arguments in support of their own side of an issue as significantly stronger than those on the other side. But what matters for purposes of this analysis is whether in-your-face politics alters the level of legitimacy accorded to the opposition. This series of items was used to create indexes indicating respondents' overall assessments of the *legitimacy of arguments for favored positions*, as well as the *legitimacy of arguments on the opposing side*. Subjects in control and treatment groups rated the legitimacy of all arguments. The scales used to tap these three dependent variables all achieved respectable levels of reliability (see Appendix B).

HOW IN-YOUR-FACE POLITICS AFFECTS AWARENESS OF AND RESPECT FOR THE OPPOSITION

Can viewing a twenty-minute television program significantly affect levels of respect for the opposition? Drawing on findings from Experiment II, Figure 3.3 begins addressing this question using the feeling thermometer ratings for each respondent's least liked candidate broken down by the four experimental treatments. A two by two analysis of variance indicated a significant interaction between civility and camera perspective. As shown in Figure 3.3, in the medium camera conditions, levels of incivility did not affect how respondents felt about the least liked candidate. However, when featured in close-up, incivility reduced the extent of warmth that viewers felt for the opposition by more than ten thermometer degrees. Interestingly, there was no significant effect of either experimental treatment on attitudes toward the candidate that each respondent favored.

These findings suggest an important asymmetry in how viewers respond. They had negative reactions to in-your-face incivility on the part of the candidate they disliked, but not in reaction to the candidate they liked. For the favored candidate, incivility was apparently seen as justified indignation; of course he was annoyed by the things his opponent was saying! But when the other candidate acted similarly, viewers thought systematically less of him for his social transgressions.

Because of the attention-grabbing powers of arousal, I predicted that recall of oppositional views would be superior in the in-your-face conditions, just as it was for overall recall. As shown in Figure 3.4, regardless of whether one considers knowledge of arguments

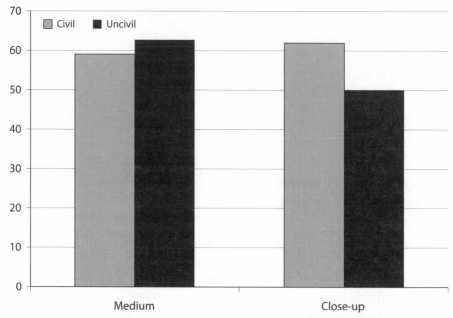

Figure 3.3. Effects of civility and camera perspective on thermometer rating of least liked candidate

Note: Two factor analysis of variance indicated a significant interaction between civility and camera perspective ($F = 4.84, p < .05$). Findings are from Experiment II.

supporting one's own or others' issue positions, the patterns are virtually identical. Recall of arguments was enhanced by the same factors that enhance arousal: incivility and a close-up camera perspective. Using a two by two analysis of variance crossing civility and camera perspective, the interaction of incivility and close-up camera perspective was significant for awareness of oppositional issue arguments ($F = 4.36, p < .05$). For awareness of arguments on one's own side, only incivility significantly enhanced recall ($F = 5.13, p < .05$), although the pattern is very similar to that seen on the left-hand side of Figure 3.4. The uncivil, close-up conditions consistently stand out in producing higher levels of recall.

Turning next to mean comparisons with the striped control conditions in the center of the panels, there is clear evidence that viewers learned something about the issue controversies from watching the program. In Figure 3.4, awareness of issue arguments on one's own side is improved by the experimental versions of the program, regardless of whether viewers watched civil or uncivil, close-up or medium versions. Those who watched knew more than those who did not. All planned contrasts between each of these groups relative to the control condition were significant ($p < .05$).

On one hand, this finding is simply consistent with previous evidence of television's capacity to inform the electorate; people learned something from watching.[25] But it also supports the notion that television may play an important role in educating the public on the views of people outside their immediate environments, and on the arguments these others use to support their oppositional positions. These findings are basically supportive of the idea that televised public discourse may play an important role in making people aware of

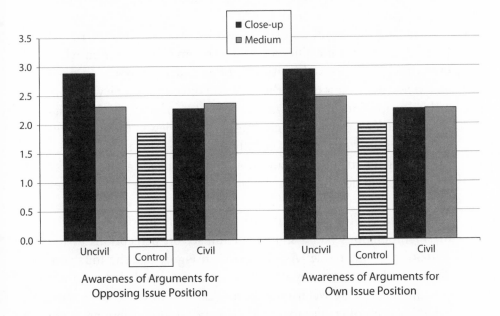

Figure 3.4. Effects of civility and camera perspective on awareness of arguments for own and opposing issue positions

Note: Based on a 2 by 2 analysis of variance, the interaction of incivility and close-up camera perspective was significant for awareness of arguments for opposing issue positions ($F = 4.36, p < .05$). For awareness of arguments on one's own side, only incivility significantly enhanced recall ($F = 5.13, p < .05$). All planned contrasts between each of the experimental groups relative to the control condition were significant ($p < .05$). Findings are from Experiment II.

oppositional issue perspectives, and possibly in legitimizing oppositional political perspectives.

Relative to the control group, the people who watched televised
political discourse came away from the experience better able to recount the other side's arguments as well as their own. One would
hope that this result translates into a sense that theirs is not the only
legitimate way to think about the political world. But open-ended
recall is clearly not the same as perceiving those oppositional arguments to be legitimate reasons. For this purpose, I compared means
for the direct assessments of the perceived legitimacy of arguments
made on both sides. For this measure, respondents were given a set
of statements arguing for various sides of these controversies, and
evaluated each one individually, and were then sorted by whether
the advocated position was consistent with or in opposition to the
respondent's own view on the issue.

Analyzing these indexes using a two by two analysis of variance,
I found no significant differences by experimental condition when
examining the perceived legitimacy of arguments supporting one's
own views. Regardless of whether political discourse was viewed from
a close or medium perspective, and regardless of whether the political advocates were civil or uncivil, respondents viewed the arguments
supporting their own side as equally legitimate. This result parallels
the finding for attitudes toward most and least liked candidates. The
treatments had no discernible effect on what respondents knew they
liked.

However, as with my findings on attitudes toward the candidates,
the manipulations had a significant impact on perceptions of the
value of the "other side." As illustrated in Figure 3.5, the four conditions within the two by two factorial design produced a significant interaction between civility and camera distance ($F = 6.41$,
$p < .05$). Levels of civility mattered a great deal to perceptions of the
legitimacy of oppositional views when subjects viewed the uncivil
exchange in one of the close-up conditions. This interaction demonstrates that when viewed up close and personal, people found the
very same arguments espoused in the civil version of the debate more
legitimate than those in the uncivil one. If viewed from a medium
camera perspective, civility made no difference.

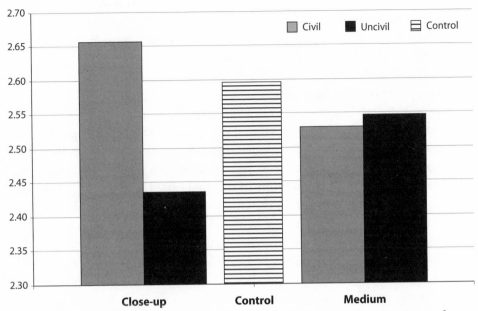

Figure 3.5. Effects of civility and camera perspective on the perceived legitimacy of opposing arguments

Note: A 2 by 2 factorial design (omitting control) produced a significant interaction between civility and camera distance ($F = 6.41, p < .05$). Planned comparisons demonstrated that the mean in the control condition was statistically indistinguishable from the means for both of the medium conditions on the right-hand side of the figure. But on the left-hand side, the mean of the close-up uncivil condition indicated significantly less perceived legitimacy than the control condition, and the mean for the close-up civil condition indicated significantly greater perceived legitimacy relative to the control condition (omnibus $F = 7.10, p < .01$; contrast between civil and control, $p < .01$; contrast between uncivil and control, $p < .001$). Findings are from Experiment II.

The presence of the control condition shown in the center of Figure 3.5 makes it possible to assess whether watching this program helped or hurt the perceived legitimacy of arguments on the other side relative to not watching at all. Planned comparisons relative to the control group suggest that the mean in the control condition is statistically indistinguishable from the means for both of the medium conditions on the right-hand side of Figure 3.5. But on the left-hand side, the mean of the close-up uncivil condition illustrates significantly *less* perceived legitimacy than the control condition, and the mean for the close-up civil condition indicates significantly *greater* perceived legitimacy relative to the control condition (omnibus $F = 7.10$, $p < .01$; contrast between civil and control, $p < .01$; contrast between uncivil and control, $p < .001$).

These comparisons make it possible to draw conclusions about the effects of viewing different styles of televised political discourse relative to not watching at all. Even though subjects in the close-up and medium conditions viewed precisely the same exchange, the perceived proximity of the politicians led to less favorable evaluations of the disagreeable issue arguments in the uncivil exchange, and more favorable evaluations in the civil one. These results nicely mirror previous findings on the intensifying effect of physical proximity in face-to-face situations. When disagreeable issue positions are espoused by a civil person in close-up, they are viewed as *more* legitimate than they otherwise would be. When disagreeable positions are espoused by an uncivil person, they are viewed as *less* legitimate than they otherwise would be.

To summarize the results of Experiment II, these findings suggest that televised political discourse—of virtually any type—does have the capacity to improve citizens' *awareness* of rationales for oppositional views. But in-your-face politics is, indeed, a double-edged sword. On the one hand, the intimacy of the television camera can enhance the perceived legitimacy of those oppositional views when they are presented in a civil manner. But when they are presented in an uncivil manner, that same intimacy convinces people that the opposition is even less legitimate than they would have thought without viewing any political television whatsoever.

Thus far the findings I have presented on oppositional legitimacy are limited to results from one large-scale experiment. Although the findings form a consistent pattern, any one set of experimental results can be subject to peculiarities in the specific treatments used, the subjects who participated, or random chance. Thus to assess the generalizability of these findings to other populations and issue conflicts, another between-subjects experiment was conducted with a different set of issues. Experiment III was designed to replicate the important between-group findings in Experiment II. To reduce the number of subjects required, participants were randomly exposed to one of only two conditions this time, either close-up versions of civil discourse or close-up versions of uncivil discourse. Given that these were the two conditions that produced consistent significant differences in Experiment II, a similar pattern of results in Experiment III would lend greater confidence to these findings. The measures used were parallel to Experiment II, with the wording changed to reflect the different issues the candidates discussed.

Figure 3.6 analyzes the results of Experiment III to see whether subjects in the uncivil/close-up condition systematically evaluated their least favored candidate more negatively than subjects in the civil/

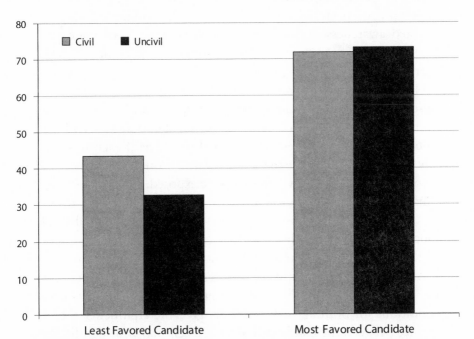

Figure 3.6. Effects of close-up/civility on thermometer ratings of preferred and least liked candidate

Note: Analysis of variance indicated no significant difference between civil and uncivil conditions for the most favored candidate ($F = 0.21, p = .65$), but a significant difference between conditions for the least favored candidate ($F = 6.17, p < .01$). The size of the gaps between individuals' evaluations of their least and most favored candidates also were significantly different by condition ($F = 5.14, p < .05$). Findings are from Experiment III.

close-up condition, as was the case in Experiment II. As illustrated, there was no difference in affect toward the candidate each subject liked the most as a result of viewing them behaving in a civil versus uncivil exchange. However, the opposition was judged systematically more negatively in the uncivil condition relative to the civil one. Uncivil behavior on the part of one's *own* side is dismissed as mere righteous indignation in the face of an uncivil opponent; but when the other side engages in similar behavior, it is a sign of their depravity.

Again using items parallel to those used in Experiment II, I next examined effects of incivility on sheer awareness of arguments for own and opposing issue positions. Here, the results using the close-up conditions demonstrated the same pattern as in Figure 3.4 for the close-up conditions. As shown in Figure 3.7, incivility significantly boosted awareness of arguments for respondents' own issue positions, and it had an especially large impact on awareness of arguments for opposing issue positions.

Next, I examined the pattern of results for recognition recall as opposed to open-ended recall of rationales for own and oppositional opinions. As described in Chapter 2, a series of quotes was attributed to each candidate, and respondents had to decide if each was actually said by that candidate in the program. The quotes were balanced across the four issues to which they were exposed, and across the two candidates, and respondents received a point for each correct answer. Recognition recall is known to be easier than open-ended recall. Once prompted with what a candidate said, respondents are more likely to remember it than if they must generate it from scratch.

Although the findings were consistently in the same direction as the open-ended result, that is, showing greater recall in the uncivil conditions for both agreeable and disagreeable arguments, the difference between the conditions did not reach statistical significance. Out of a total of forty possible correct answers, the average score was twenty-nine, so ceiling effects were not responsible for this finding. I suspect, instead, that between-group differences were not as crisp because of the way in which arousal improves memory for program content. High arousal levels may cause people to pay more attention to the program, which should improve either kind of memory. But that is not the only way in which arousal precipitates memory.

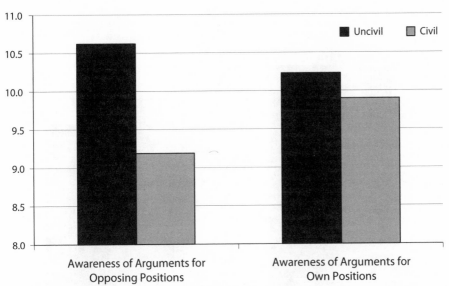

Figure 3.7. Effects of civility on awareness of arguments for own and opposing issue positions

Note: Analysis of variance indicated significant differences between civil and uncivil conditions for awareness of own positions ($F = 4.57, p < .05$), as well as opposing issue positions ($F = 6.58, p < .01$), but the gap was significantly larger in the latter case. Findings are from Experiment III.

In making information more vivid by associating it with emotional intensity, it increases the accessibility of the memory and makes it more likely to come to the top of the mind—thus improving open-ended recall in particular.

Figure 3.8 examines the direct assessments subjects made of the legitimacy of arguments that were presented to them. Arguments on their own side of the issue were consistently perceived to be more legitimate, as always. Moreover, the impact of incivility was consistent with the result of the previous experiment; in both cases, those who viewed the uncivil version of the program were significantly less likely to rate arguments supporting opposing positions as legitimate relative to those who viewed the civil version. The perceived legitimacy of arguments on their own side of the issue was not significantly affected by incivility. Relative to a civil broadcast, people come away from watching in-your-face politics thinking the opposition has even less of a legitimate basis for its differing views.

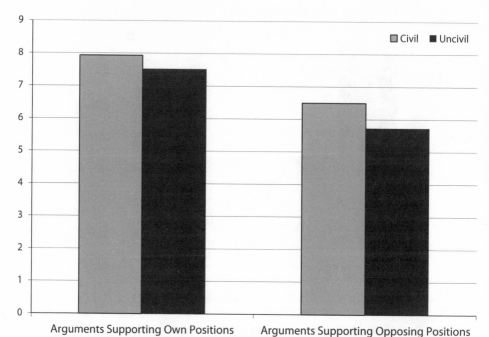

Figure 3.8. Effects of civility on perceptions of the legitimacy of own and opposing issue arguments

Note: Analysis of variance indicated no significant difference between civil and uncivil conditions in the legitimacy attributed to arguments supporting own positions ($F = 1.63, p = .21$), but a significant difference between conditions for the perceived legitimacy of arguments supporting opposing positions ($F = 3.49, p < .05$).

REMEMBERING MORE, BUT RESPECTING IT LESS

Based on these studies, people do appear to learn from political television, and this includes learning about why others hold the opinions that they do. Subjects recalled significantly more rationales for oppositional views than they would have otherwise as a result of viewing even highly uncivil political discourse. For those citizens who find it difficult to fathom how others might reasonably hold views other than their own—an increasingly sizable group according to many sources—televised political discourse is undoubtedly serving an important purpose.

These memory effects are probably encouraged by the kind of lively repartee that often characterizes today's political programs. Close-up perspectives on uncivil exchanges of political views are arousing for viewers to watch, and thus help to draw audiences to these programs, as well as to encourage attention and retention while viewing. To be sure, levels of attention are likely to be abnormally high in a laboratory setting, so the levels of recall reported here would be somewhat less impressive in real-world viewing settings. On the other hand, civil and uncivil political programs would probably not draw equally sized audiences in the real world either; uncivil programs would draw larger audiences and thus have the potential to educate more viewers about oppositional views. Generalizability issues could thus cut both ways when projecting these findings to real-world contexts.

When seen exclusively from the perspective of attention and memory, televised political discourse would seem to be in the service of an informed, deliberative body politic. People may not be conversing with friends or neighbors who hold opposing views so much, but at least they hear about them on television. As the control group comparisons suggest, any exposure is better than nothing when it comes to what people know about why the political opposition feels the way it does.

But the problem with this optimistic assessment becomes apparent when the analysis turns to people's *attitudes* toward those same candidates and opposing issue arguments. Incivility alone does not dampen enthusiasm for political advocates, nor for the arguments they make. However, when incivility and close-up camera perspectives combine to produce the unique in-your-face perspective, the high levels of arousal and attention come at the cost of lowering regard for the other side.

The intimacy of uncivil political discourse on television discourages the kind of mutual respect that might sustain perceptions of a *legitimate* opposition. Here the pattern of findings is quite consistent; close-up perspectives on uncivil discourse routinely damage perceptions of the candidates and issue arguments that subjects are already prone to dislike, that is, attitudes toward the *least* liked candidate, and the perceived legitimacy of rationales for *opposing* issue positions.[26] The same pattern of effects did not occur for attitudes toward the preferred candidate, nor for perceptions of the legitimacy of arguments for the preferred issue position. The overall effect of these two patterns is to increase the magnitude of the difference that is perceived between one's own side and the opposition.

From one perspective, this pattern might call for downplaying the real-world significance of these findings; after all, what difference does it make if people have even greater dislike for candidates or ideas that they are already inclined to oppose? But the implications are important because of the need for people to be aware of, and hold some degree of respect for, people and views other than their most preferred choices. In short, these differences matter for the legitimacy of any multiparty, pluralist system. A willingness to acknowledge that there is something to be said for the other side, even when one's own views do not prevail, is essential to the kind of legitimacy that allows a democratic political system to remain stable.[27]

Do these findings suggest that characteristics of contemporary political television may encourage mass polarization? The answer to this question depends upon how one defines polarization. The evidence does not speak to the notion of citizens endorsing increasingly extreme issue positions. But to many scholars, what these experiments demonstrate is precisely what political polarization is all about. As Wilson defines it, "Such a condition is revealed when a candidate for public office is regarded by a competitor and his supporters not simply as wrong but as corrupt or wicked; when one way of thinking about the world is assumed to be morally superior to any other way; when one set of political beliefs is considered to be entirely correct, and a rival set wholly wrong."[28] In this sense of the term, the intimacy and confrontational nature of contemporary political television does, indeed, encourage mass polarization. Citizens may not have more extreme views about their own policy preferences, but they are convinced that the opposition is completely unworthy and illegitimate. As humorist Dave Barry pondered, "Do we truly believe that ALL red-state residents are ignorant racist fascist knuckle-dragging NASCAR-obsessed cousin-marrying road-kill-eating tobacco-juice-dribbling gun-fondling religious fanatic rednecks; or that ALL blue-state residents are godless unpatriotic pierced-nose Volvo-driving

France-loving left-wing Communist latte-sucking tofu-chomping holistic-wacko neurotic vegan weenie perverts?"[29] Sadly, for many Americans, the answer to this question is a resounding yes.

These results also hint at possible historical changes in the way citizens respond to candidates and political advocates in an age of televisual politics, a topic I explore in greater depth in Chapters 7 and 8. Although there is widespread agreement among political pundits that television has changed American politics in some fundamental way, scholars have been hard-pressed to figure out and document exactly how television is different from other media in its political implications.[30] When early content analyses showed that television's political content was basically the same as that of newspapers, proponents of television's exceptionalism had to take note. Likewise, there continues to be no compelling evidence that television is more effective in persuading viewers than print media.

But the content of television is more than merely the words spoken. When viewers develop a sense of intimacy with public figures whom they have never met, and with whom they may have emphatic disagreements, strong emotions are not surprising. Visual intimacy and the arousal it brings with it serve to intensify feelings. Thus one of the legacies of political television may be to discourage the quaint notion of a "worthy opposition." To the extent that televised political discourse intensifies feelings about political advocates, it does not serve the goals of consensus or compromise.

These findings validate the important role that emotion plays in understanding the processing of political television. The effects observed in these studies depend upon gut-level affective reactions. As anyone who has been cornered by a disagreeable person at a cocktail party knows, this experience tends to be unpleasant at best. The natural reaction for most is to flee such individuals as soon as possible. It is one thing if the person is espousing his or her disagreeable views on the other side of the room, and quite another if he or she insists on doing so at close range. So although television may carry the same information as any other medium, the emotional impact of televised political discourse is probably quite different from what one would expect from a print source, and different as well from television that frames public figures at more of a distance. Television replicates the sound and sight of human experience so that today's political advocates can, for better or worse, truly be in our faces.

The appearance of spatial proximity is clearly important; however, it is worth noting that the sense of threat experienced by television viewers is not likely to be a cognitive acknowledgment of some real threat. After all, few people in the United States would claim they feel imminent danger from a politician on a television screen. Instead, it is a subconscious feeling of threat based on the perception of being physically very close to someone who is disagreeable, and who thus presents an unwelcome invasion of personal space.[31] By creating a facsimile of real-world visual experience, the visual element of television encourages "gut reactions" on the part of viewers, emotional reactions that are not mediated by cognitive assessments.[32]

Precisely because people respond in fundamentally social ways to televised human interactions, the routine violations of social norms in political television have consequences. Being polite to others is not just an arbitrary social norm; it is a means of demonstrating mutual respect. Politicians violating norms for civility and distance, even if only for the sake of more lively television, negatively influences the perceived legitimacy of the other side. So while some forms of political television at least give people more respect for the opposition than they would have otherwise, other forms actually do significant damage relative to watching apolitical programming.

CHAPTER 4

THE COSTS OF IN-YOUR-FACE POLITICS FOR POLITICAL TRUST

The consequences of in-your-face politics appear to be a mixed bag. On the one hand, it draws viewer attention and improves memory for political content. These are valuable contributions. On the other hand, it appears to make people think less of people and ideas with which they do not agree. These effects are rooted in psychological processes of which people are not consciously aware when they watch. Arousal intensifies their already negative views of people and ideas they dislike, thus creating still more intense disaffection. Interestingly, viewers and television producers both seem unaware that it matters how unnaturally close politicians appear to be on television, or that this affects people's reactions, but many of the undesirable effects of incivility are contingent upon or moderated by the sense of spatial closeness people feel to those on the television screen.

In this chapter, I suggest that people may also react to incivility for entirely different, more straightforward reasons. After all, as discussed in Chapter 1, people are all too aware of the banality of shout shows they see on television, and they have made their disgust for this practice well known. They notice that politicians don't act like normal people discussing politics in their day-to-day lives. If there is consensus that politicians and political advocates are not behaving admirably, then perhaps incivility in political discourse also affects public regard for politics and politicians more generally, despite its lack of any apparent effects on attitudes toward individual favored politicians.[1] Alternatively, it is plausible that a certain amount of rancorous debate is part and parcel of what citizens have now come to expect from political advocates on television. Watching politicians and pundits hurl insults at one another on television could be merely a harmless pastime, or it could have consequences for how people think about politics and government.

To American citizens observing the political process, politics appears to be all about acrimonious debate. If political conflict is aired openly in an uncivil fashion, can citizens be expected to maintain respect for politics and politicians? Televised portrayals of political conflict have received a particularly severe beating, with some pointing to media reports highlighting conflict as a source of greater political cynicism.[2] More general theories suggesting that television bears some responsibility for negative attitudes toward politics and politicians have received enthusiastic receptions over the years. In the 1970s, Robinson popularized the term "videomalaise" to refer to negative public attitudes that resulted from watching television news.[3] Evidence in support of the original videomalaise claim was based on a quasi-experimental study of effects from viewing one particular television program. In a subsequent study, content analyses of the three major network news programs showed that negative coverage predominated.[4] Although evidence of effects from this content remained thin thereafter, an overview of research on television and politics in the early 1980s echoed the popularity of this thesis, concluding that political television "has altered the culture significantly by intensifying ordinary Americans' traditional low opinion of politics and politicians, by exacerbating the decline in their trust and confidence in their government and its institutions."[5]

Some observers have suggested that the root of the problem is the cynicism of game-centered political news coverage; by emphasizing the strategy and tactics behind campaigns, journalists contribute to an ongoing denigration of politicians' motives.[6] Others have argued that it is the conflict-oriented, adversarial nature of political coverage that lowers public esteem for politicians and government.[7] The timing of the well-documented decline in trust toward governmental institutions initially gave these theories great plausibility, but documenting a causal link between watching political television and negative attitudes toward politics and government has proven quite difficult. Despite the widespread belief that television has something to do with low levels of political trust, evidence supporting this causal claim has been very limited.

In this chapter I hypothesize that when political actors engage in televised interactions that violate the norms for everyday, face-to-face discourse, they reaffirm viewers' sense that politicians cannot be counted on to obey the same norms for social behavior by which ordinary citizens abide. After all, to trust is to assume that a person or institution will "observe the rules of the game,"[8] and to believe that those involved will act "as they should."[9] But what does that imply in the context of televised political disagreement? Does this mean that people expect political actors who appear on television to abide by the same social norms acknowledged by ordinary Americans? When political actors violate interpersonal social norms on television, do viewers react as they would if they were witnessing the same interaction in real life?

In face-to-face settings where people disagree about politics, there are strong social norms likely to be observed for purposes of these interactions. Face-to-face exchanges are relatively polite. Although people occasionally yell at one another and stomp their feet over political differences, such behavior is far more common in mediated presentations of political views. Norms involving politeness are extremely strong;[10] in fact, most people are polite most of the time. Civil and polite exchanges of opinion do occur on television, and screaming occasionally occurs in interpersonal discussions surrounding politics, but the central tendency in media is to highlight emotionally extreme and impolite expressions, whereas the central tendency in face-to-face communication is toward polite and emotionally controlled interactions.

Polite manners and other pleasantries may seem extraneous to political trust, but politeness is particularly needed when people are expressing controversial views. Of course, my hypothesis rests on the assumption that citizens' expectations are the same for televised politicians as for when conflict is face-to-face. As Reeves and Nass argue, "People expect media to obey a wide range of social and natural rules. All these rules come from the world of world of interpersonal interaction."[11] Although people may be well aware that different social norms characterize televised interactions, my hypothesis is that they nonetheless will respond to televised depictions of politicians based on norms for "real" life.

When encountering differences of opinion in person, the tendency is for people to downplay their differences and maintain a polite, cordial atmosphere; in contrast, mediated portrayals of political conflict emphasize strong differences of opinion, at least in part to enhance dramatic value and attract viewers. I suggest that this violation of social norms should cause more negative assessments of politicians and government. People expect others to obey social norms and evaluate them less favorably when they do not. When asked for global evaluations of politicians or government, if the politicians who first come to mind are ones who have violated social norms for civility, then people's evaluations will naturally be more negative.

Does this prediction contradict the ego-defensive pattern of findings in Chapter 3, where people did not punish the politician they liked best for his incivility? As is well known, one's own congressperson is consistently more praiseworthy than Congress as a whole.[12] Likewise, people compartmentalize personal and collective-level judgments about a wide range of phenomena.[13] So despite the previous pattern of findings, global evaluations of politicians as a group (as opposed to *my* preferred politician in particular) can become more negative as a result of incivility; in this case, people have no personal or partisan investment in evaluations of the category as a whole.

Should viewing politicians engaged in civil political discourse likewise raise the level of trust in government relative to not watching at all? Given that the normative expectation from the face-to-face world is civility, I hypothesized that effects on trust should be primarily a function of negative reactions to incivility, rather than positive reactions to civility. But this is obviously an empirical question.

In the results reported in this chapter, I explore two sets of hypotheses. First, I examine the impact of civility on widely used measures of trust in politicians, trust in Congress, and trust in the system of government more generally. Second, I evaluate the extent to which people's self-reported levels of discomfort with conflict moderate the impact of uncivil political discourse on trust. Unlike the automatic reactions people have based on their sense of distance from another person, people seem to be aware of their level of discomfort with conflict, at least in face-to-face contexts. Moreover, there are substantial individual differences in how uncomfortable people are with conflict. Using scales designed to tap these individual variations, I examine the extent to which discomfort with face-to-face conflict predicts people's reactions to televised incivility.

To examine these ideas, I drew on two laboratory experiments combined with representative national survey data. The experimental designs should be familiar from previous chapters, but in this case the focus is specifically on the impact of incivility on levels of political trust. By using experimental treatments that are not only randomly assigned, but also identical in terms of the political views expressed and the candidates featured, I avoid the possibility that other characteristics of the treatments are responsible for any observed differences in political trust.

As measures of political trust, I drew mainly on widely used questions from the American National Election Studies, though not exclusively so. To address all of the various types of trust that have been linked to political television, different sets of questions were included to form three separate political trust indexes. These tapped trust in politicians, trust in Congress, and trust in the political system. Although it is customary to define different kinds of trust by virtue of the target being trusted (the political system, politicians in power, etc.), these data suggest, consistent with Citrin and Muste's findings, that while the items used to measure political trust may have different target objects, they are of "dubious discriminant validity."[14] For this reason I do not claim to have measured empirically distinct concepts, nor does my theory make differential predictions in any case. However, because indicators have traditionally been grouped by target object, the same is done here in the initial analyses, and then I subsequently provide a pooled analysis that combines these three dimensions into a single index.

To reiterate, I predict that people will be more likely to say they distrust politicians if the politicians who are most salient in their minds at the time have been uncivil in their interactions with one another—even though this behavior could be considered commonplace for political television. When political advocates do not behave according to face-to-face social norms, viewers are reminded that politicians do not feel the need to abide by the same rules as everyone else. Norm violations should generate negative reactions, much as they do when people are exposed to such violations in real life.

THE IMPACT OF INCIVILITY ON POLITICAL TRUST

I began testing these hypotheses using the simplest possible experimental design, a simple two-group between-subjects comparison in which participants were randomly assigned to watch the civil or uncivil exchanges. As shown in Figure 4.1, all three trust measures were significantly influenced in a negative direction by the uncivil exchange. Trust in politicians became more negative, even though the content of the talk show made it clear that neither Bob Lindzey nor Neil Scott currently was, or had ever been, a member of Congress ($F = 10.35$, $p < .001$). Likewise, trust in Congress also became more negative after viewing only one 20-minute exposure ($F = 6.00$, $p < .01$). Finally, attitudes toward the American political system also were significantly, though far more modestly, influenced by the civility of discourse ($F = 3.12$, $p < .05$).

I have suggested that viewers are reacting to violations of social norms by politicians. But others have proposed what might seem a far simpler explanation: people simply dislike conflict, and they see it as particularly unnecessary when the answers to many political problems seem perfectly obvious to ordinary people.[15] Perhaps, then, what we observe in Figure 4.1 is incivility in public discourse leading people to lose respect for the idea that free and open debate is an important part of our political process. If people often see poor examples of how politicians engage in political disagreement, then attitudes toward conflict and its importance to the democratic system might naturally become more negative.

Two indexes tapping attitudes toward political conflict were used to evaluate this alternative; one tapped attitudes toward congressional debate (including items such as "Members of Congress bicker a lot more than they need to"), and the second index tapped attitudes

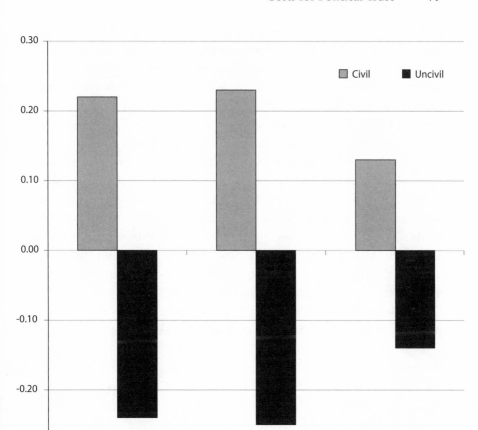

Figure 4.1. Effects of incivility on trust in politicians, Congress, and our system of government

Note: The civil and uncivil conditions were consistently significantly different in the expected direction ($F = 10.35, p < .01; F = 6.00, p < .01;$ and $F = 3.12, p < .05$). Findings are from Experiment III.

toward the importance of free and open political debate more generally (e.g., "It's very important that politicians air their differences of opinion publicly").

Surprisingly, the experimental treatment did not influence evaluations of conflict in either case. People apparently differentiated between the importance of public conflict—that is, the exchange of differing views, which remained constant across the two presentations—and the civility of that conflict, which varied significantly. Popular discussions often conflate the extent to which disagreement takes place with the civility of those interactions, thus confounding greater incivility with greater conflict. But in this study, neither the combined scales nor any one of the many individual items tapping attitudes toward conflict varied by experimental condition. As shown in Figure 4.2, the treatments had no effect on attitudes toward conflict more generally, regardless of whether I compared reliable indexes or individual survey items that seemed most likely to shift. The fact that viewers did not become more negative toward conflict lends support, albeit indirect, to the assertion that viewers' reactions stem from a negative reaction to incivility rather than disagreement, a norm that originates in face-to-face social norms, but that is applied to televised politicians as well.

In order to examine evidence bearing more directly on this hypothesis, I made use of an index of items included in the experiment

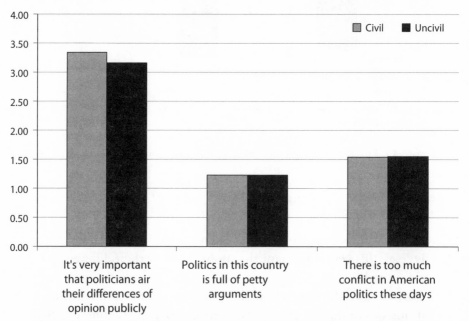

Figure 4.2. Effects of incivility on agreement with statements about political conflict
Note: The civil and uncivil conditions were not significantly different individually or as an index. Findings are from Experiment III.

pretest questionnaire as well as in my national survey data that assessed the extent to which individuals approach or avoid situations involving conflict in their everyday face-to-face discourse with others. The Conflict Approach/Avoidance Scale was developed to predict an individual's willingness to make interpersonal conflicts explicit. It is known to have high reliability levels, minimal social desirability bias, and predictive validity based on willingness to participate in conflict-related interventions, such as mediation. The scale is also sensitive to different cultural norms related to conflict-related communication.[16]

The items included in this scale tap the extent to which an individual enjoys challenging the opinions of others, feels upset after an argument, and so forth (see Appendix C for details). If people are reacting to televised political discourse in the same way they would face-to-face conflict, then this individual difference should exacerbate their reactions to incivility. But if watching politicians on television as purely a third-party observer bears no relation to how people react when they themselves are personally involved in disagreements, then reactions to televised political incivility should not be contingent on what makes them uncomfortable in interpersonal interactions.

In order to see if responses to civility and incivility are different for those with varying propensities to avoid conflict, the Conflict Approach/Avoidance Scale was divided into equal thirds of low, medium, and high levels of conflict avoidance. An analysis of variance evaluated the main effects of civility/incivility and of conflict avoidance, plus the interaction between conflict avoidance and civility. If the effects shown in Figure 4.1 are truly based on the same thing as aversion to face-to-face disagreements, then those most conflict-averse in face-to-face contexts should react most strongly to viewing televised uncivil discourse as well. For purposes of this analysis, the three measures of political trust were combined into a single index, given that they are highly correlated and generate identical patterns of results. Moreover, the reliability of the general index of political trust is higher than any of the individual indexes.

Figure 4.3 shows the differences in levels of political trust between the civil and the uncivil conditions, broken down by low, medium, and high levels of conflict avoidance. As suggested by this pattern, the analysis of variance model generated not only the significant main effect for civility that was already observed ($F = 10.37, p < .01$), but also a significant interaction between conflict avoidance and incivility ($F = 5.81, p < .01$).

As shown in Figure 4.3, the extent of difference between levels of political trust in the civil versus the uncivil condition was a function of individual differences in conflict avoidance. For those who are generally uncomfortable with face-to-face conflict, the uncivil condition generated much lower levels of political trust than the civil condition. For those with moderate levels of discomfort with conflict, there was a somewhat smaller differential. And for those who find disagreements somewhat enjoyable, the pattern was reversed in that the uncivil condition generated slightly higher levels of political trust than the uncivil one, though not significantly so. This pattern of results lends credence to my interpretation based on the impact of personally "experiencing" disagreement via television viewing. Even though viewers are obviously not personally involved in the political disagreements they view, they nonetheless react differently when others' televised disagreements violate face-to-face norms.

A second experiment was used to replicate and extend these findings. In this case, the candidates discussed a different set of four issues

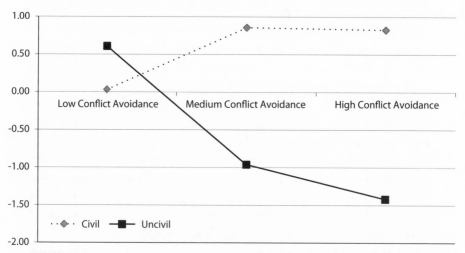

Figure 4.3. Effects of incivility on political trust by levels of conflict avoidance
Note: Means represent the size of the effect on trust (civil-uncivil presentation) by level of conflict avoidance. Findings are from Experiment III. Results from analysis of variance including civility (2) and conflict avoidance (3) demonstrated a significant main effect of incivility ($F = 10.37, p < .01$), as well as a significant interaction between conflict avoidance and incivility ($F = 5.81, p < .01$).

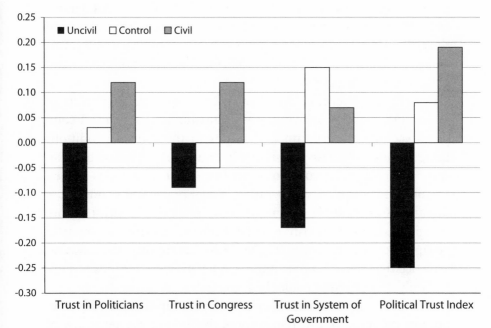

Figure 4.4. Effects of incivility on political trust

Note: Comparison of means produced consistently significant analysis of variance results: trust in politicians ($F = 3.86, p < .05$), trust in Congress ($F = 2.71, p < .05$), trust in system of government ($F = 2.96, p < .05$), political trust index ($F = 5.67, p < .05$). All uncivil and civil means are significantly different from one another at the $p < .05$ level. The only means significantly different from the control conditions are trust in system/uncivil and political trust index/uncivil. Findings are from Experiment III.

in the twenty-minute talk show to ensure that the results did not hinge on any one particular stimulus. But more important, the design was extended to include a control condition that viewed an unrelated video of the same length in addition to the civil and uncivil conditions. Using this design, it was possible to ascertain whether uncivil exchanges decrease trust in government relative to not watching at all, whether civil exchanges increase it, or both.

Figure 4.4 shows the means for the three separate indexes of political trust, plus the combined index, broken down by civil and uncivil conditions. First, it is worth noting that despite the fact that the issues discussed in these stimuli were different, the effects of incivility on political trust replicated nicely across all three indexes. The results are virtually identical to those found in Figure 4.1. The civil presentation resulted in significantly higher levels of political trust than the uncivil exchange of the same political views. This pattern extended to attitudes toward Congress, politicians in general, and the entire U.S. system of government ($F = 2.61$ and $p < .05$, $F = 3.84$ and $p < .05$, and $F = 3.13$ and $p < .05$, for Congress, politicians, and government, respectively).

In order to determine whether civility was increasing levels of political trust and/or incivility was decreasing levels of trust, I compared each of the experimental means to the control conditions using planned contrasts. As shown in Figure 4.4, although the general pattern of results for two of the three trust measures is suggestive of more positive assessments from civil presentations and more negative assessments from uncivil ones, comparisons with the control group means demonstrated that the differences from the control group were significant *only* for the uncivil conditions. There was no evidence that civil discourse improved people's impressions of politics, only that incivility made them worse.[17]

To confirm that the asymmetric control group comparisons were not just the result of low reliability in the indexes, the reliability of the dependent variable was improved by combining the three highly correlated sets of items into a single index of political trust. Even with the more reliable index, there still was no significant difference between the control condition and the civil condition, and the significant difference between the control and the uncivil condition remained the same.

This pattern is consistent with the idea that people expect civil behavior as the baseline. Although cognitively they may avow that the norm on television is incivility, their expectations are based on the world of interpersonal interaction, where civility is what is expected. Incivility creates important deviations from people's default assumptions. Thus the civil condition does not differ from the control condition, while the uncivil condition does.

More generally, my findings support the assertion that the effects of uncivil discourse on political trust are caused by television's departure from interpersonal social norms. Viewing a civil interaction leaves political trust unchanged, but viewing an uncivil interaction—even for a mere twenty minutes—significantly lowers levels of political trust relative to not viewing at all.

Based on this evidence, should one feel confident that viewers are reacting for the specific reasons posited? Does viewing an uncivil political disagreement produce more negative feelings because it violates norms for face-to-face discourse? Thus far three findings bolster this interpretation. First, this effect is most pronounced among those who try to avoid interpersonal conflict in their everyday lives, regardless of whether it is political. Second, this pattern is clearly not a function of the impact that the civility manipulation has on attitudes toward the importance of conflict per se; indeed the treatments have no effects on attitudes toward the desirability of political conflict. Even immediately after viewing a far-from-exemplary demonstration of the exchange of political differences, viewers are no more likely to see political conflict as petty, unnecessary bickering. Finally, it is incivility in particular, that is, the kind of behavior that departs from face-to-face expectations, that accounts for the negative effects observed. Unlike in Chapter 3, where civil exchanges raised the perceived legitimacy of opposition views, while incivility diminished them, when it comes to trust, the effects of incivility are clearly negative. People expect other people to act in a predictable manner, an expectation based on the world of face-to-face interaction, where civility is the norm. When political advocates do not act according to these expectations, they create negative reactions in viewers.

One simpler explanation is that incivility lowers the esteem with which viewers regard these specific candidates. Viewers think less of those who behave in an uncivil fashion, and these candidates, as representatives of the larger category of political advocates, lower the cumulative impression that viewers have of politics and politicians. As a formal test of this hypothesis, I quantified overall attitudes toward the two candidates (as measured by combined thermometer ratings for the two candidates) in both of these studies, and found that they were not systematically affected by incivility. If citizens were merely updating their views about politicians on the basis of these two men being seemingly less likable on the whole in the uncivil condition, then this is not the pattern of findings one would expect.

Instead, what appears to transpire is that when prompted to think about politicians and government more generally, citizens draw on accessible examples from recent exposure. When those examples involve uncivil exchanges that counter social norms, they think of politics as a dirtier business as a result. As shown in Chapter 3, they also think more negatively of the opposition when it acts in an uncivil manner, and this negativity may also spill over into general evaluations of politicians and government. In short, by being both attention-grabbing and memorable, uncivil political exchanges prime people to think about less savory, more strongly disliked examples of politicians and politics. This, in turn, prompts them to evaluate the whole enterprise more negatively.

My results thus far consistently suggest that incivility in televised political discourse has adverse effects on political trust. But contrary to the pattern of findings in Chapter 2, these results did not vary by camera perspective; they occurred whether the political exchange was shown through close-up or more distant camera perspectives. I suspect that this difference is because the process of influence is not gut-level and automatic when it comes to trust. In other words, people are well aware of the level of civility in the exchange they are watching, and they respond with disdain for the political system and its players more generally. Apparent distance, on the other hand, is not a treatment that respondents are cognizant of. The intensification of negative views brought on by high levels of physiological arousal happens without our awareness or engagement, whereas these effects of trust appear to be about the conscious judgments that viewers make.

DOES THE DAMAGE LAST?

The effects observed in this chapter are surprising, in part because of the brief nature of the stimulus—a twenty-minute television program. But they also defy the assumption that political trust is a more stable attribute of individuals, one that changes slowly and incrementally, if at all, or perhaps suddenly in the case of a startling news event such as the Watergate scandal in the 1970s. On the contrary, these results suggest a surprisingly high level of malleability in political trust. If even a brief exposure to political debate can produce these systematic changes, it is clearly more volatile than previously thought.

This extent of change in response to a short stimulus naturally leads to the question of whether laboratory-induced effects persist over time. Fortunately, one of these experiments provided an opportunity to examine this question. Subjects were asked at the time of their participation if they would consent to a follow-up phone call at home after the experiment itself, and just over 60 percent of the subjects agreed and provided phone numbers where they could be reached.

Roughly one month after their participation in the experiment, follow-up interviews were conducted by staff from the Ohio State University Survey Research Center.[18] During the phone call, their previous participation in an experiment was purposely not mentioned until the final debriefing at the very end of the call, in order to avoid sensitizing respondents to the questions. The telephone interview included the same battery of trust questions as in the posttest questionnaire administered in the laboratory, thus making it possible to assess the decay or exacerbation of effect size.

Given the strong effects observed in the laboratory, I anticipated that the impact of the one-shot treatments would be short-lived. The findings from this analysis basically confirmed this assumption. Figure 4.5 illustrates the extent of change in the political trust index from post-experiment to follow-up survey interview. The impact of time across all groups, both treatment and control, was highly significant; all three groups increased in levels of trust over the course of this particular month, presumably due to events affecting everyone during that period of time. If one uses the level of increased trust in the control group as a baseline expectation, then the differential change over time by treatment groups basically represents a return to the original baseline. As shown in Figure 4.5, the uncivil group that had lower levels of trust after the experiment bounced back up to the level of trust in the posttest control group by increasing in trust significantly *more* than the control group. The civil group, which tended to be slightly, though not significantly, more trusting than the control group in the posttest, also increased in trust during the interim, but it increased *less* than would be expected based on the baseline control group.

By the time of the follow-up interview, there were no significant differences by experimental condition.[19] In other words, the effects

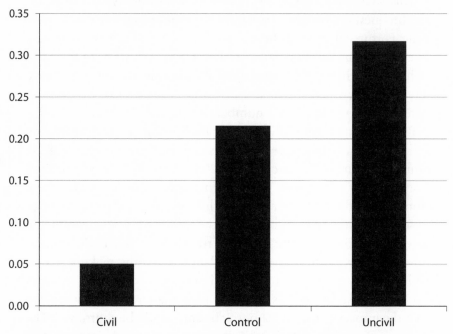

Figure 4.5. Change in mean levels of political trust from post-experiment to four weeks later

Note: Findings are from Experiment II. Means were no longer significantly different from the control group four weeks later, and were no longer different from one another in the predicted direction either. All means increased significantly in the direction of greater trust, but the uncivil condition bounced back to a greater extent than did the civil condition.

observed in the lab are transient and short-lived. But given that the brief manipulation was designed to simulate the persistent, often rancorous tenor of televised political interactions, the ongoing effects of television's tendency toward uncivil political conflict may compound in size over time. Indeed, if one envisions the cumulative impact of repeated exposure to incivility, then low levels of political trust are not surprising. On the other hand, to the extent that civil political discourse is equally prevalent and gets equal amounts of attention (a dubious proposition!), one would expect these effects to cancel themselves out.

From a normative perspective, it is fortunate that these effects do not persist because they suggest that incivility does no permanent damage to levels of trust in politicians and government. However, so long as incivility suppresses trust, and civility does not have a symmetric counter-effect, the possibility of increasing levels of trust in government and politics via civil discourse seems thin. Moreover, if incivility is more widely viewed than civility, and these "treatments" are often repeated in the real world over time, reinforcing people's negative judgments, then one would expect a net negative impact overall, one that may have already been compounded to produce the historically low levels of trust in the contemporary United States.

THE SIGNIFICANCE OF EFFECTS ON POLITICAL TRUST

In this chapter I find that the uncivil manner in which so much political disagreement is communicated encourages more negative attitudes toward politics and politicians. Nonetheless, almost 90 percent of Americans say they think it is possible for people to disagree respectfully, even in the current political climate.[20] Thus uncivil political advocates come across to audiences as nasty, boorish sorts who somehow feel they need not obey the same social norms as ordinary citizens. Incivility among political advocates thus produces systematically less trust in government than equivalent disagreements that transpire more politely. Clearly, there is something about incivility that rubs Americans the wrong way. Not only attitudes toward politicians and Congress, but also levels of support for the institutions of government themselves were influenced. Importantly, these effects occurred even though the extent of substantive disagreement/political conflict was held constant.

Although television has long been suspected to have negative effects on Americans' regard for government, there has been little empirical support for this claim outside of a few isolated studies of the effects of specific programs or events. The extent to which a common and ongoing characteristic of political television produces such outcomes should be cause for concern. Some have suggested that political conflict itself is inappropriately seen as unnecessary and distasteful: "Citizens . . . dislike being exposed to processes endemic to democratic government. People do not wish to see uncertainty, conflicting options, long debate, competing interests, confusion, bargaining, and compromised, imperfect solutions."[21] Likewise, others have noted that it is precisely when Congress is doing its job, debating and eventually resolving controversial political issues that public regard for this institution appears to decline.[22]

The highly controlled experimental findings in this chapter suggest that *incivility* in political discourse, rather than political conflict per se, may be the root of the problem of low regard for politics and politicians. In an age when politicians and political advocates play to the demands of television, and compete for relatively small audiences, incivility is often encouraged without concern for potential negative consequences. An accumulation of effects from viewing shout shows would obviously have much larger effects than documented in these experiments. These shows' audiences might be small, but those who choose not to view them at all when first aired might still see them when replayed on traditional news programs as political "news," or they might see them posted on someone's Facebook page or on YouTube. I leave discussions of the generalizability of these effects— who precisely watches such programs—to Chapter 6. But as I illustrate in Chapter 8, the intensification of political conflict on television is not limited to political shout shows; it pervades political news as well as other kinds of political programming.

Leaving aside for the moment the generalizability of these effects, what are the noteworthy consequences of declining trust in politicians and government? Why does it matter if political television has negative effects on trust? The significance of declining trust in government has been a subject of scholarly debate since at least the 1960s and 1970s. The severity of the decline was such that in 1964, 76 percent of Americans said they trusted government at least most of the time, whereas by 2008 that same number was 30 percent. Some argued that this trend portended apocalyptic consequences, such as radical extralegal political change, whereas others viewed it as simply a function of poor government performance.[23] Although views differ on its consequences, most agree that political trust is important for democratic government,[24] that it makes life less complex and more orderly,[25] and that it increases voluntary compliance with laws.[26] Trust has also been documented to have consequences for levels of citizen compliance with government demands,[27] as well as for the likelihood of supporting incumbents and third-party candidates.[28]

Widespread railing against "big government" is a common rallying cry for contemporary Republicans. Running "against Washington" is now a popular campaign strategy adopted by Republicans and Democrats alike. The huge declines in trust since the 1960s have particularly affected support for government policies that do not benefit the majority of voters: "Indeed, people do not need to trust the government much when they benefit from it. Instead, people need to trust the government when they pay the costs but do not receive the benefits."[29] In other words, when political majorities are asked to make sacrifices for political minorities, such as is the case with antipoverty and race-targeted policies, people must trust that the policy will actually make things better for everyone in the end. It is when there is no immediate personal benefit that trust in government becomes particularly important. Likewise, high levels of trust have been argued to free elected representatives from representing strictly parochial concerns.[30]

Interestingly, while many journalists are comfortable with the idea that the press should assume the mantle of adversarial watchdog, taking down government leaders when they see it as appropriate, they would probably not be comfortable with the idea that their actions specifically favor a more conservative policy agenda. Nonetheless, if incivility in political discourse harms trust in government, as documented in this chapter, then it seems likely that in-your-face politics unintentionally promotes antigovernment policies as well. Political trust "is the foundation of public support for liberal domestic policies,[31] particularly among conservatives."[32] Thus when political advocates, regardless of ideology, scream and yell at one another for the sake of enlivening political television, they may inadvertently be doing far more than drawing larger audiences. By discouraging trust in government, they may also discourage support for policies that rely on trust in the federal government. This means that incivility, whether practiced by liberal or conservative talk shows, or in a putatively nonpartisan venue, may nonetheless discourage support for policies implemented by the federal government.

PART II

WHEN DOES IN-YOUR-FACE POLITICS MATTER?

CHAPTER 5

REAL-WORLD CONTEXTS

The results in the first few chapters of this book enjoy tremendous advantages from a methodological standpoint. Because of the high degree of control over the political content of the broadcasts, the participants involved in the conflicts, and the way in which the cameras covered the dispute, it is possible to draw strong causal inferences about the impact that incivility and camera perspective have on viewers' experiences of political conflict. The problem is that in creating such a perfectly controlled environment, it is easy to overlook characteristics of such disputes that are somehow critically different in the real world from how they were presented in the lab. Although the professional production quality meant that none of the subjects voiced suspicions about the programs themselves, it is still plausible that other, unidentified differences between the real world and this exchange may have altered the outcomes.

The generalizability of these findings outside of the laboratory, outside of the collection of stimuli used in this experiment, and outside of these convenience samples of subjects warrants consideration. With respect to the experimental subjects, the findings are on stronger than usual footing for laboratory experiments because I did not rely exclusively on college student subjects. In addition, the subjects for various experiments were drawn from three different areas of the country (California, Ohio, and Pennsylvania) with varying social and demographic characteristics. They represented a range of ages, levels of education, and socioeconomic backgrounds. Moreover, within each individual study, we found no evidence of differential effects between the subjects obtained through different means of recruitment.

We used a political talk show as a realistic pretext for viewing civil and uncivil political stimuli, but not out of a desire to draw conclusions about the effects of talk shows in particular, so much as to evaluate the consequences of uncivil discourse more generally. Uncivil discourse can and has appeared on regular news programs and in political debates, as well as on talk shows of various kinds. The level of incivility demonstrated by the political actors in our program was relatively mild compared to the hostility exhibited in many of today's political talk shows, and this was purposeful. It would make little sense to produce a finding based on levels of incivility that occur only rarely. Furthermore, the requirement that viewers' perceptions of the candidates' political positions and ideology remain indistinguishable across civil and uncivil conditions meant that we were limited in the extent of incivility that would be plausible.

In addition, those engaged in uncivil repartee on national programs are not always the candidates themselves. Instead, they are often representatives of opposing campaigns or issue camps. Although candidates do at times engage one another directly, particularly at the level of local congressional politics of the kind depicted in these experimental treatments, in national politics it is more common to send a representative to skirmish for the candidate, just in case the interaction has negative repercussions. So while it is not unrealistic, the fact that it was the candidates themselves engaging one another rather than their henchmen or henchwomen could have heightened the effects on candidate-relevant attitudes, though probably not on issue-related attitudes or politics more generally. In practice, candidate representatives are more likely to risk incivility than are the candidates themselves, thus producing potentially stronger effects.

The artificiality of the laboratory could cut both ways. On the one hand, because of the laboratory setting, the subjects undoubtedly paid closer attention to the television program than they might have in a more naturalistic context. Greater attention is likely to create greater potential for emotional reactions of the kind we have observed. On the other hand, the types of issues discussed in these programs should have counterbalanced any such increase. None of the issues discussed were particularly emotion-laden relative to other possible topics. In general, one would expect issues such as same-sex marriage, flag burning, and abortion to prompt much stronger emotional reactions. Nonetheless, regardless of which subset of issue disagreements an experiment used, the findings were consistent.

All of the issues used in the program had been in the news at the time of the taping, and they remained relatively topical for the duration of the experiments. Our pretest questionnaires showed that most subjects had opinions on the discussed issues. On a few topics, such as free trade, pretest data suggested that subjects had fairly committed views, but on the whole these were not the sort of issues likely to elicit strong reactions. If the discussion had instead involved so-called hot-button issues, we would have expected much stronger reactions. Likewise, if the discussion had occurred among politicians toward whom the subjects had preexisting intense feelings, their reactions might have been stronger.

Although it would be impossible to explore all of these possible dimensions of generalizability, in this chapter I use three additional experiments to evaluate the generalizability of the findings presented in the previous chapters. In the first study, I eliminate the most obvious difference between the experimental treatments and real-world broadcasts by clearly identifying the two candidates by political party. In a second study, the videos used as experimental treatments were drawn from segments of real-world political programs that were either civil or uncivil, rather than from programs constructed for these purposes. Finally, in a third, population-based survey experiment, I use a random sample of the population as participants, and still pictures as experimental treatments rather than video.

The lack of experimental control afforded by these more generalizable designs meant that not all hypotheses could be tested within each design. For example, when using real political programs recorded off the air, the civil and uncivil conditions cannot include the same political information, so it is impossible to compare recall from one condition to another. Nonetheless, each new study offers an opportunity either to confirm findings or to refine our understanding of the boundaries of the theories underlying these predictions.

PARTISAN CANDIDATES AND PARTISAN VIEWERS

In the real world, almost all U.S. political candidates are affiliated with the Republican or Democratic Parties. This is probably less true of political advocates who spar regularly on television. But even with well-known pundits, there is typically an effort to cue viewers as to who brings what partisan perspective to the table, whether the disputants are characterized as Republicans versus Democrats or perhaps as advocates for liberal versus conservative advocacy groups.

For this reason, I attempted a replication study using the same program videos, but explicitly identifying the political party of each candidate using superimposed identifying text at the bottom of the screen when the candidate is shown. Moreover, the sample of participants in this experiment was blocked so as to obtain roughly equal numbers of Republicans and Democrats. Although I have not provided a breakdown by partisanship for each experiment, the laboratory studies conducted in Ohio tended to include slightly more Republicans than Democrats, whereas the ones conducted in Philadelphia included far more Democrats than Republicans. Indeed, for laboratory studies conducted in Philadelphia, such as this one, the dominance of Democrats over Republicans in the area meant that special subject recruitment procedures were required in order to attract greater numbers of conservatives.[1]

One might wonder whether the candidates could really be assigned Republican or Democratic labels without arousing suspicion among participants given the issue positions that they espoused. As reported in Chapter 2, the issues chosen for discussion were real issues under congressional debate at the time, but I purposely chose issues that did not have a strong or consistent partisan profile, so as not to make it implausible that a Republican candidate could favor increased spending on NASA, or that a Democrat could oppose taxing purchases made on the Internet. All positions were and continue to be within the realm of positions that candidates support within both political parties.

The videos were altered to indicate each candidate's party identification on-screen each time either candidate was shown in either a medium or close-up. Consistent with common practice on television,

"D" and "R" labels were placed after the candidates' superimposed names on the screen. Manipulation checks at the very end of the experiment confirmed that the candidate assigned the Democratic label was identified as such significantly more so than the candidate with an R, and vice versa. Although political party was measured along a continuum, rather than as a dichotomy, it was clear that participants noticed because they rated the Democrat more likely to be a Democrat, and vice versa, regardless of which candidate had which label.

Before exploring the results of this experiment, it is worth considering specific theoretical expectations: what difference is this difference likely to make? When we assign party labels to candidates, two things are likely to occur. First, the party labels should have effects on which candidate is favored by the participant, based on the correspondence with his or her own party identification. While this is a logical expectation, it has no direct bearing on the pattern of outcomes from incivility reported thus far. In other words, it might alter which candidate was most or least liked, but there is no logical reason why it should alter whether the effects of incivility are focused on the most or least liked candidate.

More important, party identification could change the experimental results by altering viewers' perceptions of the degree of civility versus incivility that the two candidates demonstrated. Given the powerful perceptual filter that partisanship provides, it is possible that in this version of the experiment, those who shared a candidate's party affiliation did not interpret the same behaviors as uncivil and socially inappropriate. In the manipulation checks shown for the previous experiments, *both* candidates were perceived by viewers as more hostile in the uncivil condition than in the civil condition, whether perceptions were analyzed collectively as an overall average, or by individual candidate. And neither candidate was perceived to be significantly more liberal/conservative or more likely to be a Democrat/Republican relative to the other. However, if perceptions of only the *opposing* party candidate were viewed as significantly more hostile, then people's perceptions of the interaction between the two candidates would be quite different, as might be the results of those perceptions.

As shown in Figure 5.1, the experimental treatments appear to have been sufficiently strong so that both the Democratic and Republican candidates were perceived to be significantly more hostile

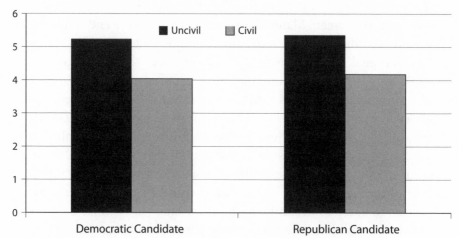

Figure 5.1. Perceptions of incivility by party of candidate

Note: Bars indicate the extent to which respondents perceived the Democratic and Republican candidates to be uncivil, measured as a combination of perceptions of each candidate along emotional-unemotional, quarrelsome-cooperative, hostile-friendly, rude-polite, and agitated-calm scales, with high scores indicating that more incivility was perceived. Both civil conditions were perceived as less hostile than uncivil conditions (Democratic candidate, $F = 4.98, p < .05$; Republican candidate, $F = 4.56, p < .05$). Findings are from Experiment V.

in the uncivil than in the civil condition. The treatment was effective for each candidate individually. The question that Figure 5.1 does not address is whether both Republican and Democratic subjects perceived the candidate of the opposing party as more uncivil than the candidate of their own party. After all, the results in Chapter 3 suggest that the effects of incivility tend to be on attitudes toward the candidate one does not like. It is thus possible that this result occurs because respondents see the other side as unnecessarily argumentative, whereas the candidate on their own team is just expressing understandable righteous indignation. The potential for a partisan lens to color interpretations of candidate behavior naturally increases once candidates are assigned partisan identities.

Did respondents judge the behavior of the candidate from their own party as harshly as the other party? As shown in Figure 5.2, respondents judged their own and the opposing party to be equally hospitable in the civil conditions, but they judged the opposing party's candidate to be more uncivil. In other words, they judged

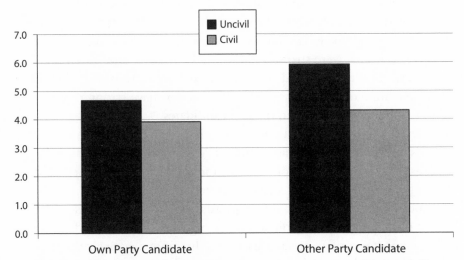

Figure 5.2. Effects of incivility treatment on perceptions of candidate incivility among like-minded and opposing partisans

Note: Bars represent the same outcome as in Figure 5.1, but broken down by whether the candidate was of the same party or the opposing political party as the respondent. A mixed-model analysis of variance with one within-subject factor (extent of own party candidate perceived incivility versus other party candidate perceived incivility) and one between-subject factor (civil versus uncivil versions of program) indicated that respondents perceived candidates in the civil and uncivil conditions as significantly different from one another as predicted (between-subjects $F = 12.54$, $p < .001$). They also perceived other party candidate as significantly more uncivil than own party candidate (within-subjects $F = 4.37, p < .05$). Importantly, there was no significant interaction between these two factors. Findings are from Experiment V.

the partisan opposition to be systematically more rude, quarrelsome, hostile, and agitated than the candidate of their own party, even when both were acting equally uncivil, as shown in Figure 5.1. To summarize, the civility/incivility treatments worked equally well in altering perceptions of candidate behavior, but the overall level of incivility perceived by viewers was substantially less if they were judging their own candidate versus the candidate from the other party.

Having established that the experimental manipulation was successful even in the presence of party identification, but that the severity of incivility was judged differently for candidates of the same party as the subject, I turned next to see whether and to what extent I could replicate the effects of incivility on trust in government that were outlined in the previous chapter. What difference might partisanship make in this context? Labeling the candidates by party meant that viewers would have easy heuristics for identifying "us" versus "them." Likewise, some participants were only weakly partisan whereas others were strongly committed partisans, and the strength of partisan identity could have important implications for whether people are likely to react with indifference or have strong reactions to rising tensions between the two candidates.

On the one hand, research suggests that weak partisans should be most susceptible to persuasive influence of various kinds, mainly because they have weaker political opinions overall. On the other hand, the type of influence that I have documented in response to incivility is not quite the same as political persuasion. Instead, the idea is that the more people see candidates behaving outside the boundaries of social norms for face-to-face discourse, the more negatively they will feel about politics and politicians in general. Strong partisans might well have the strongest reactions to norm violations in this context. In Figure 5.3, I address this research question by looking at reactions to the experimental treatments by strength of partisanship.

In Figure 5.3, incivility once again had a significant negative main effect on political trust, just as in the experiments that did not have party identification attached to the candidates. But what is most prom-

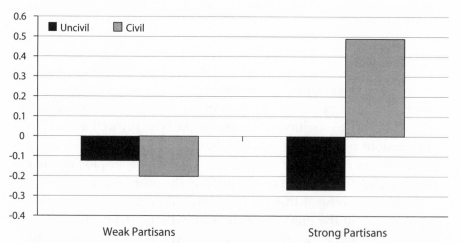

Figure 5.3. Effects of incivility on trust in government by strength of partisanship
Note: Incivility had a significant negative effect on political trust overall ($F = 6.39$, $p < .05$), and incivility also had a significant interaction with strength of partisanship ($F = 5.02$, $p < .05$). Findings are from Experiment V.

inent in Figure 5.3 is the difference between how weak and strong partisans responded to these treatments. Overall, the observed effects were due to the reactions of strong partisans. The gap in levels of political trust between the civil and uncivil conditions was vastly different within these two subgroups. Incivility made little to no difference to the trust levels expressed by weak partisans, and the means did not differ significantly. But among strong partisans, there was a substantial difference, with those in the civil condition expressing much higher levels of trust in government and politicians than those in the uncivil condition.

Overall then, it appears that strong partisans are the driving force behind this effect. This finding is particularly important because, as discussed further in Chapter 6, political discussion programs are most likely to be watched by strong partisans. If strong partisans were not affected by incivility, then its impact in the real world might easily amount to very little. However, as described at length in Chapter 8, in-your-face politics is not limited to political talk shows. And in any case, strong partisans are *more* rather than less reactive to such content.

Of course, the Republicans and Democrats in this study were not chosen as representative samples of all Republicans and Democrats; they were merely a convenience sample. As a result, it would be difficult to generalize the descriptive characteristics of these particular partisans and the effect sizes I have found to broader contexts in the United States. Nonetheless, the fact that the randomly assigned treatments interact with partisanship suggests that variations in treatment effects may arise from underlying differences between Republicans and Democrats.

In particular, when effects are rooted in very basic reactions to aversive stimuli, it seems plausible that traits associated with different underlying physiological sensitivities might come into play. Multiple studies suggest that conservatives are more physiologically responsive to threat than liberals are. It remains true even when the type of threat is completely unrelated to politics.[2] Conservative political ideology is associated with greater neural sensitivity to threat.[3] Based on convenience samples of those with strong political views, conservatives differed from liberals in their sensitivities to threatening visual images and sudden noises.[4] In the study most closely paralleling my own experiments in Chapter 2, Oxley and colleagues found that changes in skin conductance in response to threatening stimuli were much higher among those with high levels of support for "protective" policies such as defense spending, capital punishment, and the Iraq War.[5] To the extent that Republicans/conservatives are generally more sensitive to threat, one might expect them to respond more to uncivil political stimuli as well. To reiterate, even though watching television is in no sense physically threatening to viewers, the expectation is that people's brains react as if the threats they witness are real. They are likely to cognitively override any overt reaction, but they may nonetheless react differently to incivility at a neurophysiological level.

In Experiment I, in which people were hooked up to monitors of skin conductance, there were unfortunately too few subjects to compare Republicans to Democrats. However, in the experiment designed specifically to study how partisanship related to these effects, there were sufficient numbers of Democrats and non-Democrats to make such a comparison possible. Although I attempted to solicit participation from as many Republicans as Democrats, many of the participants recruited through heavily conservative organizations nonetheless identified themselves as "Independents" when in the Philadelphia laboratory, thus necessitating a comparison of how the randomly assigned treatments affected Democrats versus non-Democrats. Comparing liberals to conservatives proved more problematic because large numbers of study participants identified themselves as "moderates" and thus could not be ideologically classified either way, despite patterns of political attitudes that suggested otherwise.

The partisan candidate experiment did not include psychophysiological measures of skin conductance. However, one popular means of assessing both the valence and extent of arousal is by means of "self-assessment manikins" (SAM), a measure included in the posttest questionnaires. As illustrated in Figure 5.4, after viewing the treatment video, respondents were asked to circle one in a series of stylized depictions of a cartoon person. The first row represents valence, that is, a basic measure of whether respondents feel positively or negatively. The second row represents arousal levels, with the far

Please circle one figure on each line below to indicate how you feel at the moment.

VALENCE DIMENSION

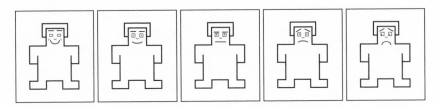

AROUSAL DIMENSION

Figure 5.4. Self-assessment manikins for measuring valence and arousal
Source: Bradley and Lang (1994).

right picture indicating low arousal, and the far left high levels of arousal. While inferior to direct physiological measures, the SAM measure of valence correlates highly with facial electromyographic measures of positive and negative affect, and the arousal measure correlates well with skin conductance measures.[6] Thus the SAM scales frequently serve as surrogate measures of arousal and valence.

In order to examine differential aversive reactions by party identification, I used the SAM measures to construct an indicator of negative emotional arousal, and then examined the effects of the incivility treatment on Democrats and non-Democrats. Those with positive reactions received zeros for negative emotional arousal, whereas those with negative reactions were assigned values consistent with the extent of their negative emotional arousal.

As shown in Figure 5.5, incivility did indeed affect Democrats and non-Democrats differently, and this was confirmed by the statistically significant interaction between party and incivility. Levels of negative emotional arousal were especially high among Republicans and

Independents who viewed the uncivil program. By contrast, the same group showed especially low levels of negative emotional arousal when shown the civil program. Democrats had indistinguishably moderate levels of negative arousal in response to both programs.

This pattern of results is consistent with those found in other studies suggesting that Republicans and conservatives may be particularly sensitive to norm-violating threats to the social structure. On one hand, this pattern is somewhat ironic because shout-show politics is often associated with conservative television talk shows. To the extent that Republicans are more sensitive to incivility, it should be extremely effective in getting their attention. Moreover, the groups most affected by incivility—strong partisans and Republicans—are probably also people who are likely to be exposed to it. I explore the demographics of viewership more extensively in the following chapter.

Overall, the fact that politicians are usually identified by political party on television does not change the basic nature of the effects observed here. It highlights who is and who is not on the viewer's

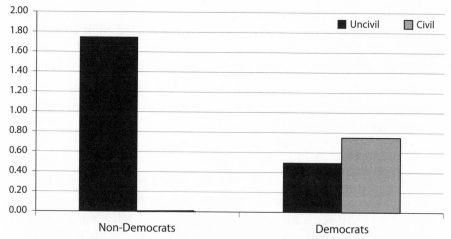

Figure 5.5. Effects of incivility on negative emotional arousal, by party
Note: Arousal and valence were assessed using self-assessment manikins on 1 to 5 scales. To create an indicator of negative emotional arousal, valence scores were coded 0 for any neutral or positive valence, and 1 or 2 for weakly or strongly negative valence. These items were multiplied by arousal on a 1 to 5 scale to create a measure of the extent of negative emotional arousal. The effects of incivility interacted with political party ($F = 5.03, p < .05$). Findings are from Experiment V.

own side, but does not change fundamental reactions to in-your-face politics. Furthermore, differences in reactions among partisan subjects suggest a pattern consistent with evolutionary interpretations of how people respond to televised images.

REAL-WORLD UNCIVIL TELEVISION

Including partisan labels made the programs somewhat more realistic, but they were still artificially constructed programs addressing candidates unknown to the audience before viewing. So yet another experiment endeavored to manipulate civility using real-world examples of civil and uncivil television. This study was done in conjunction with Eran Ben-Porath, who was interested in evaluating the effects of incivility on attitudes toward the journalists who are frequently involved in these civil or uncivil conversations. To begin this process, video clips were recorded from on-air news and discussion programs. The most promising segments for civil and uncivil discourse were then pretested to evaluate how civil/uncivil the discussions were perceived to be by student subjects. The end result was a selection of two civil and two uncivil exchanges of approximately equal length.

Participants assigned to the civil condition viewed one segment of *Hardball* from MSNBC in which journalist Chris Matthews interviewed Senator Sam Brownback and discussed abortion and judicial appointments. A second civil segment included a roundtable discussion from *This Week* on ABC between George Stephanopoulos and several journalist-experts about the Middle East. Participants in the uncivil condition viewed a different segment from *Hardball* in which Chris Matthews interviews Senator Zell Miller following Miller's appearance at the 2004 Republican National Convention. In a second segment, Chris Matthews interviews Chris Galloway of the Young Democrats and Jason Mattera of the Young America Foundation. When combined, the two civil segments and the two uncivil segments were of roughly equal length.

The point of this experiment was to evaluate whether the same effects would be found using treatments drawn from actual broadcasts, and to test the generalizability of the operational measures of key outcomes of interest. Because the civil and uncivil videos involved different political advocates and altogether different discussion topics, it only made sense to expect replication of the effects on attitudes toward government, politics, and politicians. Given that the political content of the discussions was different, and the discussants themselves were different people, it was not possible to compare levels of recall of information and issue positions, or affect toward the candidates.

As an outcome measure, instead of the traditional measure of trust in government used in previous studies, in this study respondents were asked a series of questions about how they felt about politicians and whether they were in touch with ordinary people. For example, three of the items asked respondents to agree or disagree with statements such as "Most politicians have a pretty good idea what people like me care about," "Most politicians share my values," and "Most politicians are arrogant."

If the underlying mechanism I have posited is correct, that is, viewers think less overall of people who violate face-to-face social norms for the polite expression of political differences of opinion, then the pattern of results found in earlier experiments should be true even when the uncivil people are political advocates and journalists rather than politicians themselves. Viewers are prompted to think that the political world is replete with people who are not like them. Indeed, when an experiment asked about attitudes toward civil versus uncivil journalists instead of politicians, attitudes toward uncivil journalists were also negatively affected.[7] For example, in the Chris Matthews–Zell Miller exchange described in Chapter 1 (also used as stimuli in this study), evaluations of Matthews suffered, as did those of Senator Miller. The violation of social norms contributed to a sense among viewers that politics on the whole is a dirty business and that these people are not governed by the same social norms that govern everyday people like themselves.

Did the variation in materials used for the experimental treatments and/or the differing operationalization of the dependent variable change the fundamental pattern of findings? As shown in Figure 5.6, the same general results emerged in this experiment as in the

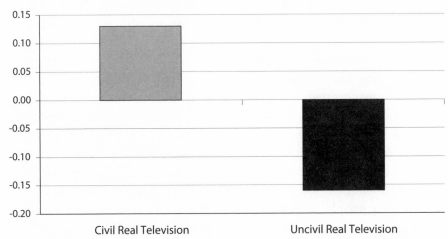

Figure 5.6. Effects of real-world civil versus uncivil media on attitudes toward politicians

Note: Means are significantly different $(F = 3.87, p = .05)$. Findings are from Experiment VI.

previous ones; watching uncivil banter may be arousing, but it leaves viewers with a bad taste in their mouths when it comes to what they think of politics and politicians. This same effect was observed regardless of party affiliation or ideology. Along with the results of previous studies using different issue disagreements, what these findings suggest is that the results observed in the previous chapters are highly generalizable; they do not depend on a particular experimental stimulus or a particular operationalization of the outcome. When people watch exemplars from the political world that violate social norms, they think less of the political world in general. Interestingly, the politicians they personally support are seldom directly penalized, but the reputation of the collective enterprise nonetheless suffers.

A REPRESENTATIVE SAMPLE FROM OUTSIDE THE LABORATORY

One final experiment was used to examine several additional dimensions of generalizability. Its purpose was to explore characteristics of the sample of subjects and the campus laboratory setting that might contribute to producing this overall pattern of findings. The experimental participants observed thus far were convenience samples of non-university-affiliated adults from communities near the campuses where the experiments were conducted and, in a few cases, students drawn from campus groups. Although I had no a priori reason to think these populations would demonstrate different reactions, they were not a representative sample.

In addition, because they took part in these studies on campuses, there could have been demand characteristics at work when being observed by university faculty. To the extent that disdaining impolite politicians is just a way to look good in front of well-educated university people, one might expect the laboratory context to cause subjects to more negatively evaluate politicians after viewing uncivil behavior on television. The rooms in which subjects participated were never marked "laboratory," and they were not aware of the experimental nature of the studies until debriefing. Nonetheless, they obviously knew they were participating in research.

Beyond evaluating the generalizability of these laboratory findings, I also wanted to explore more thoroughly the mechanism producing effects on attitudes toward politicians. Thus, as a final test of my proposed mechanism of influence, I embedded an experiment in a representative national survey sample.[8] In this case, my goal was to pare down the experimental stimuli to the bare bones of what might be capable of producing an effect on political attitudes. If the effect was simply a function of prompting people to have at top of mind unlikeable political figures—regardless of why they are disliked—then incivility is important to attitudes toward politicians because it is a common way (but certainly not the only way) that politicians come to be disliked by being shown as counter-normative and above the manners required of ordinary Americans.

In order to execute a study with these goals in mind, a representative sample of respondents was first asked to select five people that they most liked or most disliked from a list of twenty-seven political figures. Whether they were asked to select liked or disliked figures was based on random assignment to a *like* or *dislike* condition. Respondents could choose from a list of people ranging from Jesse Jackson to Jesse Helms, and from Rudy Giuliani to Ronald Reagan.

Ideally, I would have liked to expose viewers to video footage of their liked or disliked politicians. However, video proved to be prohibitively expensive with a national sample. For this reason, I was limited to still photographs framed as close-ups or as more distant visual perspectives.

Using a two-by two, between-subjects factorial design, respondents were also randomly assigned to an *image size* factor, so that they were presented either with the name of the person and a small picture of each political figure shot from far away, or with the name and a close-up picture of each political figure's face. Given that both image size and the frame surrounding an image may affect perceptions of spatial distance, this approach promoted a more pronounced manipulation of distance. After viewing a photo, respondents were asked to indicate their feelings toward each individual political figure on a feeling thermometer scale of 0 to 100, where 0 indicates feeling extremely cold, 50 means feeling neither warm nor cold, and 100 signifies feeling extremely warm toward the person.

I tested three main hypotheses in this study. First, consistent with the hypotheses in previous studies, I predicted that larger pictures would lead to more extreme evaluations of these political figures in a positive direction for liked politicians, and in a more negative direction for those assigned to disliked ones (that is, an image size by like/dislike interaction effect on attitudes toward these specific individuals). I also hypothesized that being prompted to think about disliked as opposed to liked politicians would lower viewers' overall evaluation of politics and politicians (a main effect of like/dislike on general attitudes toward politicians rather than these particular politicians). Finally, I also predicted that larger images of liked/disliked political figures would produce stronger effects on attitudes toward government and politicians (an image size by like/dislike interaction effect in influencing general attitudes toward politicians).

Do attitudes differ simply because respondents have recently viewed liked or disliked politicians from an in-your-face perspective? Although still pictures tend to be less arousing than video or flesh-and-blood humans, the results of this experiment provided some partial support for these hypotheses. Interestingly, despite the fact that the small or large still photos of the politicians were on the screen while respondents were evaluating just how positively or negatively they felt toward each, I found no evidence that people staring at larger photos felt more strongly about those they liked or disliked than those staring at smaller photos.

However, attitudes toward government and politicians were influenced as expected, although the size of the effect was quite small. As shown in Figure 5.7, those who were prompted to think about politicians they disliked shortly before answering questions about government and politics reported more negative attitudes than those primed to think about politicians they liked a great deal. In this sense, the effects observed in Chapter 4 may be simply a function of weighting people's evaluations toward what is top of mind at the moment—politicians they do not particularly like. When politicians play nice and interact politely, it naturally primes more positive evaluations of government and politicians than when they behave counter-normatively.

But as also illustrated in Figure 5.7, the size of the effect on attitudes toward government and politicians was significantly greater when respondents saw the large, close-up images rather than the small, dis-

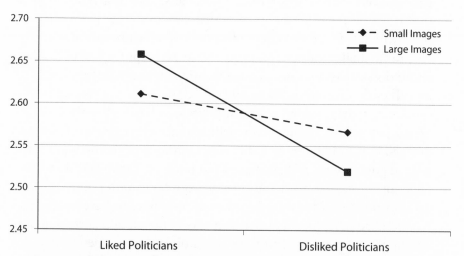

Figure 5.7. Effects of viewing liked/disliked politicians on favorable attitudes toward politics and government, by image size
Note: The main effect of liked/disliked politicians was significant ($F = 11.88, p < .01$), as was the interaction between image size and liked/disliked politicians ($F = 2.77$, $p < .05$). Findings are from Experiment IV.

tant images. Given that the thermometer ratings of these individuals were no more extreme with the large pictures than the small, this is somewhat surprising. How did image size intensify people's feelings toward the group without intensifying feelings toward the individual politicians? I can only speculate, but it is worth noting that this finding is similar to those in my earlier experiments indicating no effects of incivility on overall evaluations of the specific individuals in the broadcast, coupled with significant effects on attitudes toward politicians more generally. In most cases, the more disliked one of the two politicians was being penalized for being uncivil, whereas the most liked politicians was not. Perhaps because all politicians used in this study were well known and selected by respondents because they elicited particularly strong positive or negative feelings, it was particularly difficult to change subjects' feelings toward them. In the more artificial experiments, by contrast, the politicians were new and unknown to the respondents. The fact that in all cases the more global evaluation of politicians and politics changed tells us something about the likely mechanism. Perhaps when politicians behave badly, it brings to mind an entire category of social norm violations rather than specifically the antics of the politicians depicted.

THE GENERALIZABILITY OF EFFECTS OF INCIVILITY ON ATTITUDES TOWARD GOVERNMENT AND POLITICS

Overall, this chapter has examined the generalizability of the experimental paradigm used in Part I, with an emphasis on when findings replicate and when they do not. The experiment that assigned party labels to the candidates demonstrated that although party labels may alter which candidate a participant says he or she likes best, the basic pattern of findings is the same. Incivility is more easily observed in candidates of the opposing party than in candidates from one's own party, but greater levels of perceived incivility still register even in viewers' perceptions of the candidate of their own party.

In addition, strong partisans registered much larger reactions to incivility than did weak partisans. Contrary to what one might expect, strong opinions do not insulate viewers from reacting to incivility; instead, they exacerbate it. This finding is noteworthy because of what it suggests about whether the kind of people who watch political programs are susceptible to its influence. I explore other dimensions of who watches in Chapter 6, but the fact that political programs have highly partisan audiences clearly does not stand in the way of effects from in-your-face politics. Moreover, to the extent that shout shows tend to attract more conservative audiences, in-your-face politics has much stronger effects because most such influence appears to be accounted for by those who are conservative and/or Republican, and by strong partisans in particular.

The experiment using civil and uncivil content that was taken directly off the air nicely replicated the earlier pattern of findings. Although relinquishing control over the program content in some of these studies meant that it was not possible to evaluate levels of recall for specific arguments within the programs, the overall pattern of outcomes remained very predictable. Trust in politics and government was consistently harmed.

Some of these insights go beyond mere replication to help explain patterns of findings in earlier studies. For example, if incivility is more easily perceived in the partisan opposition, this may help explain why those on the opposing side are punished for their violations of social norms, while those on one's own side are not. Because television is particularly good at eliciting emotional reactions to politicians, factors that make a viewer susceptible to strong emotions facilitate its effects.

To further evaluate generalizability, I moved outside the laboratory setting and gathered representative national survey data on program viewership of the most popular political television programs. Despite extensive efforts in the population-based survey experiment discussed in this chapter, I found no evidence that characteristics of the national sample conditioned participants' likelihood of effects. This is perhaps because these effects were more muted with still pictures. Some evidence suggests that static images of faces in particular are not as arousal-inducing as dynamic facial expressions.[9] Faces are most critical to emotional expression, and static faces may simply produce weaker experimental treatments when manipulating incivility. Regardless, extensive data dredging produced little additional evidence suggestive of heterogeneity of effects. This was true despite the fact that the large, representative, national sample facilitated relatively powerful comparisons, much more so than the laboratory experiments with smaller sample sizes.

Next, in Chapter 6, I use survey data on program viewership to address generalizability from yet another angle. The focus of this chapter is on who watches in-your-face programming in the real world. To the extent that personal characteristics that predispose people to experiencing effects from incivility also predispose them not to watch this kind of television, this may moderate the potential for negative effects on the American public. I also focus on individual differences that seem most theoretically promising as sources of heterogeneity in the extent of watching in-your-face politics, differences in individual attitudes toward conflict.

CHAPTER 6

WHO WATCHES THIS STUFF ANYWAY?
THE AUDIENCE FOR IN-YOUR-FACE POLITICS

One of the central paradoxes explored in this book is why people watch in-your-face politics when they supposedly find it so unpleasant. The answer to this question is central to understanding how market-driven political television persists with programming of this kind. It is also an important question to answer for purposes of assessing the generalizability of the laboratory findings shown in the previous chapters. If the people who showed up in the lab and were affected by these programs are the kind of people who would never watch this kind of program in the real world anyway, the effects may not be generalizable outside the laboratory.

The purpose of this chapter is to provide an exploratory account of who watches programs with a high degree of in-your-face incivility. Scholars knew a great deal about who watched traditional television news, and viewership followed a highly predictable pattern: older, well-educated, wealthier, and more politically interested people were more likely to watch the traditional evening news. But importantly, most of these observations were based on analyses of audiences for evening news programs *before* there were any alternatives to evening news programs. Now that the varieties of political television on offer have increased tremendously, viewers who want to hear about politics can choose among dozens of options for political programming across a variety of formats. In addition, there are always many channels carrying fictional or entertainment programming rather than news, so political programs face stiff competition from a wide variety of nontraditional political formats as well as from nonpolitical fare.

One would presume that the patterns of news consumption mentioned above still hold to some extent; in particular, that people who watch political television are those most interested in politics, the most partisan, and so forth. However, the greater variety of available political programming means that some of these demographic correlates may have changed. In addition, in this era of many television choices, an increasingly large proportion of the American population has opted out of political television viewing altogether, thus further complicating assessments of who watches political television.

My particular interest in who watches what goes beyond knowing what kind of people consume political television in the more diverse political information environment of today. More specifically, my question is what kind of people expose themselves to "in-your-face" political television. To answer this question required a multistep approach that allowed me to quantify both the characteristics of individual programs, as well as the kinds of people who watched them. Toward that end, I designed an extensive content analysis to document the degree to which various programs emphasized in-your-face characteristics, and I combined this information with national survey data on program viewership from the National Annenberg Election Panel Study from 2008.

I begin this chapter by describing the process of characterizing individual programs along the dimensions of incivility and close-up visual perspectives. Next I analyze program-level data and explore which programs including political content are most uncivil and most visually close-up in their style of presentation. Third, I evaluate the implications of these findings for the generalizability of my experimental results. Next I turn to representative national survey data and match viewers with the characteristics of the programs they watch in order to understand what kind of people are drawn to in-your-face political programming. These data are then used to resolve the question of whether those who watch are also those likely to be affected.[1]

CHARACTERIZING POLITICAL PROGRAMS

In order to characterize political programs as generally more or less uncivil in their political discourse, and to ascertain the extent to which they are typically shot using intimate or more distant camera perspectives, coders were asked to watch multiple episodes of each program. As they watched each program, they filled in coding sheets asking about civility as well as the sense of visual closeness to the humans on the screen. A sample of ten episodes of each program was saved to a digital video recorder, and three coders were assigned the task of watching these episodes, with at least two independent coders assigned to each program.[2] Having recordings of the episodes made it possible for coders to rewind and reexamine content as needed for purposes of answering extensive questions on the coding forms.

For purposes of this analysis, both civility and camera perspectives were considered to be continuous attributes rather than simple dichotomies. As detailed in Appendix D, the coding scheme asked many of the same questions about the program that subjects were asked in the experimental studies. For each episode that was viewed, coders judged the interactions using the exact same civility scales as in the experiment. For example, coders were asked, "Overall, how would you describe the discussion and disagreement on this program?" and they located each episode on scales anchored by end-points labeled quarrelsome-cooperative, hostile-friendly, rude-polite, and agitated-calm. In addition, a summary question asked whether the overall tone of the program was extremely friendly and warm (1), mostly calm, polite, and civil (2), a mix of polite disagreement with some heated interactions (3), or mostly heated interactions (4).

For purposes of coding the sense of visual closeness conveyed by each episode, two additional questions probed visual aspects of the episode. Coders first located the episode on a scale asking about the most *common* camera shot used in the program: "During the time when people are shown on the screen, how much of each individual person is generally visible?" This scale ranged from *whole body* (1) to *face only* (9), with a midpoint labeled *head and shoulders*. As shown in Appendix D, to increase reliability, the scale on the coding form was labeled using television screen images illustrating points along the spectrum from extreme close-ups to whole body shots, with the standard head and shoulders shot as the midpoint.

Coders were subsequently asked about the tightest, that is, the most close-up, shot in the episode, of those shots that involved one or more people talking during the program. In this case they reported what proportion of the TV frame was taken up by the talking faces. This scale ranged from *less than 1/4 of the screen* (1) to *all or almost all of the screen area* (6). These two items were combined into a single indicator of perceived visual closeness.

Each of ten episodes of the thirty-six programs was scored, and these scores were then aggregated up to the program level by averaging across all ten of the episodes of each of the programs that were coded. At this point, a single score summarized the extent of incivility to be expected from a given program, and a separate score summarized the perceived visual closeness of people on the program. Although variation is certainly to be expected from episode to episode, my goal was to obtain a general characterization of each program.

The standard program format used in each program episode was also noted. From a list of seven common formats, coders were asked to select the three most commonly used formats in the episode they had just watched, including whether face-to-face interaction among participants was involved, a monologue by a host, out-of-studio video clips, a face-to-face interview, split-screen interviews, and so forth. Coders ranked the three most frequently used formats. My goal in ascertaining this information was to determine whether certain program formats are associated with greater or lesser incivility and greater or lesser close-up camera perspectives.

Because camera setups and format decisions tend to stay the same from episode to episode of any given program, this approach is likely to accurately characterize a program in all but exceptional episodes. Levels of civility probably also vary from episode to episode of a program, depending upon the issue at hand, the tenacity of the guests, and so forth. Nonetheless, ten episodes seemed a reasonable basis for roughly assessing which programs tended to be more or less in your face as a matter of habit.

WHAT KINDS OF PROGRAMS ARE MORE IN YOUR FACE?

The results of the content analysis were roughly what one would expect based on casual knowledge of many of these programs. Figure 6.1 arrays the thirty-six programs along these two dimensions. The least hostile program with political content was the ever cheerful *Good Morning America*, and the standard morning and evening news programs such as *ABC World News*, *CBS Morning News*, *CNN Newsroom*, and *The Today Show* all fell into the most civil quartile as well. Near the median were programs such as *Dateline*, *Anderson Cooper 360*, and *20/20*. The most uncivil programs at the time were *Hannity & Colmes* and *Hardball*, followed by *Morning Joe*.

To evaluate whether certain formats or types of programs are more conducive to in-your-face politics, I first analyzed these data at the level of individual programs. Although this approach produces a relatively small sample size, it allowed me to answer some obvious preliminary questions. First, do the two dimensions I use to define in-your-face politics—incivility and up-close visual perspectives—go hand in hand with each other on political programs, or is this combination the exception, as it is in the real world, where incivility and greater physical distance are far more likely to coincide?

Second, are conservative political programs more uncivil than liberal ones as is often popularly claimed? Fortunately, this same list of television programs had already been subjected to an extensive coding process to categorize them by ideological leanings.[3] So in order to test this hypothesis, I borrowed these measures of whether a program was generally perceived to be left-leaning/Democratic, right-leaning/Republican, or neither, in order to evaluate the relationship between partisanship and in-your-face characteristics.

My third question was whether there are program formats that are more or less conducive to in-your-face politics. To examine this question, I used summary indicators of the extent to which each program emphasized up-close visual images and incivility and looked at their relationships with the dominant format used by the program. My fourth and final question was whether programs that are more heavily political in content (though not necessarily *partisan*) are also more uncivil. To answer this question, the coders categorized the

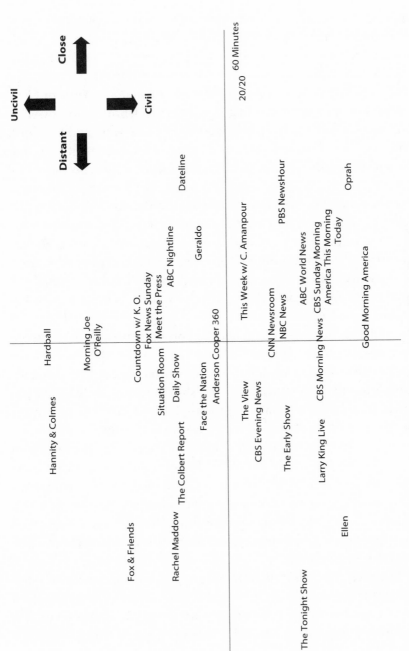

Figure 6.1. Political programs plotted on civility-incivility and close-distant dimensions

episodes into one of three categories: programs with content that was almost entirely political in nature (e.g., national news broadcasts, political discussion programs), programs that included political content regularly, but not to the exclusion of nonpolitical content (e.g., morning news programs such as *The Today Show* or *Good Morning America*, or shows that incorporate celebrity news as well as political content, such as those hosted by Larry King and Geraldo), and programs that very seldom include political content (e.g., *The Tonight Show with Jay Leno*, *The Late Show with David Letterman*, etc.).

Interestingly, as can be gleaned from the plot of results in Figure 6.1, there is no significant relationship between the up-close camera perspective and the level of incivility in any given program. These two characteristics are, if anything, somewhat negatively correlated, but not strongly so within this sample of programs. So the combination of incivility with up-close visual perspectives is not a "natural" for producers of political television any more than it is for human beings in everyday life.

To address the relationship between program partisanship and the in-your-face presentation style, I looked at partisanship as it related to the two independent dimensions of in-your-face politics. Interestingly, I found no significant relationship between the left-right political leanings of programs and their level of incivility or camera perspective. However, as shown in Figure 6.2, programs with some partisan leaning—in either direction—were significantly more likely to involve high levels of incivility. Moreover, these were likely to be the programs with heavy doses of political content rather than ones that only occasionally dabbled in political topics. As also shown in Figure 6.2, partisan programs were somewhat less likely to emphasize up-close visual perspectives, although this pattern was only marginally significant.

To answer my questions pertaining to program formats, I examined the format characteristics as rated by multiple independent coders. To what extent did the programs use formats such as face-to-face discussion in which people were in the same physical environment? To what extent did they involve discussions between people who were not physically in the same room? In particular I hypothesized that incivility would be more likely when the people discussing politics

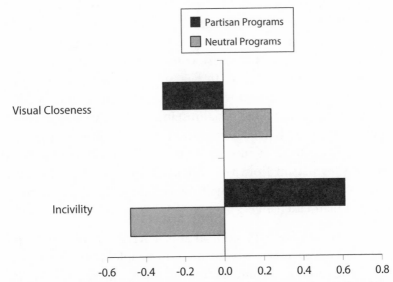

Figure 6.2. Visual closeness and incivility of political programs, by partisanship
Note: Bars represent means by program categories. Partisan programs are significantly more likely to involve high levels of incivility relative to neutral programs (t = 3.88, $p < .01$). Visual closeness was only marginally greater among neutral programs (t = 1.57, $p = .13$). Based on an analysis of 36 political programs.

were in different physical locations, whether via a split-screen format, or the Ted Koppel–style format, in which the interviewer is in one location and the interviewee is in another physical location.

Anecdotal evidence as well as research on interpersonal interaction suggest that incivility is far easier when one is not face-to-face with one's target. Consistent with this idea, Ted Koppel, the longtime host of ABC's *Nightline*, regularly refused to have guests appear with him in the same studio. When guests conditioned their *Nightline* appearance on appearing face-to-face with Koppel, he most often refused. Why is it guests fight for the privilege of appearing in the same studio rather than in the one next door? The lack of face-to-face contact tends to give Koppel an upper hand. As one observer of Koppel's technique described it,

> When you're interviewed on *Nightline*, normally you sit in a studio, in Washington or anywhere else in the world, a listening device in your ear, facing a camera. You don't even have the comfort

of seeing the image of Ted Koppel. The producers do not provide a monitor for you to watch the likeness of your inquisitor. . . . So there is no eye contact, not even your eye to image-eye, no instantaneous recognition of the interlocutor; rather a sequential passage of words through your ear. In fact, it places the interviewee in a foreign perceptual world where the guest no longer has the benefit of two dimensions—spatial/instantaneous as well as temporal/sequential. Using language, you still possess the power of analysis, but you cease to react automatically, as the human animal. By removing his person from you, Koppel cunningly deprives you of your animal instinct, of the will you could muster in an eye-to-eye mano-a-mano exchange.[4]

The artificial physical separation that is described here may be precisely what makes it easier to be hard on people when they are not in the same room. Communication technology makes it possible to interact while physically distant from another human being, but a desire for more hard-hitting, sparks-flying television makes this format more desirable for the interviewer who wants an edge over his or her interviewee, particular when it is asymmetric with respect to who can see whom.

In the political programs I studied, the extent to which a program incorporates uncivil exchanges is indeed correlated with interviews that take place between those who are physically separated ($r = .44$, $p < .01$). In other words, the absence of face-to-face contact facilitates greater incivility. It is easier for an interviewer or political advocate to be aggressive toward someone who is not actually physically present.

Some of the most talked-about shout fests, such as the one between Zell Miller and Chris Matthews after Miller's speech at the 2004 Republican National Convention, have occurred between people who were not physically in the same room. In this often replayed encounter, Chris Matthews goes after Senator Zell Miller for having deserted the Democratic Party and the Kerry campaign, and Miller ultimately reaches a level of extreme frustration. Only technological advances in communication have even made it possible to shout at someone who is not in the same room. People are more comfortable doing so under these conditions because close physical proximity makes shouting at someone seem far more inappropriate and uncomfortable.

Uncivil exchanges tend to be located in studios because they make it possible to "beam in" another person from a distant location. In fact, the incivility of program content is negatively correlated with the use of out-of-studio footage ($r = -.46, p < .01$). Outside of the studio, in the real world, the stylized incivility common on talk show sets would seem quite strange indeed. It is difficult to imagine a setting in which people would argue with one another without facing each another, and instead would both be facing a third party—in this case, the television audience.

But the format itself—often split screens with multiple people talking from inside individual "boxes" on the screen—has reached a level of popularity that borders on absurdity. Sometimes as many as six different heads talk from within boxes on a single television screen. And sometimes the artifice of the split screen is painfully obvious. Recent CNN coverage of the escape of three women kidnapped and held hostage in Cleveland for many years illustrates the bizarre way that technology has changed the treatment of spatial distance on television. As shown in Figure 6.3, two news anchors viewed in split-screen format conduct a satellite interview from the same parking lot, a point that becomes obvious when the same bus passes behind both anchors at roughly the same time. When a shot of a person or event is remote and brought into a studio via satellite, one can see how this approach makes some sense. But in this case, the two women could have stood right next to each other to talk to one another. Face-to-face exchanges are obviously no longer the preferred mode of television discourse. Moreover, the formats made possible by new technologies have unintended consequences for the civility of television discourse.

To answer the fourth question posed, whether incivility is more common in programs heavily or only occasionally emphasizing politics, I used the three-level categorization of a program's political emphasis and evaluated its relationship with the level of incivility in the program as well as close-up camera perspectives. As shown on the left side of Figure 6.4, overwhelmingly the most uncivil programs were also the most political in emphasis, and the less hostile programs tended to mix politics with other topics. In other words, what some might call the "soft news" approach tends to be warm

Figure 6.3. The split-screen obsession: "Nancy Grace and Ashleigh Banfield hold split-screen interview in same parking lot"
Source: http://www.theatlanticwire.com/national/2013/05/nancy-grace-ashleigh-banfield -cnn-parking-lot/64965/.

and friendly, whereas so-called serious political programs are associated with greater toughness and incivility. Thus a highly political program of the kind used in my experiments would tend to be the most uncivil in the real world.

As shown in the center panel of Figure 6.4, close-up visual perspectives do not follow a predictable pattern. Programs with moderate and high levels of political content indicated greater use of close-ups relative to those with low levels of political content. Combining the two measures as shown on the right-hand side of Figure 6.4 indicates that programs with extensive political content are far and away most likely to carry the joint characteristics of in-your-face politics: uncivil repartee combined with unnaturally close visual perspectives.

Perhaps programs that are exclusively political in content must gain broader public attention by means of an uncivil style of interaction, given that their substance is of interest to narrower audiences. In the post-broadcast era, people who are not interested in politics are not likely to watch much political programming when they have so much else available. Unless the programming is exciting in its own right, there are always better options for those only marginally interested.

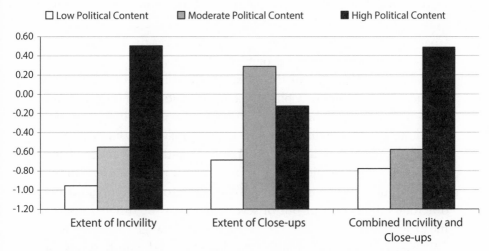

Figure 6.4. Incivility and intimacy of visuals by extent of political content in programs

Note: Bars represent standardized means. Separate analyses of variance on each of these dependent variables indicated significant differences among means for extent of incivility ($F = 8.43, p < .01$) and for the combined measure of incivility and intimate visuals ($F = 7.18, p < .01$). Post hoc comparisons indicated that the important mean differences were strictly between the high political content programs and the other two categories.

Having examined characteristics of a wide range of the most popular real-world political programs, I turn next to examine how these programs compare to the programs used in my experiments. To what extent were they representative of incivility and civility as it exists in real-world political programming?

IMPLICATIONS FOR THE GENERALIZABILITY OF EXPERIMENTAL TREATMENTS

To what extent are the experimental treatments I used as civil and uncivil programs representative of what one might actually see on television in the United States? If these programs are unique or extreme, they threaten the extent to which one would find similar effects in response to real-world programs. By design, the scales used to evaluate civility in the laboratory experiments were identical to those used to code on-the-air political programs, so it was possible to identify real-world programs that were in the same general range as the civil and uncivil experimental stimuli. As described briefly in Chapter 2, the uncivil program was nowhere near the level of intensity of chair throwing on a program such as *The Jerry Springer Show*, nor was the civil program the most civil possible; because the two candidates were purposely pitted against one another in not one, but a series of four issue discussions in which they consistently took opposing views, there were limits on how civil or uncivil they could appear.

The incivility of real-world programs was judged by coders using a series of 9-point scales ranging from *civil* (low) to *uncivil* (high). Across all of the various versions of the laboratory experiment using different subsets of four out of seven possible issue discussions, the mean levels of civility for the civil programs ranged from 3.78 to 3.96 based on the manipulation checks, whereas the mean levels for the uncivil programs ranged from 5.21 to 5.55 based on the average assessments of the experimental participants who watched these programs. If one were to select real-world programs that were coded as roughly in that same range of civility, the civil experimental treatment was on par with *The Situation Room*, *Face the Nation*, and *This Week with Christiane Amanpour*. Notably, many of the programs that would count as "civil" based on my laboratory experiments are nonetheless above the median horizontal line for incivility in Figure 6.1. In other words, the civil programs in my experiments were neither as civil as the most civil programs on the air, nor even as civil as most of those above the median in civility.

The uncivil experimental programs reflected roughly the same level of incivility as programs from *Fox News Sunday* through *The O'Reilly Factor*. Although these programs scored above median in terms of incivility, they are also clearly not the most uncivil political programs on the air. Figure 6.1 combined with the manipulation check means from the experiments suggest that the civil and uncivil experimental stimuli represented not extreme opposites in terms of civility levels, but rather relatively subtle differences. In this light, the consistent pattern of results seems especially surprising.

Manipulation check measures within each of the individual experiments confirmed that even when the political content was held constant, and only the manner of interaction between the candidates changed, the civil and uncivil programs were indeed perceived as significantly different. Yet in the real world, both television programs would fall on the uncivil side of the spectrum. Had I instead mimicked the friendly tenor of morning television news programs, for example, the differences between civil and uncivil conditions would have been more stark. On the other hand, in the real world these types of programs are quite different in content as well as in civility, so it would be difficult to mimic the camaraderie and friendliness of a morning news format with the same degree of substantive disagreement between the politicians as occurred in the experimental program.

Although the treatment programs were clearly within the range of what is commonly viewed, and did not represent unusual extremes in levels of civility or incivility, still other aspects of the experiment may also produce generalizability issues. For example, did the laboratory setting produce social desirability pressures to respond in certain ways? Although this is always possible, it seems unlikely for several reasons. First, it is unclear what effects the setting would have beyond increasing the audience's level of attention to the content. In addition, most of the designs were between-subjects experiments in which subjects could not know they were in one of several possible experimental conditions. Debriefings did not indicate any relevant suspicions about the purpose of the studies that might have confounded the results. Further the psychophysiological measures were consistent with results based on self-reports. Finally, the experiment recounted in Chapter 5 occurred outside of a laboratory, and reinforced the same pattern of findings. I turn next to survey data to investigate the generalizability of findings based on characteristics of the participants in the experiments relative to real-world viewers. Who is most likely to be exposed to in-your-face politics in the real world?

WHO WATCHES?

As mentioned at the beginning of this chapter, what has been known in the past about who watches political programs comes primarily from surveys examining how much people watch the nightly

national or local news, and perhaps a few other well-known programs. Because few studies have incorporated as comprehensive a
list of political programs as the National Annenberg Election Panel
Survey (NAES) in 2008, it is unclear to what extent these same patterns should be expected when examining a wider range of political
programming.[5]

The criteria for programs to be included in the survey involved
having some degree of political content or categorization as a news
or public affairs program for purposes of Nielsen television ratings.
As explained in greater detail in Dilliplane, Goldman, and Mutz, programs with the largest audiences were included up to the total number of programs that fit into the allotted survey time, which turned
out to be just over forty programs.[6] Because some of these programs
were not viewed regularly by any respondent in this extremely large
sample, we were fairly confident that we had captured the bulk of
political television viewing.

The 2008 NAES Panel Survey had several key advantages for purposes of tapping specific types of viewership. First, as mentioned
above, this study included an extensive battery of items asking respondents to indicate from a list of over forty specific programs which
ones they watched regularly, defined as at least once a month. This
was far greater detail on political program viewership than had been
available in any prior survey. In an era when respondents no longer
share a common definition of political news, and when audiences for
individual programs are quite small and fragmented, this approach
nonetheless allowed us to tap into a broad range of political programs.

In addition, although most self-reported measures of the frequency
of media exposure are notoriously suspect, these particular items
proved to be unusually reliable and valid indicators of political television exposure. Based on three waves of panel data using these same
items, they demonstrated high true-score reliability, as well as strong
predictive validity in predicting political knowledge gains over time
in relation to changes in political television exposure.[7] Rather than
relying on viewing measures of questionable reliability and validity, these measures have the advantage of having been validated in a
separate study.

Third, the 2008 NAES panel also had the distinct advantage of being an extremely large probability sample; over twelve thousand respondents participated in the three waves including measures of political television exposure. A large sample is helpful when studying contemporary political television viewership because a relatively small percentage of people watch political television of any variety these days. For example, 51 percent of the 2008 sample reported that they did not watch *any* of the political programs listed during the initial wave of data collection late in the 2008 primary season; predictably, as the election drew near, this number fell to roughly 45 percent as interest grew by the time of the election. Nonetheless, this means that as a practical matter, when analyzing television viewership, one loses roughly half of the sample because they do not watch any political television.

Starting from an initial representative national sample, I first eliminated the large percentage of the sample who reported watching none of the forty-two most widely viewed programs incorporating political content. This is obviously an important analytic decision when only half of the population reported watching *any* of these programs regularly during an election year. However, because my interest is not so much in what drives people to watch political television, as in what encourages them to watch *in-your-face programs in particular* when they do watch, the people who watch none at all were not of interest. Fortunately, the remaining sample of 4,920 people who reported watching one or more shows regularly was sufficiently large to allow characterizations of who views in-your-face content. By using the coding of civility and visual perspectives for each program in conjunction with survey data on viewership, it was possible to match individual respondents with the characteristics of the political programs they watched regularly.

Based on the content analysis, each program was assigned a mean for the extent of close-ups, a mean for the extent of incivility, and the product of those two measures as an indicator of overall "in your faceness" by program. Given that the audience for any individual political program is fairly small in the age of fragmented television audiences, I combined these individual measures for all political programs that were watched by any given individual to create a summative indicator of the total number of political programs watched, the percentage of programs over the median level of incivility, and a third measure indicating the percentage of programs with high percentages of close-ups. Because the total number of programs watched may well set boundaries for the amount of content of a particular kind to which any given individual is exposed, I included the total number of programs watched in many of the analyses.

There are two distinct ways of addressing the question of who is most exposed to in-your-face politics. The most simple and straightforward is to ask the question in descriptive terms: what are the people like who watch programs with high levels of incivility and up-close visuals? I begin with this simple bivariate approach. For each of a variety of characteristics, I examined how they were related to the overall number of programs viewed as well as to the percentage of those programs that were uncivil or that were shot from a close-up visual perspective. A second, multivariate, approach asks how these various characteristics independently contribute to viewership while simultaneously taking into account all of the other characteristics. For this analysis, I used a series of multivariate regression equations. Neither approach is expected to provide a causal account of what leads people to watch in-your-face politics; however, given that we know little about who watches political television programs in general these days, let alone who watches in-your-face politics in particular, an exploratory analysis seems most appropriate.

Bivariate Associations

Older people have traditionally been the heaviest viewers of standard evening network news programs, and indeed this remains the case. Even when taking into account the much broader array of political programs available today, older people still watch a great deal more political television than younger people. As shown on the right-hand scale in Figure 6.5, the total number of political programs watched goes up steadily with age. But interestingly, the proportion of those programs that is over the median level of incivility goes *down* with age, while the percentage with high levels of close-up visuals remains flat. Older Americans continue to be steadfast viewers of political

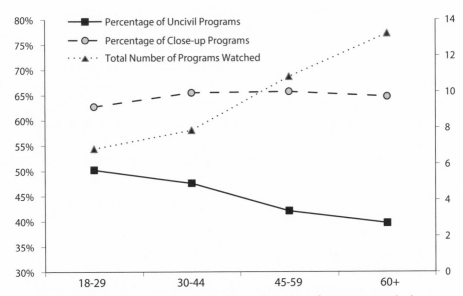

Figure 6.5. Relationship between age and total number of programs watched, proportion of uncivil programs and proportion of close-up programs

content, but they are clearly not drawn to the incivility of in-your-face politics; in fact, precisely the opposite appears to be true.

Strong partisanship traditionally goes hand in hand with political television viewership as well. Interestingly, Figure 6.6 shows a more muted pattern in this regard. Although strong partisans view more programs than independents, these differences are relatively small, and Democrats at all levels of partisan strength watch more programs than the Republicans of corresponding partisan strength. What is particularly interesting in Figure 6.6 is that strong Republicans are by far and away the heaviest viewers of incivility, and strong Democrats are the least likely to view incivility. As noted earlier in the chapter, partisan programs are more likely to feature incivility, but no more likely whether they lean Republican or Democratic. Nonetheless, if one conceives of the political television diet of each group as a whole, Democrats are exposed to a larger group of programs, a small proportion of which are uncivil; Republicans are exposed to fewer programs, a much larger proportion of which are uncivil. Incivility is clearly a much bigger part of the average Republican's political television diet. Moreover, as shown in Chapter 5, Republicans are also more affected by uncivil political content.

Why are Republicans drawn to more uncivil content? Based on qualitative evidence, Sobieraj and Berry argue that it is because uncivil partisan programs offer validation and political companionship to conservatives that is missing in their day-to-day lives: "In other words, we suspect conservatives feel that they are in a more precarious position than liberals when it comes to political talk."[8] Based on nationally representative data on conservatives' political discussion networks, I am skeptical of this explanation. Conservatives have highly homogeneous political discussion networks, so there is no reason they should lack safe havens for face-to-face discussion. If anything, conservatives have more conversations with like-minded others than do liberals.

The pattern with respect to the proportion of programs viewed that involve close-up visual perspectives is less obvious, but it nicely mirrors the pattern for the dotted line representing the overall extent of

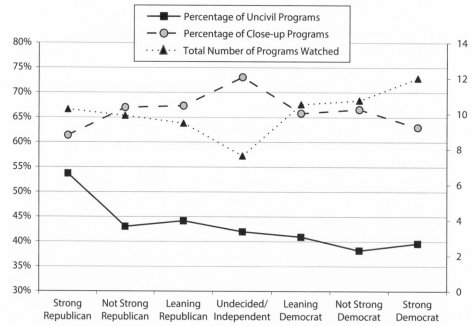

Figure 6.6. Relationship between party identification and total number of programs watched, proportion of uncivil programs and proportion of close-up programs

viewing. Those who watch the most programs watch a lower proportion of visually close-up programs, whereas those who watch fewer programs tend to watch a higher proportion of programs with close-up visual perspectives. In descriptive terms, strong partisans tend to watch a lower proportion of close-up shows relative to those who are less partisan.

As a last look at purely descriptive patterns of viewership, Figure 6.7 illustrates viewing in relation to patterns of political interest. Political interest is obviously one of the most widely used surrogates for viewership. And indeed, the pattern for the total number of programs watched is exactly as one would predict: the total number of programs viewed increases in a clear linear pattern with increasing levels of political interest. However, the percentage of programs that involve close-up visual perspectives declines in precisely the opposite fashion: those very interested in politics are substantially less likely to have close-up visuals in their programs relative to those not at all interested. This is likely to result from the fact that the kind of programs emphasizing a more intimate camera perspective are also the more friendly, less intensely political programs, such as morning news shows with lower levels of political emphasis. Most interestingly, the proportion of uncivil programs forms a curvilinear pattern in which both those very interested and not at all interested in politics view a higher proportion of uncivil programs. For the highly interested, people who watch large numbers of programs, they may well be driven to include uncivil programs in their political television diet because they tend to watch virtually everything. But Figure 6.7 also suggests that incivility is particularly attractive for those with less interest. This pattern would make little sense if people truly abhorred incivility; if people are only watching a few programs anyway, there are certainly plenty of civil choices one could watch instead of the uncivil ones. Instead, it seems plausible that people at different ends of this spectrum watch in-your-face politics for two distinct reasons; they watch in-your-face politics either because of an intense interest in politics, or because they have relatively little interest, but appreciate the drama of in-your-face programs.

Thus far total political program viewership seems to follow predictable patterns, despite the greater range of programs on offer.

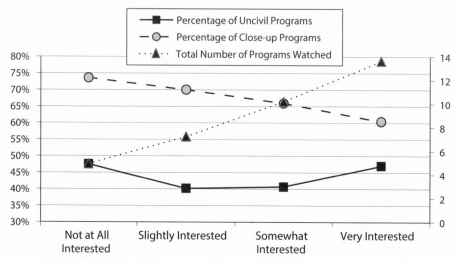

Figure 6.7. Relationship between political interest and total number of programs watched, proportion of uncivil programs and proportion of close-up programs

Given that there are no previous studies of who views in-your-face political television, I have offered exploratory evidence suggesting that Republicans, young people, and those most and least interested in politics are most drawn to uncivil political content. Close-ups follow a pattern in which those least interested and involved tend to watch more programs involving up-close visuals. Because close-ups and incivility are, if at all related, negatively correlated in political programs, just as they are in the real world of human interaction, they do not go hand in hand with a particular viewer profile.

Multivariate Analyses

To fill in the rest of this picture, I turn next to more complex multivariate analyses. Because the national survey included not only demographics, but also a large number of other variables that may help to characterize viewers of in-your-face politics, I drew on many of them for purposes of multivariate analyses. These included basic demographics such as age, education, race, gender, household income, paid employment, whether respondents lived inside or outside of a metropolitan area, and whether they lived with a spouse or partner. In addition, another set of variables represented levels of involvement in politics, such as whether they were registered to vote at their current address, whether they voted in the midterm elections, and their self-reported level of interest in politics. Another measure of political interest more directly tied to political television viewing was created based on Prior's indicator of relative news versus entertainment preferences when viewing.[9] The procedure for calculating relative entertainment-news preferences involved asking respondents to rank order their preferences for a number of types of television programs, from most liked to fourth most liked.[10] On this 5-point scale, the lowest scores for relative entertainment preference went to those respondents who ranked news programs as most preferred, followed by those who ranked them second, third, and fourth, respectively. Not surprisingly, the bulk of respondents did not rank news at all among their top four types of programs. Those respondents received the highest score on relative entertainment preference.

Yet another group of measures tapped political preferences, including party identification and ideology. In addition, variables indicating whether the household had home Internet access and access to cable television via either cable or satellite were also taken into account. Finally, I also included what might loosely be dubbed lifestyle measures including how often respondents attend religious services, whether they have one or more guns in the household, and union membership.

The full results of these analyses are shown in Table 6.1, where I compare the most important predictors of three different types of viewing: (1) the total number of political programs watched, (2) the extent of viewing uncivil programs, and (3) the extent of viewing uncivil programs that combine in-your-face visuals with incivility. I do not analyze predictors of viewing programs with close-up visuals separately, because the effects found in Part I of this book depend upon either uncivil content alone or uncivil content in combination with up-close visuals. None of the effects was driven by close-up visuals alone.

Table 6.1. Predictors of Total Amount of Political TV Watched, Total Amount of Uncivil TV Watched, and Amount of Uncivil and Close-Up TV, among Those Who Watch Some Political Television

	Total amount of political TV watched		Amount of uncivil political TV watched		Amount of uncivil and close-up TV watched	
	b	*SE*	*b*	*SE*	*b*	*SE*
Demographics						
Age	0.10	0.01***	−0.02	0.00***	−0.11	0.02***
Education	0.11	0.14	−0.27	0.06***	−1.20	0.27***
White	−2.35	0.27***	0.33	0.13**	1.68	0.52**
Female	1.10	0.23***	−1.05	0.11***	−4.79	0.44***
Household income	−0.05	0.03	0.05	0.02**	0.20	0.07**
Live with spouse/ partner	−0.18	0.25	0.06	0.12	0.22	0.49
Metro vs. rural	−0.32	0.31	0.17	0.15	0.99	0.60
Employed for pay	−1.00	0.24***	0.11	0.11	0.38	0.47
Political involvement						
Voted in midterm	−0.08	0.28	0.28	0.13*	1.00	0.55
Registered to vote	−0.01	0.40	−0.26	0.19	−0.79	0.77
Political interest	2.02	0.14***	0.39	0.07***	1.36	0.27***
Relative entertain- ment preference	−0.90	0.08***	−0.29	0.04***	−0.98	0.15***
Political leanings						
Republican	−0.07	0.28	0.25	0.13*	0.84	0.53
Democrat	−0.73	0.33*	−0.29	0.15	−1.16	0.64
Ideology (conservative)	−0.72	0.14***	0.69	0.07***	2.84	0.27***
Lifestyle						
Gun owner	−0.21	0.24	−0.08	0.11	−0.24	0.46
Attend religious services	0.06	0.07	−0.10	0.03**	−0.44	0.14**
Union member	0.39	0.33	−0.01	0.15	−0.12	0.63
Media access						
Have cable or satellite TV	1.40	0.30***	1.13	0.14***	4.45	0.58***
Have home internet access	−0.67	0.40	0.04	0.19	0.20	0.78
R^2		.25		.16		.15
(n)		3,618		3,599		3,599

*$p < .05$. **$p < .01$. ***$p < .001$.

Total Number of Political Programs Watched

Predicting who watches the most programs that include at least some political content turns out to be the easiest of these three tasks. Consistent with evidence on viewing traditional political news, as shown in the first column of Table 6.1, older people and those with high levels of political interest are most likely to view large numbers of programs. Also consistent with predictions, those with particularly strong preferences for entertainment programs are much less likely to watch political programs.

Demographically, what is most surprising is that when including this much broader range of political programs, women are *more* rather than less likely to watch political programs. Also unexpected was the large negative impact of being white and non-Hispanic relative to all other racial/ethnic categories. In the past, findings have suggested that women and minorities are less likely to view political programs. Although minorities have been documented to be heavy television watchers in the past, they have not typically been heavy viewers of news and public affairs programming. But again, the news and public affairs landscape is quite different now from when most of those conclusions were drawn. The other significant demographic pattern was a negative relationship between being employed for pay outside the home and total viewing. Perhaps because of the greater number of potential viewing opportunities for those who are not at an office, not being employed boosts viewership of these programs overall.

Politically, the multivariate findings were also surprisingly different from the descriptive relationships. In purely descriptive terms, both Republicans and Democrats watched more programs than those in the middle, although Democrats watched more programs overall. However, once other forms of political interest and involvement are taken into account, Democratic identification was associated with viewing fewer programs overall (excluding leaners). Because this finding was unanticipated, I double-checked to make sure collinearity was not a problem in this model. Although partisanship is certainly correlated with interest, it appears to be interest that is driving exposure rather than partisanship per se. Democrats watch less all else being equal, and conservatives watch significantly more political programs than liberals.

Finally, one of the most powerful predictors of amount viewed was simply having cable television access. Although having cable gives one access to a huge amount of entertainment programming, it also provides access to far more political programming, and this is reflected in the number of political programs cable subscribers view.

Extent of Exposure to Uncivil Political Programs

As shown in the second column of Table 6.1, the pattern of results for exposure to uncivil programs was not the same as for the total number of programs. To be sure, some predictors were similar; for example, having cable television access increased exposure to uncivil television, as did political interest, and preferring entertainment programs over news significantly reduced exposure to uncivil programs, while those who voted in midterm elections were more likely to have been exposed to incivility. And in a similar pattern, Republicans and conservatives were more likely to be exposed to uncivil programs, despite the lack of relationship with right-leaning partisanship at the program level of analysis.

Demographics, however, followed precisely the opposite pattern as they did when predicting total amount viewed. Older people were significantly *less* likely to be exposed to uncivil programs, and whites were significantly *more* likely to expose themselves to uncivil programs. And again, contrary to overall patterns of viewership, women were *less* likely to view incivility, even though they watched more programs overall. Socioeconomic variables such as income and education were unrelated to total amount viewed, but education negatively predicted exposure to uncivil content, while income increased exposure. Those who attend religious services regularly were less likely to expose themselves to incivility.

Extent of Exposure to Close-ups of Uncivil Exchanges

Overall, the pattern of results for the complete package of in-your-face politics—up-close portrayals of incivility—is very similar to the patterns for exposure to incivility more generally; as shown in the final column of Table 6.1, younger, poorly educated, conservative white males are more likely to expose themselves to such content, particularly if they have cable TV and a decent income, and are interested in politics to some extent.

Overall, these results suggest that it is quite difficult to predict who watches in-your-face politics. While around 25 percent of the variance in total amount watched was explained by these models, predicting uncivil or uncivil/close-up exposure was substantially more difficult; these models predicted only around 15 to 16 percent of the variance, even with a large number of predictor variables.

In interpreting these findings relative to previous work, it is important to keep in mind that by eliminating all of the people who do not watch any political or public affairs programming, I have changed the structure of the variance in these analyses. It is certainly possible to include those who watch no programs whatsoever, but because they represent roughly half of the population, they have excessive influence on the pattern of results. Because my focus is not on what creates political interest so much as what leads people to choose one type of political program over another, eliminating them seemed most appropriate.

THE GENERALIZABILITY OF EXPERIMENTAL SUBJECTS

The generalizability of any given result does not end with realistic treatments or neutralization of social pressures in the laboratory. Characteristics of experimental subjects are also of concern. If there are characteristics of people that make them particularly susceptible to these effects—for example, conflict aversion makes people more susceptible to the effects on political trust demonstrated in Chapter 4—and those kinds of people are seldom ever exposed to in-your-face programming anyway, then this pattern suggests a limited likelihood that these effects will be problematic in the real world. Other evidence of heterogeneity appeared in Chapter 5, where it was demonstrated that Democrats were less likely to react to incivility than Republicans.

Outside of these two exceptions, there was very limited evidence of heterogeneity of effects. I regularly tested for interactions between the civility and close-up treatments with age, education, gender, and strength of party identification. With null effects, one can never be certain if this occurs because heterogeneity is simply not there or because of the limitations of sample size in identifying significant interactions. Thus in a few cases, where I had a good theoretical reason to expect heterogeneity of effects, I pooled subjects across multiple experiments in order to do a better job evaluating potential heterogeneity.

As mentioned in Chapter 5, due to laboratory locations in largely academic communities and liberal urban areas, conservatives tended to be underrepresented in my laboratory samples, despite purposeful efforts to recruit subjects from organizations known to be conservative. Given that conservatives appear to be more sensitive to these experimental treatments than liberals, this pattern suggests that one might find even stronger evidence using more representative subject pools.

My most concerted effort to examine heterogeneity of effects centered on gender because of the seemingly logical possibility that women would respond more strongly to incivility than men. This possibility was raised virtually every time I presented these results publicly, and it seemed intuitively logical to me, as well as to my audiences. Given that most politicians are male, and male candidates were used in my incivility experiments, it seemed predictable that female subjects would react particularly negatively to what they might see as simply "men behaving badly."[11] This logic was further recommended by studies suggesting that women are more risk-averse than men, although there is, in this case, no actual economic risk of the kind usually intended in such comparisons.[12] Nonetheless, to the extent that the implied threat of incivility is more aversive to women than men, one would expect stronger reactions from female viewers.

Thus I evaluated interactions between gender and experimental treatments in each and every experiment executed, and while some findings looked to be headed in the anticipated direction, with females responding somewhat more strongly to in-your-face incivility, none of the findings reached conventional levels of statistical significance. To make sure this was not a sample power problem, I next pooled all of the experimental results and looked for an interaction between incivility and gender, again with no results. Although the experiment in Chapter 4 including conflict avoidance measures confirmed that the female participants were more conflict-avoidant than the male participants, an interaction between incivility and gender was not significant in that experiment either, indicating that gender was not an adequately clear-cut marker of tendencies toward conflict avoidance.

This puzzle prompted me to look further into what is known about gender differences in conflict avoidance. The scale I had used for conflict avoidance was one dimension of a multidimensional scale designed to measure interpersonal conflict communication styles.[13] The tendency to approach or avoid conflict was tapped by five questions tapping agree-disagree responses to items such as "I enjoy challenging the opinions of others" and "I hate arguments."[14]

The non-finding was initially very puzzling to me. After all, so much of in-your-face politics consists of men violating social norms in seemingly aggressive ways. But the further I looked into the matter, the less clear-cut this expectation seemed. Although it is true that women tend to be more conflict-avoidant by many measures, findings have not been entirely consistent.[15] In particular, when it comes to the expression of emotion as part of conflict-related communication, women tend to be more comfortable with it than men.[16]

Regardless, none of the psychological studies of conflict-related attitudes used representative samples of men and women, thus making their conclusions difficult to generalize. Conflict avoidance was the basis for the heterogeneity of effects that I had observed, but I next examined all four validated dimensions of conflict avoidance within a representative national sample. People's attitudes toward conflict-oriented communication can be characterized along four different dimensions, only one of which was reflected in the Conflict Approach/Avoidance Scale used in the earlier experiment.[17] The three other dimensions are also potentially relevant to attitudes toward viewing in-your-face politics. These included (1) a six-item subscale with questions addressing whether people dislike face-to-face confrontation in particular (e.g., "I feel more comfortable having an argument in person than over the phone," "I dislike when others have eye contact with me during an argument"), (2) a four-item subscale assessing a preference for private over public conflict (e.g., "I feel uncomfortable seeing others argue in public," "I don't mind strangers arguing in my presence"), and (3) an index of six items addressing discomfort with emotional expression during disputes (e.g., "Everything should be out in the open in an argument, including emotions," "It shows strength to express emotions openly"). In the national sample, these four dimensions of conflict orientation were internally consistent, all with respectably high Cronbach's alphas. The four separate dimensions were also positively intercorrelated with each other, but only very weakly so (see Appendix C).

To begin, I examined simple mean differences in each of the dimensions by gender. Women were consistently more anticonflict on three of these four dimensions. As shown in Figure 6.8 and as intuitively expected, American women were more averse to face-to-face confrontation than American men. Likewise, women were more likely to say that conflicts should be aired in private rather than in public, and to score higher on the Conflict Approach/Avoidance Scale that I had used as a moderator in the previous experiment.

However, as also shown in Figure 6.8, on one dimension of conflict communication orientation, the avoidance of emotional expression, men scored significantly higher than women. The expression

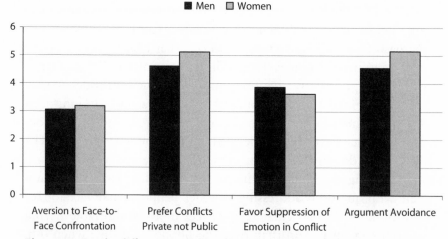

Figure 6.8. Gender differences in dimensions of conflict avoidance
Note: All gender differences are significant. From left to right, t values were $t = 5.79$, $p < .001$; $t = 16.03$, $p < .001$; $t = 10.75$, $p < .001$; $t = 21.57$, $p < .001$, respectively.

of emotion, which is frequently an important component of uncivil exchanges, is significantly more comfortable for women than for men. So one might argue that women are not, across the board, more averse to conflict in all of its dimensions; when it comes to emotional expression within conflicts, men are more averse than women. Given that television is a particularly strong medium for conveying emotion, and arousal and the emotional reactions that follow from it are part and parcel of what draws people to in-your-face politics, these factors may help shed additional light on who watches and why.

Of course, what draws a person to a program involving in-your-face politics need not be the same thing that predisposes them to be affected by it. Nonetheless, the fact that people who are averse to conflict were most reactive to my experimental treatment suggested a potential generalizability problem: if conflict-avoidant people also avoid in-your-face political television, then there would be few opportunities for effects. If those most affected by it seldom ever watch it outside of a forced laboratory situation, then generalizability is a clear concern.

To investigate this possibility, I included these four conflict orientation indexes as additional predictors of the extent of exposure to in-your-face political programming in a multivariate model, extending the analysis begun earlier in this chapter. As shown at the bottom of Table 6.2, three of the dimensions of conflict orientation are negatively signed, as would be predicted, but none reach statistical significance as suppressors of exposure to in-your-face content. Whether entered individually or simultaneously, they do not predict exposure. Only the index indicating preferences for avoidance of emotional expression was a significant predictor, and surprisingly, it is positively signed; in other words, the more a person is uncomfortable with emotional expression, the more he or she likes watching political programs that are teeming with emotion.

This was not what I had predicted. As a result, I went back to the original data, checked all of the coding, and reran each analysis, but the finding remained. Although I can offer no easy post hoc explanation that would be convincing, it seems plausible that those uncomfortable with the expression of emotions nonetheless like to watch others' emotional displays. Uncivil exchanges may be particularly

Table 6.2. Predictors of Exposure to In-Your-Face Politics, among Those Who Watch One or More Political Programs Regularly

	b	SE	t-value	Sig.
Demographics				
Age	−0.076	0.019	4.108	.000
Education	−1.183	0.266	4.443	.000
White	1.036	0.525	1.975	.048
Female	−3.943	0.458	8.604	.000
Household income	0.156	0.066	2.348	.019
Live with spouse/partner	0.243	0.483	0.503	.615
Metro vs. rural	0.903	0.596	1.516	.130
Employed for pay	0.116	0.465	0.250	.803
Political involvement				
Voted in midterm	0.992	0.537	1.847	.065
Registered to vote	−0.811	0.763	1.062	.288
Political interest	1.989	0.279	7.134	.000
Relative entertainment preference	−1.257	0.150	8.391	.000
Political leanings				
Republican	0.863	0.525	1.644	.100
Democrat	−1.400	0.627	2.232	.026
Ideology (conservative)	2.535	0.268	9.461	.000
Lifestyle				
Gun owner	−0.346	0.451	0.767	.443
Attend religious services	−0.392	0.138	2.840	.005
Union member	−0.034	0.619	0.055	.956
Media access				
Have cable or satellite TV	4.902	0.571	8.585	.000
Have home internet access	−0.004	0.764	0.005	.996
Conflict orientation				
Averse to face-to-face conflict	−0.354	0.259	1.367	.172
Suppression of emotion in conflict	0.897	0.277	3.236	.001
Conflict avoidant	−0.278	0.248	1.118	.264
Prefers conflicts private	−0.214	0.211	1.011	.312
Total amount of political TV	−0.331	0.032	10.455	.000
R^2		.18		
(n)		3,595		

arousing and riveting for those who generally dislike them in their own lives. Moreover, the fact that people who report that they dislike displays of emotion are nonetheless drawn to it on television is very similar to the conundrum from Part I: people say they dislike incivility, yet they like to watch it because it is not boring. I will need to leave it to future researchers to understand this particular contradiction. But overall, there is no suggestion in Table 6.2 that the kind of people who will be affected by incivility will avoid exposure to it.

Two other coefficients in Table 6.2 are also worth noting. One is that gender remains a strong predictor of exposure, even after all of the controls for political interest, conflict orientations, and so forth. Women are unlikely to be in the audience for in-your-face politics, yet this does not appear to be due to general conflict avoidance. In addition, at the very bottom of Table 6.2 we see that the total amount of political television viewed is negatively related to how much a person views in-your-face politics; the more a person watches political television, the less likely he or she is to watch much of the in-your-face variety. This finding suggests that people are not just watching in-your-face politics as part of a political junkie media lifestyle; these programs, in particular, are watched probably because of, rather than in spite of, their uncivil content.

LIMITATIONS IN ADDRESSING GENERALIZABILITY

Before moving on to new findings in Part III, it is worth pausing to take stock of the extent to which Part II has thoroughly addressed concerns about the generalizability of the experimental findings. Generalizability issues can pertain not only to the experimental setting and subjects, but also to the treatments and dependent measures. The internal validity of the experimental findings benefits from both the replications and modifications offered in the six experiments discussed thus far. In these controlled settings, it was possible to establish not only that incivility was successfully manipulated, but also that the political opinions expressed and the perceived ideological extremity of the candidates were not inadvertently manipulated. The experiments used combinations of different civil and uncivil exchanges, in order to ensure that no one experimental treatment was responsible for the findings. In Part II, I demonstrated that the same pattern of findings obtained when including party identification in the experimental paradigm and when using real-world television content. Parallel findings were also obtained in a study using a large, representative national sample of subjects. Furthermore, even when the outcome measures used somewhat different instrumentation, the same pattern of findings emerged.

Nonetheless, the most difficult generalizability issue that I have explored can at best be only partially addressed. Are the kind of people affected by in-your-face politics also those who watch it in the real world? To some extent I know the answer to this question to be yes, because conservatives are both especially drawn to this content and clearly react to it as well. Moreover, I find no evidence that the type of conflict avoidance that predisposes people to stronger effects prevents them from viewing more content of this kind.

But of necessity, I have explored only a few dimensions of heterogeneity that might be involved in drawing people to in-your-face politics, and none of the measures I used was particularly strong as a predictor of attraction to this content. It remains possible that some other, as yet unexamined, characteristic limits the potential influence of in-your-face politics in the real world. However, as explored in Part III, in-your-face politics has increased in intensity even within the highly civil programs discussed in Part II. It is a far more general and mainstream trend in television content, one that is not limited to partisan talk shows.

WHO WATCHES AND WHY IT MATTERS

Based on the analyses in this chapter, conservatives and Republicans are particularly likely to expose themselves to in-your-face programs in the real world, and based on the experimental results, they are also especially likely to be react once exposed. In addition, the experimental treatments overall tended to be quite civil relative to the levels of incivility found in real-world programs. This confluence of findings suggests that in-your-face impact is probably alive and well in the real world, not just in the laboratory, and perhaps to an even greater extent than I have documented in Part I.

My analyses of who watches the most in-your-face politics among those who watch political television at all met with only limited success. In my exploratory analysis, some of the "usual suspects" such as political interest, relative entertainment preference, and access to cable television were consistent predictors in obvious directions, but many others were not. The people most likely to watch such programs tend to be young, less educated white men with higher incomes. Conservatives in particular are drawn to these programs, even though there is plenty of incivility on offer in programs of both leanings for liberals who would like to partake. Those who are religiously involved tend to avoid such programs, contrary to the stereotypes that have been suggested about the religious right wing.

In Part III, I turn my attention to the historical implications of in-your-face politics, addressing the question of whether the same theories should be expected to hold in other media. In addition, drawing on visuals from television over many decades, I examine how political television itself has changed during its relatively brief history.

HISTORICAL IMPLICATIONS FOR POLITICAL TELEVISION

CHAPTER 7

DOES THE MEDIUM MATTER?

Having demonstrated several effects of televised in-your-face politics, the logical next question in my mind was whether these effects were specific to television. Could other media such as radio or newspapers produce some of these same effects? Thus far in this book, I have framed in-your-face politics as a theory about the effects of television, but incivility in political discourse can obviously occur on the radio, to be sure, and at times even within newspapers. Furthermore, the Internet has become a particular locus of concern with respect to the civility of political discourse in recent years.

Of course, there is no analogue to the close-up camera perspective in these other media, although newspapers can carry photographs, and radio can be used to convey a sense of intimacy as well. To what extent are the effects of in-your-face politics tied to the emergence of television? This is an important question for understanding the mechanisms underlying the effects, but it is even more important for purposes of understanding the potential historical importance of in-your-face politics. If uncivil political discourse is simply business as usual in American politics, then the effects of in-your-face politics have been with us for a very long time. However, if it matters *how* American citizens are exposed to incivility, then what people experience now may indeed be quite different from in the past, even if the level of incivility in political discourse has not changed at all.

To explore this question, I begin by reviewing arguments evaluating whether television is, indeed, unique as a medium of political communication. Then I turn to the same experimental paradigm used in Chapters 2, 3, and 4 to explore whether any of these same effects occur in response to incivility in political discourse that reaches audiences through other media. My results confirm that television is uniquely powerful in conveying emotional intensity; this capacity translates into important differences between how audiences understand conflictual political discourse via audiovisual media versus through other media. Finally, I draw on these findings to explain the widespread perceptions of decline in civil political life in America.

WHAT'S SPECIAL ABOUT TELEVISION?

It is commonplace to claim that the advent of television fundamentally changed everything about how American politics is conducted. Among academic researchers, however, that hyperbolic claim was dropped soon after the rise of television news. The political content of television turned out to be not all that different from what newspapers covered, although television news necessarily covered less material given its time constraints. By the mid-1970s, questions also were raised about whether this supposedly all-powerful visual medium was really so influential after all. Patterson and McClure's seminal book, *The Unseeing Eye: The Myth of Television Power in National Politics*, casts further doubt on the distinctiveness of television, arguing that the mythological status of television far exceeded its actual impact.[1]

In Part I of this book, I documented several different kinds of effects from in-your-face politics, so it is important to consider what role, if any, a specific medium might play in each of them. Interestingly, past theories linking declining political trust to media have not specified television per se as the cause. Instead, theories originally about "videomalaise" were broadened into more general claims about effects of political journalism, claims that transcend television, newspapers, and virtually all political media. For example, some have suggested that negative commentary from journalists naturally leads members of the public to think ill of politicians and the system in which they are embedded.[2] Journalistic narratives emphasizing the ulterior, self-interested motives of political actors also have been widely blamed for public negativity. The shift toward general theories of "mediamalaise" does not mean that television has been given a complete reprieve from its putative responsibility for all that ails American politics. Instead, the argument has evolved to blame television journalism for *initiating* the deleterious shifts in tone and content that subsequently spread to other political media. Because of the need to compete with television, print media began to mimic television's tone, at least so the argument goes.[3] Whatever the rationale, few scholars have contended that political television, as it currently exists, presents a unique perspective on government and politics.

The few exceptions are studies suggesting that television, by virtue of its visual nature, draws attention to certain dimensions of candidate evaluation over others. As one journalist summarized, "Television makes the candidate of today a human being at one's elbow, who is going to be judged on the same terms as a man greets any new acquaintance."[4] The sensory realism of television is also widely believed to convey a sense of intimacy with political actors that citizens were unlikely to encounter in the past, even in face-to-face meetings with politicians.[5]

Nonetheless, evidence of television's unique impact has proved elusive. For example, content analyses have repeatedly suggested that television and print media present very similar information about candidates.[6] Moreover, perceptions of candidates' personal qualities do not vary based on people's sources of information,[7] although there is some evidence that candidate appearance influences vote choice among the uninformed.[8]

Despite the fact that television is by now considered an "old medium," scholars have only begun to understand the consequences of the fact that political candidates and advocates of political ideas appear on television as actual human beings rather than as a series of disembodied words or voices. The sense of personal intimacy that viewers have with people appearing on television is obvious at one level, but research to date has not explored how and why it matters if these people appear to be physically proximate human beings to their citizen-viewers.

Research within social psychology confirms that print and pictures are indeed processed differently: "Differences in the processing of pictures and words emanate from the physical similarity of pictures, but not words, to the referents."[9] Print is the preferred mode of communication for both psychologically and spatially distant referents, whereas pictures are preferred for things that are spatially close and concrete.[10] Likewise, things we can see with our own eyes tend to be processed as if they were spatially and psychologically close.[11] Psychologists suggest that this occurs because, audiovisual media notwithstanding, most things humans can see are, indeed, spatially close, making this specialization highly adaptive outside the world of media: "Pictures thus impart a sense of closeness to the referent objects . . . whereas words do not convey proximity."[12]

Interestingly, evidence suggests that different kinds of distance— social, psychological, temporal, and spatial—are linked in the human mind.[13] It is no mere accident that "long ago and far away" seem to fit together much better than "long ago and nearby." Likewise, different conceptions of distance can influence one another such that targets thought to be far away are also perceived to be more psychologically distant.[14] Sensitivity to physical distance information is thought to be most basic because it is "built into the design and function of the human brain," and then becomes the basis for understanding other kinds of distance as well.[15] Interestingly, politeness is also greater when addressing a spatially distant rather than a proximate target.[16]

Thus far, research on what is unique about television relative to other media has been limited to the extent to which televised politics heightens the importance of certain kinds of information over others. For example, perceptions of candidates' personal qualities were found to be no different based on which medium people used, but personal qualities were more important to voters who obtained political news from television.[17] Another study suggested that television primes people to rely more on personality perceptions when evaluating candidates.[18]

In the case of in-your-face politics, however, I explicitly argue that television's effects are not due to differences in the political *content* provided by one medium versus another, but rather differences in how audiences *experience* that content. Precisely because watching, more so than reading, feels more like being there, people may internalize expectations from the world of face-to-face discourse to a greater extent with television than with other media. Thus television's violations of norms of civility may be experienced more acutely and uncomfortably than they would be in print.

Would trust in politics and politicians improve if the public simply did not witness so much uncivil political disagreement in video form? By creating an impression of closer proximity, I suggest that televised political disagreements exacerbate the "intensification of feeling" that Walter Lippmann so despised in politics.[19] This theory offers an entirely different rationale for why incivility may intensify negative attitudes toward government and politicians.

In the experiments in Part I, I examined the impact of televised examples of uncivil political discourse. I did so for three reasons. First, although incivility is not limited to television, television is still the dominant medium through which citizens are exposed to political controversy. Second, and more important, I chose television because its images and sounds more accurately mimic conflict as experienced in interpersonal situations. These visuals contain a lot of information about social relations between speakers, and between speakers and viewers.[20] Because visuals focus attention on primitive social cues, political television's violations of the usual social rules should be especially salient. Third, these social cues are easily and effortlessly communicated in visuals, without changing the political content of a program. This makes television especially likely to generate reactions even among inattentive audiences: "Pictures, because they look like the things they represent, require less mental effort to translate between referent and reality. Pictures give information that is more familiar and easy to process."[21]

Of course, just because televised incivility seems especially likely to generate reactions based on violations of social rules does not mean that other media could not also do so. Whether such effects are specific to televised exposure to incivility is a complex question. For example, a print version of this same program—even a direct transcript—might not be perceived as demonstrating the same extent of incivility as the television program, in which viewers witnessed nonverbal and paralinguistic cues such as Bob sneering at Neil, and Neil shaking his head ruefully while Bob was speaking. In a study manipulating civility versus incivility using print manipulations, Funk found results in the general direction one would expect, but the effects were not statistically significant.[22] Interestingly, she predicted that this null finding would have been significant had she used televised variations in civility, although she was not able to test this hypothesis.

Overall, the theoretical framework I have offered suggests that television is likely to exacerbate effects of incivility, even if this effect is not necessarily limited to televised incivility. It seems doubtful, for example, that reading about a heated political controversy in the newspaper would cause the same extent of heightened physiological arousal as watching that same conflict on television. It is also plausible that only television causes the in-your-face paradox: what rankles viewers about watching incivility on television is a sense of close proximity to uncivil conflict rarely found in untelevised life. Despite the fact that most viewers might acknowledge, at a purely cognitive level, that incivility is the norm for televised political debate, viewers react as if norms are being violated.

THE CROSS-MEDIA INCIVILITY EXPERIMENT

In order to evaluate whether the medium matters when it comes to the effects of political incivility, I created print, radio, and television versions of civil and uncivil political exchanges. I began with the television talk shows used in the earlier experiments. Given that I already had civil and uncivil versions of the exact same televised political discourse, I used these as the basis for producing civil and uncivil radio and newspaper versions. For the radio version, I used the soundtrack from the videos and played them for participants using a combination radio/cassette deck.

Producing print versions of the very same civil and uncivil exchanges was somewhat more challenging. As a template, the debate transcript format used by the *New York Times* was emulated in order to avoid the need to construct a news story about the debate that would deviate more from the actual event. A news story, for example, would entail journalistic selectivity with respect to what to emphasize as well as omission of some of the material. If a newspaper printed only a few highlights of the exchange, or commented directly on the tone of the exchange, then it would be difficult to assess whether the medium itself or this additional commentary was the cause of any cross-media differences.

Figure 7.1. Newspaper version of the civility/incivility treatment

To avoid the possibility that variations in political content might account for any observed effects, the entire civil and uncivil versions of the debate were transcribed word for word in their entirety, as illustrated in Figure 7.1. The exchange was printed on newsprint and formatted in columns exactly as previous presidential debate transcripts have been printed in the *New York Times*. In this case the newspaper (as indicated at the top of the printed page) was the *Indianapolis Star*, an appropriate newspaper of record for a congressional race in the state of Indiana. Photographs of the two candidates (two still images from the television program) were also included in the story so that the candidates' physical appearances were held constant.

It is important to consider what can and cannot be made "equal" in a cross-media experiment of this kind. Video footage inevitably includes information that goes beyond the specific words that are spoken. There is information to be gleaned from details of the room in which the participants are seated, the candidates' dress, their body language, how they are oriented toward each other spatially, their facial expressions, and so forth. In this sense it is impossible to perfectly equate the television version of the exchange with the radio and print versions. Likewise, the radio version includes voice cues that could alter listeners' interpretations of the political content.

Because these differences are essential to what is different about experiencing political discourse via one medium versus another, they were necessarily included when manipulating cross-media differences. As a result of characteristics inherent in these media, television viewers are exposed to more nuances of facial expression than are radio listeners; and because of radio's unique characteristics, listeners are exposed to tone of voice cues that are not accessible to those experiencing the same exchange via print.

Combining civil and uncivil versions of the newspaper, radio, and television versions produced a three by two factorial design with six possible experimental conditions. Around one hundred subjects were randomly assigned with equal probability to this between-subjects design. As in the previous studies, subjects were brought into the laboratory one by one to answer pretest questions before exposure to the stimulus, followed by a posttest questionnaire.

Notably, although the civil and uncivil treatments of the televised version had been validated as different through manipulation checks in several prior experiments, the civil and uncivil treatments of the radio and print versions had not been previously validated. Thus as a first step I analyzed the same posttest index of perceived civility/incivility discussed in the original manipulation check in Chapter 2. To reiterate, this index tapped the extent to which discourse was perceived to be calm-agitated, hostile-friendly, rude-polite, and so forth, and it created a highly reliable index in this sample as before.

However, when I attempted to validate the civil-uncivil treatment with the index of perceived civility-incivility, the results were problematic. As shown in Figure 7.2, the manipulation check findings from the previous television versions of the experiment replicated nicely in this experiment with the uncivil condition perceived as significantly more uncivil than the civil one. But the civil and uncivil radio versions were only borderline significant with respect to perceived differences in the extent of incivility ($p = .10$), and the newspaper versions were nowhere near significantly different in perceived levels of incivility. In short, the manipulation check demonstrated that the civility manipulation was working as intended only in the case of television.

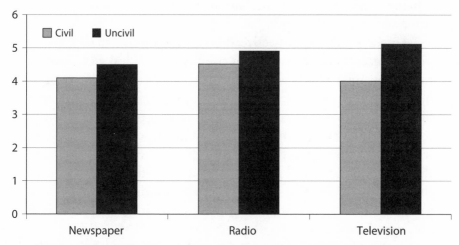

Figure 7.2. Effects of incivility treatments on perceived incivility by medium
Note: Tests of mean differences for civil versus uncivil conditions within each medium suggested a significant manipulation check for television ($F = 6.36, p < .01$), a borderline result for radio ($F = 2.60, p < .10$), and a nonsignificant difference for newspapers ($F = 0.62, p = .44$). Findings are from Experiment VII.

Although it was not my original intent to study the relative effectiveness of these experimental treatments by medium, this finding was quite fascinating. Apparently the civil/uncivil treatment was being carried by the tone of voice and visuals of the candidates, not by the words that they uttered. In the condition where participants read the exchange in a newspaper, there were no detectable differences in civility whatsoever between the two conditions. This suggests, above and beyond a failed manipulation check, that the same political content would not be viewed as the same by audiences who experienced it via different media. In other words, a newspaper account of the same event would probably not come across as equally uncivil, nor would a radio version.

Furthermore, Figure 7.2 also suggests that the main differences by medium in perceived civility versus incivility occur because of the uncivil conditions. In other words, the three civil conditions are roughly equal across the three media, but the three uncivil conditions are different in the extent of perceived incivility with television producing the greatest perceptions of incivility, followed by radio and then by newspaper. Given the importance of facial expression in perceiving and interpreting emotions, this is not surprising. The same statement without facial cues and/or voice tone simply does not come across the same way.

Taking a historical perspective, this finding suggests that when audiences received their news about conflicting political views strictly from print media, they were unlikely to perceive the same level of hostility as they are now when most such information comes to audiences via television. In one sense then, it does not matter whether today's politics and politicians are any more uncivil than they ever were. Even if they act the same as they always have and say the same things, the audience will perceive them as more uncivil. By virtue of the audiovisual cues that television provides, audience members are privy to more of the emotional content of political discourse than they were before.

Of course, by virtue of forcing the candidates/actors to stick to the same basic script and voice the same issue positions, they were artificially constrained in ways that are not true in the real world. It is possible to imagine, for example, a different version of the newspaper version of this debate in which the words themselves carried more emotional content and the writing was such that the reader could better discern the level of emotional intensity in an exchange. Historians have observed that the development of the "modern newspaper" brought with it a change in writing style that has been described as moving from the highly descriptive account with "Hollywood's exaggerated touch" to a dry, boring account of who said what to whom.[23] Without any interpretive commentary, it seems unlikely that incivility in political discourse would register in news audiences' minds, except in the most extreme cases such as a story about a political duel or physical confrontation. Barring situations in which the story was focused on incivility as its topic, it seems unlikely that readers would perceive high levels of incivility in a written account of any given political confrontation.

Since the uncivil versions of the radio and newspaper coverage did not survive the manipulation check, it made little sense to look for differences in levels of political trust and other outcomes by incivility condition. Nonetheless, a lingering question remained: if newspaper coverage did, indeed, convey heightened incivility, would this medium produce the same kinds of consequences that uncivil television does? Granted, this manipulation might be far harder to accomplish in print, but do the consequences of in-your-face politics require actual faces and thus depend on television per se?

CAN NEWSPAPERS PRODUCE IN-YOUR-FACE EFFECTS?

In order to answer this question, the print stimulus materials needed to be revised. To produce print versions that differed in levels of perceived civility, I sacrificed some experimental control over the political content of the discussions. Although the candidates retained the same issue positions as in the televised versions, they responded to one another more strenuously in words than in the original versions, and there were more cues for readers as to the tone of the exchange. This was accomplished by altering both versions of the text to emphasize either incivility or civility. First and foremost, in order to avoid making the candidates' issue positions more extreme, the moderator's comments were used in the print version to call attention to the nature of the interaction. For example, in the new, more extreme uncivil print version, the moderator makes reference to mudslinging and the fact that the candidates are shaking their fists at one another. At another point he references the need to "cool the discussion down a bit."

In addition to direct references by the moderator to the tension (or lack thereof) in the exchange, the candidates' language was also altered to sound more severe. For the example, the "huge price tag" attributed to NASA in the original uncivil version became a "ridiculously high price tag" in the extremely hostile version. More extreme modifiers, such as "absolutely," "extremely," and "definitely," were added to their language. A candidate described by his opponent as "wrong" about an issue in the original version was now "completely and utterly wrong" in the enhanced account. Direct accusations were also made in the extra-hostile version. For example, Neil exclaims, "You are not being honest, Bob!" and Bob accuses Neil of interrupting him in midsentence.

In contrast, the extremely civil version was revised so that the candidates went out of their way to acknowledge the other candidate and his views. For example, Bob begins a defense of his own position by saying, "Neil's points are well taken, but. . . ." Neil likewise asserts that they have "the same goals in mind." They compliment one another on minor points, and emphasize general areas of agreement, via statements such as "Bob and I obviously agree that we need to protect those most vulnerable" and "These are complex questions." By making the uncivil version more uncivil and the civil version even more civil, my hope was to obtain a significant manipulation check for the civil versus uncivil newspaper versions and thus be able to answer the question of whether incivility—*if adequately perceived in sources other than television*—would produce the same salutary and harmful effects.

With the newly strengthened newspaper versions in hand, I initiated yet another experiment, this time trimmed down to the four conditions formed by crossing newspapers versus television with extremely civil and extremely uncivil political exchanges. A total of 109 fresh participants were randomly assigned to these four conditions. Not surprisingly, the first order of business in analyzing the data was to determine whether the extremely civil and extremely uncivil versions were, in fact, perceived as significantly different from one another in the print and television versions.

As shown in Figure 7.3, the new newspaper versions accomplished my goal; the extremely civil and extremely uncivil print versions were now clearly significantly different from one another in levels of perceived incivility for both media. However, the revisions to the stimuli appear to have created a significant interaction as well. The civil-uncivil manipulation is now significantly stronger for the newspaper conditions than for the more subtle television ones. To be clear, the civil and uncivil means were significantly different for both media, just more so for newspapers. As a result, it is difficult to compare the size of the incivility effect from one medium to another. But it is at least possible—unlike in the previous experiment—to see whether uncivil discourse carried by newspapers produces any of the same effects.

I began by attempting to replicate the findings from Chapter 3 on attitudes toward the opposition. Was incivility damaging to how audiences felt about the opposition with print versions of incivility?

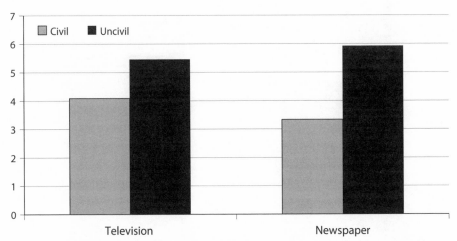

Figure 7.3. Effects of incivility treatments on levels of perceived candidate incivility by medium, using extreme uncivil and extreme civil newspaper articles

Note: The altered versions of the newspaper articles succeeded in producing a significant manipulation check ($F = 45.03, p < .001$) such that both uncivil conditions are perceived as more uncivil than the civil ones. However, by boosting both civility and incivility in the newspaper versions, a significant interaction was also created indicating that the civility manipulation was significantly stronger for the newspaper condition than the television condition ($F = 4.23, p < .05$). Findings are from Experiment VIII.

The answer appears to be probably not. As shown in Figure 7.4, liking for the least liked candidate was significantly influenced by the extreme incivility treatment just as in the previous television-only experiments; in other words, the main effect of incivility was significant. However, this effect was driven almost entirely by the civil and uncivil television conditions, which produced a large gap in liking for the least liked candidate. A modest suggestion of a similar difference occurred between the civil and uncivil newspaper versions, but the newspaper means were not significantly different from one another as they were for the two television conditions. It is worth noting that this cannot be a result of a weaker manipulation of incivility in the newspaper conditions. As shown in Figure 7.3, the manipulation was significantly *stronger* for the newspaper versions than for the television ones. Nonetheless, television produced stronger effects.

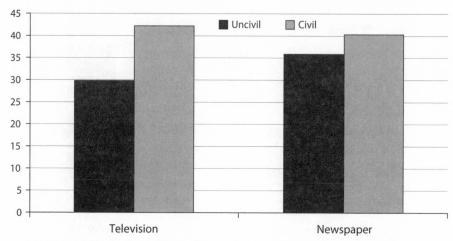

Figure 7.4. Effects of incivility on feeling thermometer ratings for least liked candidates by medium, using extreme uncivil and extreme civil newspaper articles

Note: Bars represent the feeling thermometer score for each respondent's least liked candidate. Results indicated a significant main effect of civility on candidate liking ($F = 3.78, p < .05$). However, the means were not significantly different for the newspaper conditions alone. Findings are from Experiment VIII.

Next I attempted to replicate the effects of incivility on recall. As shown in Chapter 2, political content that was presented in an uncivil fashion tended to be better remembered than content presented in a civil fashion. For newspapers, however, I found no evidence of any significant difference in recall between the civil and uncivil conditions. Thus a second finding based on the emotional intensity of televised incivility failed to replicate for newspapers.

The final replication that I attempted involved the effects of incivility on political trust. Do print versions of uncivil political discourse produce less trust in government and politicians the same way that televised incivility appears to suppress levels of political trust? Figure 7.5 shows the results of this analysis. Here, at last, there is some evidence that incivility does have a parallel effect for newspapers. Both the television and print uncivil conditions were significantly lower in trust than the corresponding civil conditions. Moreover, the much larger gap for newspaper conditions seems to reflect the much larger difference in perceived incivility levels between these two conditions.

What does this overall pattern of findings suggest? The effects of incivility on outcomes such as recall and the intensity of emotional reactions to those one does not like do not replicate well for newspapers. On the other hand, the effects of incivility on political trust appear to replicate well so long as the newspaper version adequately conveys incivility to its readers.

The reason for this discrepancy is likely to be differences in the process of influence that results in the effects in Chapters 2 and 3 (recall and legitimacy of the opposition) as opposed to those in Chapter 4 (political trust). The reason political trust declines after viewing uncivil political discourse on television or reading about uncivil political discourse in a newspaper is that readers and viewers find such shenanigans distasteful, and ask themselves why politicians can't just act like ordinary people when it comes to discussing politics. Normal people would not shake their fists at one another or put each other down. I suspect that this particular form of influence is quite mindful; that is, if asked, experimental subjects in the uncivil conditions

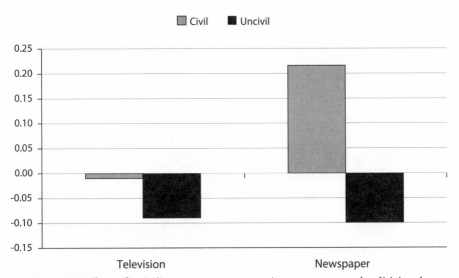

Figure 7.5. Effects of incivility treatments on trust in government and politicians by medium, using extreme uncivil and extreme civil newspaper articles
Note: The effects of the incivility treatment were significant ($F = 3.32, p < .05$) as a main effect. Findings are from Experiment VIII.

would probably indicate that the politicians they watched behaved less than admirably. Although participants were not evaluating those particular politicians when answering the political trust questions, their bad behavior reminded audiences that politicians and government seem to operate outside the bounds of the social rules that govern the lives of ordinary people.

In contrast to this highly cognitive process of influence, I suspect that the effects of incivility on recall and on the intensity of people's dislike for the opposition operate below the level of individual awareness. In other words, the increased arousal produced by incivility is not something audiences are cognizant of; nonetheless, arousal heightens their level of attention to content and intensifies their emotions. Newspapers are simply less likely to produce this same reaction and thus also less likely to produce consequences that flow from such heightened arousal.

Contrary to many popular impressions, television is a highly arousing medium. It provokes involuntary attention as well as a host of physiological responses indicative of heightened attention.[24] It is precisely because of these arousal-producing qualities that television use is associated with sleep problems in both observational studies— where sleep problems are positively correlated with time spent viewing—and experimental studies, where reducing television viewing has been shown to reduce sleep disturbances in adolescents.[25]

It is difficult to envision a critical test of whether reading is generally less arousing than watching television given that so much would depend on the type of content being read/viewed. Should such a test compare reading the actors' words to viewing them spoken on television, or a full description of the event relative to viewing the televised account? Or should the experiences be equated in length of time in addition to content? A spicy novel full of intrigue might well produce high levels of arousal, but congressional candidates—and indeed most political news content—is not of that ilk. One need only recall prominent exceptions, such as the Starr Report from the Clinton impeachment trial, to realize that most political content does not approach pulp fiction. In this particular experimental study, it is fairly uncontroversial to assume that television viewing of uncivil political conflict is more arousing than reading about it in a newspaper. Recall from the early chapters of this book that the arousal-based effects occurred primarily when conflict was both uncivil and shown in close-up. Only under highly arousing conditions— circumstances that are not typically replicable with newspapers— will one find the effects that depend on arousal.

WHY THE MEDIUM MATTERS

On the whole, my findings suggest that the arousal-related outcomes of in-your-face politics are probably television-dependent. They require heightened arousal to trigger higher levels of attention and recall, and emotional intensification of audience attitudes. Not all of the effects of in-your-face politics rely on television, however, as demonstrated by the fact that newspaper accounts of incivility, when extreme, may affect levels of political trust.

Nonetheless, it is important to acknowledge that producing a newspaper account of an event that includes enough cues so that readers comprehend that uncivil political discourse is transpiring is quite difficult. What this suggests is that given the occurrence of a particular political event involving a moderate degree of incivility, people reading about it in a newspaper would perceive the political participants as more civil than would those viewing the event on television. The combined facial expressions and tone of voice cues that are present only on television make this medium particularly well suited to conveying the emotional tenor of an exchange. When that tenor is uncivil, as frequently occurs in cases of partisan political conflict, incivility will be much more visible to audiences of television viewers than to newspaper readers. The exceptions will be cases where print reporters go out of their way to convey to their readers the incivility displayed by political advocates.

These findings are of particular importance when considered in historical perspective. Those who have in recent years decried the rise of uncivil political discourse are responding to an impression that many share, but for which there is little empirical evidence. It may or may not be the case that politicians today are less polite in their discourse than they were in the past. As historians are quick to point out, politics in the new American republic was hardly docile or polite.[26]

And as I noted in passing in Chapter 1, when Aaron Burr and Alexander Hamilton dueled on the banks of the Hudson River, no one witnessed it in person. And even if there had been a reporter present, he would have struggled to provide a written account that could produce the same intensity of emotion as a video of the event. Today the American public has ringside seats to almost any political squabble, however minor. Moreover, because political news is no longer limited to a few evening news broadcasts, there is constant demand for new material.

IN-YOUR-FACE INTERNET?

Given that these effects appear to be specific to television, perhaps the effects of in-your-face politics are essentially a thing of the past, or at least on their way out. After all, the often proclaimed "death of television" and its replacement by the Internet suggests that the effects that I have documented could be irrelevant in the near future. Although broadcast television as we once knew it may be a thing of the past and cable boxes are probably not long for most living rooms, the kind of audiovisual content commonly referred to as "television" by the public is, if anything, more popular than ever. The content may reach our homes via streaming Internet, but the content is largely the same. Indeed, news content is increasingly similar across print, television, and Internet platforms.[27]

Thus the death of television is essentially a myth if what one means by this is that audiovisual content is going the way of the dodo. Television content is not disappearing so much as it is migrating to multiple platforms. What some refer to as "media convergence" refers to the tendency for content to be available on multiple platforms. Television programs can now be watched on computers via the Internet, and Internet content and movies can be streamed through one's television. Digital content moves more or less effortlessly from one platform to the next, so when it comes to content, the distinction among television, movies, and the Internet is no longer meaningful.

There is little chance that digital audiovisual fare will disappear from our media environment anytime in the near future. There are, nonetheless, many changes afoot with implications for in-your-face politics. Many of these developments suggest that the extent of in-your-face politics will expand in the coming decades, while other trends suggest perhaps some moderation of this phenomenon. I review these changes focusing first on the *content* of audiovisual online fare, and second on the nature of the *viewing experience* for audience members.

Content Differences

From its inception, the Internet has been a text-intensive medium. And as demonstrated earlier in this chapter, text is especially poor at transmitting a sense of incivility in political discourse. Even when text is strongly worded enough to convey incivility, it is unlikely to have the same extent of effects on its readers that uncivil video has on its viewers. This pattern would seem to suggest that the shift away from traditional television toward the Internet would produce less exposure to incivility.

However, a number of factors mitigate against the likelihood that incivility has or will decline due to the demise of traditional television as the major news source. First, as the speed of Internet connections has increased, the amount of video material online has grown, and the Internet has begun to look more like television. Although it is difficult to predict just how video-centric it will eventually become, technological capacity no long seems to be the issue. As studies document the effectiveness of video online, there is likely to be still more of it.[28]

By far the greatest reason to expect an exacerbation of uncivil political discourse online is rising competition for media audiences. When so many different sources, both online and offline, are all competing for the same audiences, any characteristic that draws attention is likely to become increasingly prominent and valuable. The availability of video on demand means that there are fewer captive audiences, and instead people have greater control over the content they see. Thus in-your-face content will continue to appear regularly as part of the competition for viewer attention. Traditional limitations on the amount of space in newspapers or the amount of airtime on television are no longer important given the huge capacity of the

online "news hole." The unlimited time and space online has encouraged less gatekeeping, opening the doors to still more incivility.

Drawing conclusions about the overall extent of incivility on the
Internet is difficult because of its mixed modes of communication,
and its lack of clear boundaries. Indeed, most figures put the percentage of the Internet that has been indexed by Google as far less than
one tenth of a percent. Currently, the political content that is consumed the most comes from mainstream, so-called legacy sources,
the same news outlets that generate the print and television news
that Americans have long consumed.[29] Even in the realm of new
media, old media sources still dominate for the moment. For this reason, if we characterize the Internet based on the content most people
consume, it is probably no more or less uncivil than other media.

However, two forms of Internet-specific content have attracted particular attention as potential sources of incivility. These include partisan blogs and audience/user comments that are posted in response
to news stories or commentary. Because of its mix of text, still photos,
and audiovisual material, it would be atheoretical to make a blanket
statement about the probable effects of incivility on the Internet. All
else being equal, uncivil Internet content that is audiovisual should
be expected to have effects like those of television. Quite a lot of
televised incivility can be found on YouTube, where excerpts of especially hostile political encounters often get posted for those who
missed them on air.

Other Internet content, such as audience comments, appears in the
form of text, and should thus have more limited effects. Perhaps with
the more extreme forms of incivility that sometimes occur in user
comments, levels of trust should suffer, but it is difficult to say trust
in precisely whom or what. The most logical answer might be trust
in the political opposition, but based on my experimental evidence
using print treatments, even more extreme incivility in print form
did not affect recall or attitudes toward the opposition, although it
harmed levels of trust in politicians and government.

Empirical evidence on this question is only beginning to emerge,
and thus far it has been focused primarily on how incivility affects
the credibility of online content.[30] Other outcomes of interest have
included risk perceptions, political trust, and political efficacy. For ex-

ample, Anderson and colleagues found that uncivil blog comments polarized perceptions of the risks of nanotechnology relative to civil blog comments, and Borah suggested that news frames may interact with incivility to affect trust.[31]

The jury is still out on whether the Internet promotes greater mass exposure to political incivility and/or whether such incivility has effects; evidence remains very limited at this point.[32] But most of the studies that have examined the impact of incivility thus far have not included measures to establish that incivility was manipulated independent of other factors such as the partisan extremity of the communication source. This makes it difficult to know how much of any identified effect is style, and how much is perceived political substance. Is it the manner in which views are being exchanged that is important, or does the extremity of the views produce any given outcome? To isolate the effects of civility from political substance requires a manipulation check to ensure that incivility was manipulated *and* another check to demonstrate that the extremity of the political views was not altered in the process. In other words, only the manner of interaction should differ, not the perceived substance of the political views expressed. This latter point is especially critical because incivility in political discourse is frequently confounded with ideological extremity by observers and pundits. When advocates express viewpoints that are clearly in opposition to one another, it is easy to mistake extremity for incivility—particularly when one does not agree with the views being expressed!

Interestingly, incivility has become an even greater bête noire online than on television. The "notoriously unruly and rancorous" online public conversation has led many to question the value of online political dialogue.[33] Its defining characteristic is "rampant incivility," which is encouraged by the capacity to post comments anonymously.[34]

Although televised incivility on political talks shows has been widely decried in the past, on the Internet the problem has been viewed as even more severe. For example, reader-contributors to the websites of U.S. newspapers are frequently highly uncivil in their commentary.[35] Likewise, uncivil YouTube videos provoke still more incivility in viewer commentary.[36] Most of these complaints are about the text-based comments made by audience members. As I have argued, even though this kind of online commentary often puts television shout shows to shame in its violations of norms of civility, I remain unconvinced that it has the same kinds of effects as videos where people treat one another uncivilly. Nonetheless, it probably draws attention.

Beyond audiovisual content that is produced by industry professionals to be accessed online, the Internet also attracts perhaps more than its fair share of amateur audiovisual incivility. The widespread availability of cell phone video recording allows virtually anyone to record and upload video for all to see. This component of new media means that more "back stage" behavior that was meant for a specific social context and audience will, nonetheless, be viewed by those outside of that context.[37] For example, in the 2012 presidential race, Mitt Romney's comment that 47 percent of voters paid no taxes was intended for an elite group of donors at a private fund-raiser. However, new technology brought what was supposed to be back stage behavior to the front stage of America. Once the video of this event was posted on the web, it could be seen by all and became fodder for political talk shows. Likewise, when Vivian Stiviano recorded Donald Sterling, owner of the NBA's Los Angeles Clippers, making remarks disparaging blacks, she transformed a private conversation into a public controversy. Because many incidents of incivility occur in private, and technology has made it easier for private individuals to create their own audio and video recordings, new media may make audiences cognizant of still more incidents of incivility than ever, thus furthering the impression that today's public figures are less civil than their forerunners, who may have behaved quite similarly in private.

If the need for audiences were not enough to encourage incivility online, there is yet another incentive for incivility built into the structure of network-based communication. As mentioned in passing in Chapter 2, emotional arousal not only changes the way viewers process media content, but also makes them more likely to *retransmit* the content though their networks. Because arousal drives virality online,[38] incivility in political content is increasingly important for a message to reach large audiences. Arousal produces attention to the original content of political discourse, but it also impacts the breadth of a message's distribution. Although there is no consensus as to whether positive or negative emotions are better at driving virality,[39] it seems clear that messages generating strong affective responses lead to greater diffusion.[40] Although this pattern is true offline as well as online, the Internet makes it much easier to quickly redistribute to millions.

The Viewing Experience

The nature of the audience's experience matters, so changes in the audience's perspective on uncivil content also matter in an age of new media. Not just what people watch, but also how they watch it is important. So how have new media altered this experience?

We know that people pay more attention to faces on larger screens,[41] and that larger screens are more conducive to the kinds of effects I have documented.[42] For example, attractive faces are viewed as even more attractive on larger screens.[43] Likewise, incivility is experienced more intensely watching a large screen. Moreover, as Bracken and Botta note, "Most of the technological developments of television have moved the medium increasingly towards being more immersive or capable of grabbing viewer's attention and keeping it. This trend is true for larger screens, surround sound, improved image quality, and higher numbers of pixels."[44]

Although televisions of all sizes remain available, consumers have increasingly been purchasing larger televisions. Technological advances have made large sets more affordable. Although there are no figures on *average* consumer television size that have been consistently available since the advent of television, the best-selling models are known for most years.

As shown in Figure 7.6, screen sizes have increased significantly. Interestingly, although the "recommended viewing distance" for large screens is further away (and this might compensate for the larger image size), it seems unlikely that the size of people's living rooms has kept up with the pace of increased screen size.[45]

Although the best-selling television size has clearly increased, more recent trends also include viewing video on small portable devices such as mobile phones, tablets, and iPods. Even though smaller

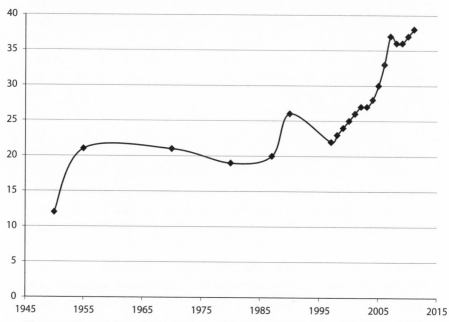

Figure 7.6. Increasing television size, 1950s to the present
Note: Best-selling screen size, analog and digital sets combined.

screens are generally viewed from a closer distance, they seem unlikely to create the same sense of immersion as large screens. Not surprisingly, the sensation of being involved in the action one is viewing
is reduced with portable consoles.[46] On the other hand, much more
of today's viewing occurs without abrupt commercial interruptions,
thus improving people's sense of immersion.

Scholars studying virtual reality originally coined the term "telepresence" to describe the sense of "being there" when immersed in a
mediated environment.[47] This "illusion of non-mediation" produces
reactions as if the viewer were in the actual presence of the people
shown on the screen.[48] Studies of the iPod suggest that smaller screen
sizes also reduce sensations of spatial presence among viewers.[49] In
general, portable consoles evoke lower levels of physiological arousal
when used for video games or movies, thus suggesting that one
would experience less of an impact from incivility if viewed in this
fashion.[50] To summarize, studies suggest that while people like the
convenience of small consoles, they generally prefer large screens.

Personal computer screens also serve as popular viewing devices, and are in between these size extremes. Computer screens tend to be smaller than televisions, but they have also increased in size, and people tend to view them from quite close, thus filling their fields of vision more easily. So although technological trends have been toward images that increasingly look like the real thing and that are responded to by viewers as such, small screens may cancel out any differences in how viewers respond.

Overall, this discussion should make it clear that figuring out the implications of new technologies for in-your-face politics is complex. On the one hand, there is no reason to expect political incivility to abate anytime soon given the vast competition for audiences, the capacity for conflict to attract viewers, and the viral advantages of highly arousing video. On the other hand, changes in how people watch televisual exchanges of political views—on screens that are both smaller and larger, with technology that is continuously improving its ability to represent humans on the screen, and with greater control over interruptions—do not suggest a clear direction in terms of the extent to which viewers will feel themselves to be in political advocates' faces.

If the medium indeed matters, as this chapter has demonstrated, then the visual content of television matters a great deal. This suggests that we should pay particular attention to situations where incivility is coupled with intimate visuals of political advocates because these exchanges are likely to do the most damage. In the chapter that follows, I further pursue the potential historical significance of in-your-face politics. I turn my attention next to how the visual component of politics on television has changed since the advent of television broadcasting, with a focus on how that content is likely to be experienced by its audiences.

My findings recommend leaving aside the historical debate over the tone of political discourse, because this may not be the most essential question to answer. Whether or not contemporary American politicians are more hostile toward one another, it seems clear that the way we as ordinary Americans experience their disagreements has indeed changed dramatically. The impression that political discourse has become more bitter and uncivil is fed by the way we now experience those disagreements.

CHAPTER 8

HOW POLITICS ON TELEVISION HAS CHANGED

In the previous chapters I have suggested that television is unique. As an audiovisual medium, it has effects that the same content would not produce if conveyed purely through audio or print. Because more people experience politicians and political advocates through television now than was the case fifty years ago, we are naturally bothered by political incivility than we were before. So regardless of whether politicians are any more rude and unpleasant than they were before, viewers experience incivility in a way that is far more noticeable and influential than it once was. Americans now see and experience political conflict from a perspective that was impossible in the past, and this change has consequences for the reactions people have to politicians and their ideas.

But the rise of political television is not the only way in which the American experience of exposure to politics has changed. In this chapter I conduct an analysis of the visual content of television over a forty-year period to establish whether and in what directions the visuals we see on television today are different from the ones seen during television's early history. I conclude that even within its relatively brief history, political television has become increasingly "in your face" due to technological changes as well as to increased competition for television audiences.

THE VISUAL CONTENT OF POLITICAL TELEVISION

Audiovisual technology has changed dramatically since the early days of television. Given the huge technological changes that have transpired since the 1960s, it would be surprising if television's visual content had not changed as well. Cameras that were once large, unwieldy, and more or less stationary have given way to light, portable video cameras that can easily be taken anywhere. Black-and-white has given way to color and now to high definition television, home theater systems, and 3D viewing.

Unfortunately for my purposes, historically oriented content analyses have tended to focus on the verbal content of television rather than its visual content. This is for understandable reasons; the content of broadcasts is much easier to analyze and quantify than the visual aspects of political television. But as a result, scholars know little about how the visuals within political television have changed over the years.

My goal in this chapter is to assess changes in the way political conflict is portrayed on television, with a focus on the characteristics that make politics appear more or less in your face to its viewers. Some of these changes are more obvious than others. For example, one obvious change occurred with the explosion of cable television programming. Viewers may now watch numerous different forms of political television that did not exist in television's early days or even in the 1980s. Given that political talk shows are now a prime venue for in-your-face exchanges of political views, the devotion of more airtime to political talk shows has meant greater availability of in-your-face politics.

With the expansion of airtime made possible by cable television and around-the-clock news channels, televised interview programs have become natural low-cost time fillers. As Ben-Porath describes this now pervasive format, "Rather than news organizations and their journalists providing the audience with a single narrative account of a day's events, the news is now increasingly delivered by way of conversation between news personalities, their sources, and other experts, all competing over their claims of factuality."[1] On the one hand, these interviews appear to be observations of interpersonal communication; but on the other hand, they are clearly intended for mass audiences. Moreover, interviewing is largely confrontational, and thus violates the usual norms for interpersonal social exchanges.

Political talk shows often involve an odd juxtaposition of intimacy and incivility. It is an especially odd combination when journalists speak to elected officials because the norms of politeness and deference are even stronger when addressing those of high status. When an interviewer is not polite in speaking with a politician, he or she implies that this person is not to be respected.

An interaction that involves physically proximate exchanges that are not polite is particularly jarring to viewers. In the world of real interaction, greater spatial distance generally corresponds to greater politeness in communication; intimacy is reserved for those close to us, both physically and attitudinally. Because various dimensions of distance tend to go together—psychological distance, physical closeness, attitudinal closeness, and familiarity[2]—conflict in close proximity violates social norms along multiple dimensions. By showing visuals of people in close physical proximity who clearly do not agree, talk shows may challenge the regularities of experience that people have come to expect in daily life.[3]

Although the rise of talk shows as a form of political television has undoubtedly had an important impact, changes in the visual characteristics of television are not limited to political talk shows or to cable television. Political television is subject to far more competition for audiences today than it was in the past. People have more choices, so producers must compete more intensely for audience attention.

Two kinds of increased competition are important. First, political news no longer has a monopoly on viewing at a particular time of day as it once did when the evening news broadcasts occurred simultaneously on all network channels. Political television must now compete with entertainment programming such as Hollywood movies, dramas, and sitcoms. In addition, there are now far more political programs than even the most politically inclined individual could possibly watch. As a result, more choices among various political programs must be made.

Increased competition for audiences means that political programming should gravitate toward attention-grabbing strategies of various kinds. Television producers' knowledge of what those strategies are is obviously imperfect. Nonetheless, aspects of form and content that enhance viewer arousal and attention should become increasingly common in such a competitive environment.

Analyzing changes in the presentation of political television is constrained by the fact that few political programs have had long tenures. We have visual records of even fewer programs that are still in existence. As television production has shifted from film to video, little has been archived consistently over time. Only network television news broadcasts have existed continuously since the earliest days of television. For this combination of reasons, for my own historical sample, I relied on the Vanderbilt Television News Archives, which has retained the visual record of television news programs from the earliest days of television to the present.

Starting from 1969, I sampled news broadcasts using a random selection of business days of the week that were not federal holidays. I chose 1969 as the first year for coding because it is the first year for which the Vanderbilt Television News Archives maintains a complete year of broadcasts for the three national networks. Although the three networks are not believed to differ much in style and content, I chose NBC in particular because it is the only network for which Vanderbilt has actual video footage for all broadcasts, as opposed to transcripts, which it maintains for all three national networks. Because watching the actual video was essential to understanding differences in how the news is presented visually, it was essential to have video of the original broadcasts.

The goal of the visual content analysis was to look at how characteristics relevant to in-your-face politics had changed over time. Toward that end, multiple human coders used a systematic coding scheme that focused on the visual characteristics relevant to in-your-face politics. Rather than attempt to characterize each and every year of broadcasts through this extensive coding process, the sampling scheme was designed to provide an in-depth look at the news at ten-year intervals. I wanted to identify long-term trends, so this strategy made it possible to watch and code the visuals in a larger number of broadcasts in order to more accurately characterize each sampled year.

Using the same randomly selected dates each year,[4] I sampled ten broadcasts every ten years from 1969 through 2009. All told, coders watched and coded over 650 unique news stories in fifty different news broadcasts. One hundred stories were then double-coded for purposes of evaluating intercoder reliability. Appendix E includes the complete coding instructions and coding forms used. Because coders had digital recordings of the original broadcasts, they could stop, start, and rewind as needed to complete the complex coding process.

Coding for each broadcast was quite extensive, and the process was subjected to numerous rounds of revision before achieving acceptable reliabilities (defined as intercoder correlations of .70 or greater). As a first step, coders were asked to identify unique conflicts within the broadcasts, whether ongoing or resolved. A conflict was defined as any controversy involving two or more parties who disagree, including conflicts between people, groups, organizations, institutions, or any combination thereof. Coders were instructed that a politician simply announcing new policies (relating to, e.g., war, Medicare, etc.) did not qualify as a conflict unless some opposition was explicitly discussed or shown.

Furthermore, conflicts were limited to conflicts within the United States in order to prevent the timing of international conflicts from unduly affecting the analyses. Internal domestic conflicts about international wars were counted as conflicts, however. For example, if the president discussed his policies on the war in Iraq, the simple fact of the war's existence did not qualify the news story as being about a domestic conflict. Only when differing views on the war in Iraq were presented did the story count as a conflict. In total, coders analyzed visual aspects of television coverage from just under two hundred unique conflicts.

Coding of visual content took place at multiple levels of analysis. For each conflict, coders recorded many different characteristics of each individual human face that was shown in an identifiable fashion. "Identifiable" in this case meant that if one already knew what the person looked like, he or she was recognizable from the photo or video, whether explicitly identified or not. For each individual shown as part of a conflict, up to five different camera shots of that person were coded. Information on each camera shot included the proportion of the television screen taken up by the human body on a 6-point scale ranging from less than one-fourth of the screen area to all or almost all of the screen. In addition, the level of realism of the human image was coded as the least realistic drawing (1), a still shot or photograph (2), a standard studio video (3), a video including people outside a studio (4), or a handheld video in the real-world environment (5). In addition, each shot was coded for whether it was framed as a full human body (1) down to a close-up of just the face (9). Finally, coders also recorded whether the individual shot involved a human moving toward the camera (1), away from the camera (−1), or neither (0).

Other characteristics were coded with respect to the conflict as a whole. For example, each story was assessed for its overall pace as slow (1), medium (2), or fast (3). In addition, coders assessed the level of intensity of the conflict that was presented. According to coding instructions, a low-intensity conflict (1) was one in which the opponents in the controversy remained calm and civil and did not act visibly angry, whereas a high-intensity conflict (3) was one in which the opponents in a controversy yelled, or otherwise raised their voices (via chanting, threatening, etc.). The highest code (4) was reserved for instances in which violence or the direct threat of physical violence was involved.

HAVE TELEVISION VISUALS BECOME MORE AROUSING?

The visual characteristics that were coded were purposely selected because they have been associated with increased arousal. Because of increased competition for political television audiences, I expected that characteristics associated with more arousing programs should increase over time. Thus what kinds of things should change within the context of television news? First, the content in general might shift toward a greater emphasis on conflict. Given that conflict is arousing and attention-grabbing, there should be more of it, and coverage should emphasize its intensity.

Beyond the actual content of broadcasts, structural elements of these productions can also increase levels of viewer arousal. For example, fast-paced productions are known to be more arousing than those with fewer cuts. Thus I expected the pacing of news programs to speed up over time. Productions with many cuts produce orienting responses (indexed by greater arousal) and increased levels of attention, which ultimately also contribute to higher recall.[5] It is possible for a video to become so fast-paced that it causes viewers to become overloaded and remember less, but for better or worse, political programs seldom if ever reach that level of excitement.

In addition, I predicted that as a result of both competition and technological change, television news would feature more human images that appeared close to the viewer by virtue of taking up larger proportions of the television screen. Powerful camera lenses and movable cameras make in-your-face close-ups easier to shoot than ever before. Moreover, as photography has become easier with digital photos transmitted electronically, realistic photographs of humans should also replace drawings, graphics, and artist renderings as the primary means of illustration. Furthermore, human faces should figure increasingly prominently in the news, as should close-ups.

One final visual aspect of news that might also have become more frequent is the kind of camera shot in which a person moves toward the camera. Attention to images is encouraged when visual images move. Even though movement toward the viewer is an illusion, it should be interpreted by "old brains" in the same way that a person would react to an actual person coming closer. When people invade our personal space by coming toward us, levels of arousal go up and we naturally orient toward the motion in order to ascertain what is happening. This response happens regardless of our cognitive understanding that the person is not actually coming toward us. Changing the apparent distance between the viewer and the person on the screen by starting with a long shot and then slowly moving in closer can be an especially effective means of exaggerating closeness.[6]

To analyze these data, I used analysis of variance and tested for significant linear trends over time in the predicted direction. Without a priori hypotheses about the specific timing of these changes, I hypothesized that these in-your-face characteristics would increase significantly with time, rather than that they would differ between any two decades. Given the many difficulties of coding visual aspects of television, it was possible to produce at best a rough approximation of the timing of changes as they occurred.

HOW CONFLICT ON TELEVISION NEWS HAS CHANGED

To assess how television news has changed visually from the 1960s to the present, I began by evaluating whether there were more conflicts per broadcast shown on television news in the 2000s relative to what was shown in television's early days. In fact, I found no evidence whatsoever of a trend toward more conflicts by decade, whether analyzing the total number of conflicts per broadcast or the number of conflicts relative to the total number of news stories or total airtime. The average number of stories per broadcast has decreased over this fifty-year period, as has the number of stories involving conflict. But the proportion of conflict-oriented stories per broadcast has remained roughly the same. At the same time, individual stories have become longer on average, reflecting the fact that there are fewer news stories per broadcast. Thus my first hypothesis was not confirmed. Television news has always and continues to include many conflicts, and conflict has remained stable as a proportion the total number of news stories.

The hypotheses addressing changing structural aspects of television news fared far better. For example, as shown in Figure 8.1, by the late 1980s, the pacing of television news had increased. Whereas the average news story involving conflict in the late 1960s was characterized by coders as slow-paced, by the late 1980s the average story was coded as medium in pace. The intensity of conflicts increased at roughly the same point in time. Although the intensity of conflicts shown on television news remained, on average, on the low end of the intensity spectrum, consistent with what one would expect, the mean nonetheless rose significantly by the late 1980s and has persisted at this level ever since.

The way in which human actors and their bodies are shown on television news likewise reflected changes in the predicted directions. As

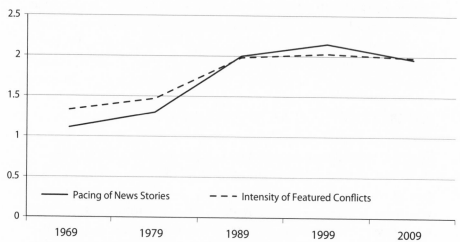

Figure 8.1. Pacing and intensity of televised conflict, 1969–2009

Note: Means for pacing by year are significantly different ($F = 23.78, p < .001$), and the means demonstrate a significant increasing linear trend ($F = 69.14, p < .001$). Means for intensity by year are significantly different ($F = 4.19, p < .01$), and the means demonstrate a significant increasing linear trend ($F = 7.77, p < .01$).

shown in Figure 8.2, the realism of human images shifted from low to high. Higher numbers on this scale reflect more camera shots that include human images shown in video rather than still photographs or drawings. As video cameras have become increasingly portable, news has steadily come to include more video, and especially more video involving people outside of the studio. In this sense, the representations of human beings offered by news coverage are increasingly similar to real-world experiences.

In addition, as shown by the broken line in Figure 8.2, humans now take up a larger proportion of the television screen than was true in the 1960s. Because the metric used in Figure 8.2 includes proportions that are summed over multiple camera shots for any given story, it is difficult to interpret it as a precise scale. Nonetheless, what it tells us is that space on the television screen is now more often taken up by humans and their bodies. People are being exposed to other people for an increasing proportion of the time that they watch television news.

Figure 8.3, which shows a standard shot of the NBC news anchor in 1969 and then in 2009, provides a nice illustration of this difference. Notice first that both anchors are shown using a head and shoulders shot. In 1969 we see Chet Huntley speaking in front of an artist's drawing of Ky, the vice president of South Vietnam, and the drawing remains static on the screen throughout the story. On the right-hand side of Figure 8.3, we see Brian Williams in 2009 reporting a story on unemployment. After Williams introduces the story in front of a graphic, the video quickly changes to out-of-studio video footage.

In addition to the shift from drawings to actual talking human beings, what is particularly interesting to note in Figure 8.3 is the way the two anchors are captured by their respective cameras. Despite the fact that both Huntley and Williams are shown in the same head and shoulders shot, Williams's body has the appearance of being closer to the viewer because it takes up a larger proportion of the television screen. By appearing larger, he thus also seems closer from the perspective of the viewer than did Huntley, despite the similar camera angle. In this sense even television anchors are now shown more intimately than anchors from the past. To the extent that the appearance of physical closeness on the television screen increases viewer arousal, viewers should experience greater "in your faceness" from the social presence of the news anchor relative to in the past.

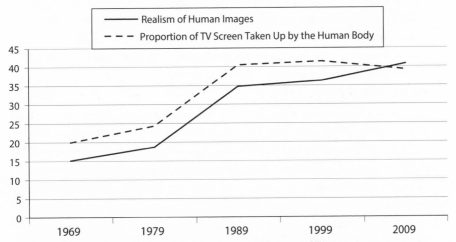

Figure 8.2. Exposure to the human body on television news, 1969–2009

Note: Means for proportions of TV screen taken up by the human body by year are significantly different ($F = 67.39, p < .001$), and the means demonstrate a significant increasing linear trend ($F = 149.71, p < .001$). Means for realism of images by year are significantly different ($F = 7.10, p < .001$), and the means demonstrate a significant increasing linear trend ($F = 25.83, p < .001$).

Figure 8.3. Comparison of standard camera perspective on news anchor, 1969 versus 2009
Source: Vanderbilt Television News Archive.

For each story involving a conflict that was shown as part of the evening news, coders were asked whether or not there was one or more identifiable face shown, other than the news anchor. In order to qualify, a face did not need not to be identified by name, but it had to be shown in a way that the viewer could identify the individual if he or she could already recognize the person. Crowd shots thus did not qualify unless at least some individuals were shown close enough to identify them.

As shown in Figure 8.4, the conflicts in television news stories are now almost always illustrated in terms of identifiable individuals. Over half of stories involved identifiable individuals back in the 1960s; now a conflict that does not include one or more identifiable face would be highly unusual indeed. News is now more than ever about identifiable human beings in conflict, at least that is how it looks to viewers on the television screen. Because institutions or other abstract entities do not generally make interesting television, cameras focus instead on the people behind these abstractions in order to produce interesting concrete visuals.

The final two characteristics of television news stories analyzed were chosen because of their demonstrated relevance to in-your-faceness and the arousal levels experienced by viewers. We know that up-close camera perspectives increase arousal, and intensify emotional reactions to content. As shown by the solid line in Figure 8.5,

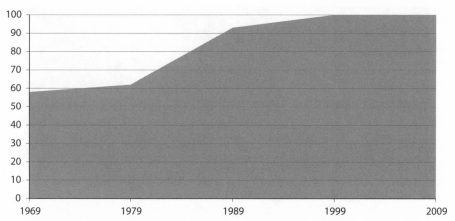

Figure 8.4. Percentage of conflicts featuring identifiable faces, 1969–2009

Note: Means by year for the percentage of conflicts per broadcast that include identifiable individual faces differed significantly ($F = 10.48, p < .001$), and the means demonstrate a significant increasing linear trend ($F = 35.08, p < .001$).

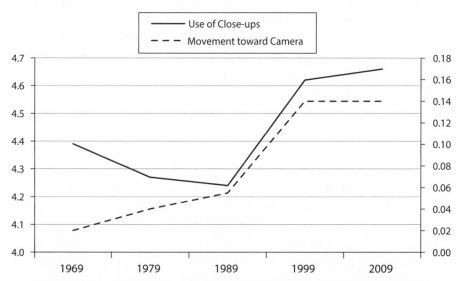

Figure 8.5. Use of camera close-ups and movement toward the camera, 1969–2009

Note: Means by year for movement toward the camera are significantly different ($F = 4.93, p < .001$), and the means demonstrate a significant increasing linear trend ($F = 17.06, p < .001$). Uses of camera close-ups by year are also significantly different ($F = 3.42, p < .05$), and the means demonstrate a significant increasing linear trend ($F = 9.64, p < .01$).

Figure 8.6. Illustrating a story on unemployment in 1969 and 2009
Source: Vanderbilt Television News Archive.

the use of close-ups is higher in 2009 than it was in 1969. The pattern in this case is less of a purely straightforward linear increase, however. The trend toward greater use of close-ups did not begin until the late 1980s, but it then increased dramatically over the ensuing decades.

In Figure 8.6, two television news stories on unemployment illustrate this difference. In 1969, as shown on the left, a crude graphic showing Akron, Pennsylvania, provides the visual as Chet Huntley discusses the problem using this particularly hard-hit town as an example. In 2009, the news story on unemployment leaves the studio immediately after its introduction by the anchor in order to feature a close-up of a recently laid-off federal worker who talks about the difficulties of unemployment while a tear rolls down her cheek.

In addition to close-ups, camera shots that involve a human moving toward the camera/viewer also have become increasingly common over the decades, as illustrated in Figure 8.5. When cameras were large and stationary, movement toward them was limited to what could occur in a studio. Now, however, it is very common for out-of-studio video to accompany a story. These shots often include a person appearing to come toward the viewer. This is important because it creates the feeling of even closer proximity. When someone appears to come toward the viewer, this orients attention and increases arousal.

THE INCREASED VISIBILITY OF POLITICAL CONFLICT

Based on the results in this chapter, the trend toward in-your-face politics has been aided and abetted by several factors. Although I used a talk show format as a convenient context within which to systematically alter levels of incivility and camera perspectives, in-your-face politics is a broader, far more general phenomenon. The rise of political talk shows is relevant, but it is far from the only context in which people experience in-your-face visuals. Even the highly traditional network news program has shifted its practices in ways that produce more arousing content. Thus in the less frequent situation where incivility makes the network news, it is more likely to be viewed by the public in a way that violates face-to-face social norms. To be clear, I am not suggesting that news producers purposely turn to tactics that will make viewers think less of politics and politicians. But attracting viewers and educating the public on matters of political importance is their job, and they cannot do their job unless they are successful at attracting audiences. So it should not be surprising that technological advances should be put toward the purpose of more attention-grabbing television.

Many developments have pushed American citizens toward seeing more uncivil, impolite political discourse in their political worlds. First, television became the dominant medium that political elites used to communicate with the American mass public. At the end of the day, it is unclear whether elite political discourse is truly any less civil now than when duels settled differences.[7] Nonetheless, the dominance of television as a source of exposure to politics suggests that, at the very least, the extent of the mass public's visual exposure to uncivil political discourse has increased.

As was illustrated in Chapter 7, it is one thing to read about political pundits' or candidates' contrary views in the press, and quite another to witness them directly engaged in vituperative argument "in person." People respond to the medium of television in fundamentally social ways because the pictures appear to be actual things, and are easily processed as real. Thus people respond more strongly to televised political incivility than to incivility that appears in print.

In addition, even within the genre of television news, visuals have changed in important ways. As a result of increased competition for audiences, political television content is increasingly produced with an eye toward what draws viewer interest and attention. Although I find no more conflict in television news these days than in the past, conflicts are now portrayed with greater intensity. Furthermore, visuals have become more in your face in recent decades through greater visual emphasis on living breathing humans on the screen as opposed to still photographs or drawings. Human bodies also now take up more of the television screen, and appear closer to viewers as a result. Close-ups and shots that involve people moving toward the camera/viewer are also more common, and these changes should further facilitate social reactions to television.

Because the level of arousal produced by a message tends to both attract audiences and improve recall,[8] one might well celebrate these efforts to keep American television audiences attuned to political life. But because there are also negative externalities from the in-your-face approach to political television, this topic requires more thoughtful consideration. I turn to this task in the next and final chapter.

CHAPTER 9
MAKING POLITICS PALATABLE
POLITICAL TELEVISION IN AN ERA OF CHOICE

Words ought to be a little wild, for they are the
assaults of thought on the unthinking.
—John Maynard Keynes, 1933

If one takes stock of the evidence on incivility that I have provided,
the path forward remains frustratingly unclear. Incivility appears
both necessary and detrimental to the audience for political television. Some of the empirical findings are encouraging, while others
are considerably less so. In Part I of the book I used a series of well-
controlled laboratory experiments to establish causal effects that
flow from incivility in televised political discourse. It is worth emphasizing that these effects are *purely* from incivility; they were not
a function of partisan programs, or of polarized issue positions. The
political substance remained the same, just the extent to which political advocates exchanged these views politely differed. In Part II
of the book I examined the generalizability of these findings, drawing on real-world programs and tracking viewership of in-your-face
politics in a representative sample of American political television
viewers. Finally, in Part III, I considered the historical implications
of my findings.

In order to draw meaningful conclusions from this collection
of results, I begin this final chapter by reviewing the key findings
throughout the book, in an attempt to systematically evaluate both

sides of the ledger. Next I consider the roads not taken, that is, the many questions raised by this research that remain unanswered. Third, I reconsider whether there is truly serious cause for concern. Is incivility really worth all of this hand-wringing? Fourth, I consider the most logical targets of blame for the current state of affairs. In the fifth and final section, I provide a series of practical suggestions about how to improve the future prospects for political television.

It is tempting, based on the evidence in this book, to simply join the legions of anti-incivility crusaders calling for a kinder, gentler civil society. After all, one meets little opposition in doing so. But as I learned throughout the course of these many studies, the issue is actually far more complex than the widespread pro-civility consensus makes it seem. Thus it is also deserving of deeper scrutiny.

THE IMPACT OF IN-YOUR-FACE POLITICS

Based on the experimental results, several consistent patterns emerge. By far the most robust negative effect on political attitudes from in-your-face politics is on trust in government and politicians. Incivility, in particular, lowers public evaluations of government and politicians. This impact does not depend on close-up camera perspectives. People watching uncivil repartee among political advocates come to think of politicians and government officials as unbound by the rules of civil behavior. Put simply, incivility breeds distrust; they are clearly not one of us.

A second negative impact of in-your-face politics is more subtle. When incivility is combined with up-close camera perspectives that make political advocates seem genuinely close and in our faces, viewers are apt to punish the person with whom they disagree and demonize the opposition. Both the least liked politician and the opposing issue positions espoused were regarded less favorably as a result of the combination of incivility and the appearance of physical proximity.

This effect is a logical consequence of two factors. First, in-your-face television heightens levels of physiological arousal. When viewers watch uncivil discourse that has the appearance of being up close and personal, the impacts of spatial proximity and incivility are compounded to produce particularly high levels of arousal. Arousal is widely known to intensify people's attitudes, even when the target of the attitude is not the source of the arousal.

As a result, in-your-face television causes viewers to dislike the politicians they did not like to begin with even more intensely. From the perspective of winning elections, this finding is inconsequential; the viewer who disliked the candidate was never going to vote for the politician anyway. But from the perspective of governing a country, it matters a great deal how supporters of the losing candidate feel about the one who won. To the extent that the opposition becomes demonized in the eyes of the losers, it harms the public's willingness to adhere to policies they do not necessarily support. In the end, democracy depends upon the consent of the governed, so even those who did not personally consent to a given leader or policy must be willing to go along with the outcome.

Interestingly, I do not find a parallel effect of intensified liking for the preferred candidate as some face-to-face studies of distance have found. It seems plausible that this is a function of perceptual bias, and the fact that viewers tended to perceive the opposing party's candidate as more uncivil than the candidate of their own party. If the politician were a well-known and much-liked leader to whom a viewer was already committed, then perhaps the effects would be more symmetric. Regardless, the outcome is an even stronger sense among viewers that the opposition is illegitimate, ill motivated, and not to be taken seriously.

Further delegitimization of the opposition is not what American politics needs at the moment; greater polarization and disrespect for the other side can make compromise still more difficult for political leadership, and political life more tense for ordinary citizens. But aside from the many studies examining polarization, is there any other evidence that respect for the opposition is flagging? Using the American National Election Studies data, I created a difference score representing the average evaluation of one's own and the oppositional party, and broke it down by partisanship. Because some years asked about the Democratic or Republican Parties and other years asked simply about Democrats and Republicans, who tend to be evaluated more favorably than their parties, for each year I calculated the difference between evaluations of own party and other party, with the assumption that the effects of wording should cancel out in any given year.

During the rise of in-your-face politics, there has been a historical change in how Americans feel about the *other* party relative to their own party. As shown in Figure 9.1, the gap between how one feels about one's own and the opposition party has clearly increased in size. Of course, people evaluate their own party more favorably, but they do so by an additional ten points now relative to the 1960s. When the separate components are analyzed, it becomes clear that people have not changed much at all in their feelings toward their *own* party, but attitudes toward the opposition have clearly suffered, thus increasing the size of the gap. It is impossible to know exactly how much in-your-face television has to do with these trends as opposed to other factors such as polarization, but the pattern is similar to what was seen in the experiments, and provides cause for concern. Interestingly, the timing of the increase appears concentrated around the same time as the changes in television that were noted in Chapter 8.

Because of the rush to condemn incivility, it is particularly important to take stock of its benefits. On the positive side of the ledger, it is important to remember that based on these results, all programs, regardless of which version was watched, informed viewers about rationales for and against the candidates and issues, so viewing educated people about their options. Viewers even learned a significant number of rationales for oppositional issue positions, regardless of what version of the program was viewed. And despite the forced attention of the laboratory setting, people were much more likely to accurately recall information if they watched an uncivil, close-up version of the program. High levels of arousal went hand in hand with greater attention to and recall of program content. In an "attention deficit democracy," getting people to pay attention and focus on political information is no mean feat.[1]

Watching in-your-face political television thus serves an important informational function. Some may worry that partisan programs tend to misinform viewers more than they inform.[2] But on

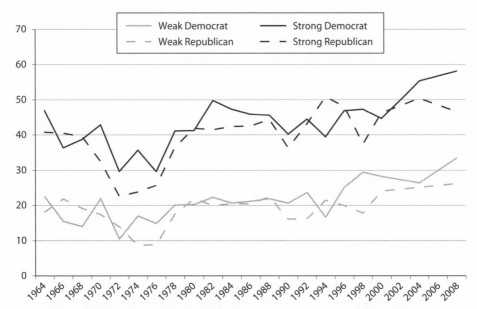

Figure 9.1. Difference between affect toward own party and affect toward other party, by year
Note: Vertical axis represents difference between evaluations of own party and other party on 100-point thermometer scales.
Source: Data are from the American National Election Studies.

the whole, they seem to increase viewers' knowledge of candidates and their issue positions.[3] So it is still better from this viewpoint if people watch in-your-face politics than if they watch no televised politics at all. In these studies, as in so many others, emotion turns out to be central to the way citizens function in the political world.[4]

Although the experimental findings make it clear that arousal plays a positive role in encouraging recall and political learning, these findings probably underestimate the real-world importance of the arousal offered by in-your-face politics. In addition to encouraging memory for content, what the laboratory findings could not demonstrate is the importance of highly arousing programs in attracting viewers to watch. Outside the laboratory, a number of things happen that make incivility central to many successful political programs. For one, political television must compete with other activities in people's lives. Furthermore, it must compete with highly arousing programs whose sole purpose is to entertain. These programs nearly always include something that political coverage does not have: a good storyline. As Plotz describes the problem,

> Any tale that you care about arcs from beginning to middle to end. But the campaign doesn't manage to tell any story at all, and that is the fatal blow. This is a story: A young orphan discovers that he has magical powers and sets off to a school for wizards. He learns that the evil wizard who killed his parents is back, looking for a magic stone. Through a series of tests and puzzles, the orphan vanquishes his nemesis and is celebrated as a hero. This is not a story: Al Gore gives a speech in Clayton, Mo., on children's health; Al Gore gives a speech in Niles, Ill., on health care; Al Gore gives a speech in Bridgeville, Pa., on women's health. Wash, rinse, repeat till November.[5]

The monotony and predictability of election coverage make it unsurprising that television producers have turned to incivility as a way to generate more excitement among viewers.

Yet another advantage of incivility is that the number of people reached by uncivil messages is likely to be far greater because the probability of retransmission is higher. So not only will uncivil comments receive more attention to begin with, as discussed in Chapter 2, they are also more likely to be propagated via social media, email, or YouTube. Arousal drives both attention and retransmission. Without arousal in some form, it seems unlikely that many people would watch televised politics. So while the negative externalities of in-your-face politics are unfortunate, one could argue that arousing political television content is absolutely necessary. The question I turn to in the final section of this chapter is whether arousal might be generated by other means.

It is also worth recalling that, relative to not watching political television at all, the civil conditions in close-up *boosted* the perceived legitimacy of oppositional views. Polite exchanges encouraged people's sense that the other side had legitimate arguments on its side, if not what they perceived to be the most legitimate arguments. In other words, television in some of its forms has the capacity to remedy the very problems to which it contributes—that is, if people will actually watch it.

When all else was held constant in the experiments, including partisanship, content, and so forth, my findings highlighted that people find the uncivil programs far more lively and entertaining than the civil ones. Despite the fact that so many people claim to be disgusted by incivility, this finding should not be all that surprising. After all, we have always had civil political programs on the air, such as *PBS NewsHour*, but audiences are not exactly clamoring to watch them.

One final pattern of note is the extent to which conservatives stand out in these findings. Conservatives appear more sensitive to the arousal generated by in-your-face presentations. In general, I find stronger effects of incivility among those with strong ideological positions. But conservatives are especially drawn to watch in-your-face programs and are especially likely to react to it when exposed. Because one of the central effects of in-your-face politics is to discourage trust in government, and this is a tendency that already characterizes conservatives to a greater extent than liberals, conservatives' attitudes toward government may decline to an even greater extent as a result.

WHAT REMAINS TO BE SEEN

Despite the many experiments and analyses in this book, I have not come close to exhausting all of the questions that I would have liked to have answered, and there are undoubtedly many others that have not yet even occurred to me. Nonetheless, I thought it useful to note at least some of the paths I have not taken, whether for practical reasons or because my results suggested these paths would probably not be fruitful.

Whenever I have presented these experimental results, my audiences have frequently had questions about the role of candidate gender. Most wanted to know what would happen if the candidates were both female, or if one candidate were female and the other male. The honest answer is that I do not know because I did not have the resources to produce multiple versions of these civil and uncivil exchanges so that mixed candidate pairings and female versus female encounters could be subjected to similar experimentation. I chose a male versus male race to begin my research because most political races remain man versus man.

Without any data to support my predictions, I would venture that politeness should be deemed particularly important in female candidates due to the fact that aggression is perceived as more socially acceptable for men. Thus, I would expect the negative effects of incivility on perceptions of the opposition to be especially strong when female candidates violate social norms for politeness. At the same time, I would expect female-on-female incivility to be an especially big audience draw due to its relative infrequency. Female mud wrestling draws large audiences in part because it is unusual to see women fight one another and get dragged through the mud. I have no doubt that any highly uncivil exchange between two female politicians would be exciting enough to audiences to be posted on YouTube and to be widely commented upon by the press.

Aside from gender issues, another question that remains to be answered is whether the highly contentious style I dubbed the "boxed debate" in Chapter 6 is processed the same way as when people are shown physically inhabiting the same space, as in a television studio. If I had to venture a guess, I would surmise that they are processed similarly, if only because the notion of people shoulder to shoulder on the television screen, but literally hundreds of miles apart in real space, is not something to which our brains can easily adjust. But obviously this would be an important kind of stylized interaction to study given that it is not only common, but also the most uncivil format in which politics is discussed today. Not being in the same room as one's adversary appears to make it easier to be uncivil and demanding as an interviewer, because it releases us from the demands of face-to-face civility, the conventions to which we are most accustomed.

My audiences have also wondered about the results of a similar experiment if one candidate were to discuss their differences in a consistently civil manner, while the other did not. The civil versus uncivil candidate pairing was indeed seriously considered because it was a simple matter of reediting the issue exchanges to create a civil-uncivil condition in which the two candidates switched off playing the civil and uncivil roles. Once created, however, no one who viewed the civil-uncivil exchanges was in favor of running an experiment using them because the programs came across as highly unnatural. When one person speaks in a calm, friendly tone, the other person typically responds in kind. Likewise, it is natural to raise one's voice in response to another person doing the same. The pairing of uncivil discourse with civil responses resulted in a highly unrealistic exchange, one our viewers could not imagine occurring in real life. Because no one believed the results would generalize to any real-world situation, this variation was dropped.

Earlier plans considered an Internet version of the experiment, but once the print version failed to generate recognition of civil and uncivil versions with the content held constant, it became clear that I would not be able to execute such an experiment without eliminating rigorous levels of control over political substance. So much of the emotional content of human interaction is carried by faces, that the rise of a print-centric new medium like the Internet probably has, if anything, a dampening effect on arousal levels. To be sure, there are plenty of uncivil bloggers and commenters online, and perhaps the sheer extremity of their uncivil behavior will allow them to produce some similar effects on their readers. But at this point in time, the format is not particularly conducive to the effects of in-your-face politics. The strong partisanship of some blogs may produce intense emotional reactions, especially when viewed by those on the other side, but the effects of partisan media may occur via another set of mechanisms.

IS INCIVILITY TRULY A PROBLEM?

Given the huge number of initiatives under way to improve levels of civility in American politics, it seems fair to say that there is an overwhelming consensus that American politics has gone too far. Civility advocates do, nonetheless, have a few detractors, although their voices have been largely drowned out by enthusiastic champions of civility. There are at least four quite sensible arguments suggesting that this whole affair has been blown greatly out of proportion.

The most prominent argument in this vein points to the numerous historical examples of extreme incivility and violence in American politics of the past. I generally concur that the claim of a historical decline in the civility levels of politicians is fantasy, a mere romanticization of the past. Such lamentations are especially common around the turn of a century. In the end, I think it is unwise to claim concern on the basis of an undocumented hypothetical trend among political elites. The key difference between nasty politicians then and now is that we as citizens witness far more of their misbehaviors. What's more, via the wonders of audiovisual media, we watch them up close and personal, as if we were actually physically there with them. This not only heightens levels of public awareness of incivility, but also intensifies the emotional reactions that viewers have to it. So while there may not have been any increase in the incivility of our leaders, there has clearly been an increase in the proximity of the incivility that citizens experience. As the phrase "in-your-face politics" suggests, we witness more incivility from a more intimate perspective than ever.

A second basis for suggesting that civility is overvalued in public life today suggests that such advocacy is essentially a lot of hot air, and a distraction from more important matters. As Sandel argues, "In politics, civility is an overrated virtue. The problem with civility is the very thing that tempts politicians to extol it: it is uncontroversial."[6] If incivility is simply the malaise of the day, and promoting civility is akin to loving Mom and apple pie, then it becomes a lot like supporting education or being anticrime—it is safe and uncontroversial, unlike promoting a specific approach to improving schools or combating crime. It is also superficial and unrelated to anything politically substantive. The potential harm done in focusing time and resources on incivility is that it distracts from the substantive issues that deserve our time and attention.

I would agree that incivility is "just a process value,"[7] but processes are important because processes have consequences. To the extent that incivility leads people to trust government less, and thus promote only policies that do not require government involvement, it influences the political substance of our country. And to the extent that incivility discourages compromise by convincing people that the opposition has no legitimate basis for its views, it will be increasingly difficult for government to accomplish anything.

Some suggest that calls for greater civility are about class warfare.[8] Promoting civility is really about keeping the powerless docile and quiet, so their political claims cannot be heard: "The 'new incivility' needs to be recognized ... for what it is: a flat out, justified rejection of leader-class claims to respect."[9] The suggestion here is that civility basically means deference to authority. By demanding that people be civil in political discourse, we perpetuate status quo inequalities between those in positions of power and those who are not. Likewise, some have argued that the very notion of politeness connotes a power deferential; to be polite to someone is to show subservience to a superior. I would have presumed precisely the opposite; the reason we encourage our children to follow the same rules of politeness with everyone from the grocery store checkout person to their elected representatives is to convey that all people are deserving of a certain amount of courtesy and respect. Power differentials do not give people a right to be impolite or dismissive of one another.

As my comments suggest, I have mixed reactions to this argument because I am not convinced of its underlying assumptions. I do not think the uncivil voices most widely heard today come from those who are powerless and have no other way to be heard. Instead, the political incivility that people are complaining so much about comes from corporate-driven news organizations eager to maintain their audiences, or mainstream politicians eager for media coverage. These are not powerless or underprivileged people by a long shot.

On the other hand, I agree that there are times when incivility is necessary in order to draw attention to causes that are not being championed by those with power, and thus are simply not being heard. Randall Kennedy points out that nineteenth-century advocates of civility indicted abolitionists for their incivility: "The people who marched under the banner of civility, the people who were the compromisers, the people who ... were afraid of being labeled as radicalists and extremists, were the people who were willing to allow slavery to continue."[10] Likewise, civil rights advocates, supporters of the Equal Rights Amendment, and other agitators for change have also used incivility as a tactic to draw attention to their causes.

Incivility is bipartisan these days, used by leaders of both the left and right, although watched far more by the right, as we saw in Chapter 6. Advocates of the status quo have used incivility as have more radical political advocates.[11] Incivility charges have been leveled at people of all classes and political stripes; thus the fact that the opponents of slavery were charged with being uncivil does not make incivility the political tactic of choice for all groups challenging authority. It would be difficult to argue that the success of abolitionists was due to their willingness to engage in incivility any more than the lack of success of other causes can be attributed to too much civility.

To accomplish major societal change requires a level of passion and commitment that, not surprisingly, goes hand in hand with intense convictions. So it is possible that successful political movements and incivility in the expression of political opinions are spuriously related because strongly committed advocates drive both outcomes. It is also worth remembering that civility and nonviolence have also been important tactics in successful social movements.

The bottom line is that political movements require mass public attention and the ability to motivate others in order to succeed. Both of these requirements are fueled by high arousal levels, so incivility has become one of the favored means of producing the attention, arousal, and motivation to make things happen politically. Without emotional arousal, mass politics would founder. Before exploring this problem in greater depth, I turn next to defend those who have been most widely blamed for the current "crisis" of incivility.

WHOM NOT TO BLAME AND WHY

For better or worse, most discussions about the uncivil state of American political discourse assume wrongdoing and focus on whom to blame for this undesirable state of affairs. I find most of these arguments overly simplistic in their understanding of the problem because of their narrow focus on profit motives, polarized politicians, or less than ideally motivated citizens. I review the basics of these arguments, and then offer my own recommendations.

By far the easiest finger to point is directed at the most immediate cause of incivility—the commercial television producers who produce uncivil television programs. In 2004, Jon Stewart bitterly admonished *Crossfire* hosts Tucker Carlson and Paul Begala for their uncivil dialogue while making a guest appearance on their program: "It's not so much that it's bad, as it's hurting America. . . . Stop, stop, stop, stop hurting America."

Although my evidence suggests that Stewart may be correct about incivility's detrimental effects, his finger pointing does not seem entirely fair. After all, *Crossfire* competes for the relatively small audience of people interested in political talk shows. It is considered journalism/political news, and is expected to tackle serious issues of the day in a thoughtful manner. *The Daily Show* relies on comedy as a means of attracting audiences, and is not held to the same standards as "serious" political programs. Stewart defended himself to Carlson and Begala, claiming, "You're on CNN. The show that leads into me is puppets making crank phone calls. . . . You have a responsibility to the public discourse, and you fail miserably."[12] As Stewart implies, he does not feel he has the same responsibility to public discourse that serious journalists do. And frankly, for him that is a tremendous advantage. He need not worry about accuracy, fairness, thoroughness, or any of the traditional professional journalistic norms. He can use humor to attract audiences, without worrying about whether it is too crude or obscene for a "real" news program.

More generally, it is common to argue that commercial pressures are to blame for the current state of political television. After all, public television's political coverage rarely contains uncivil discourse. Freed of the need to attract audiences and profits, political television is quite civil indeed. But before jumping to blame the profit motive, it is important to remember that even if market forces were ignored and political programming adhered to face-to-face, highly polite social norms, it is doubtful such programs would attract large audiences. The effects of civil political discourse will matter little when no one is watching. Ultimately we are left with the dilemma of how to create political programming that is both interesting and informative to watch, yet not likely to damage public attitudes in a significant way.

The advent of hundreds of cable channels has produced far more competition for political audiences, which were not terribly large to begin with. In the days of the three networks, many people watched these programs simply because they were on at the time, not out of interest, and there were few other options. Viewing today involves far more choice. Commercial pressures force producers of political content to labor even more for their relatively small audiences. After all, people can always turn to entertainment programs, sitcoms, dramas, and the like if political programming is too dull. And as Chapter 2 of this book demonstrated, in-your-face politics is anything but dull.

But it is precisely for this reason that one cannot fairly blame the commercial structure of American media for the rise of incivility on the air. If one imagines, instead of our present system, that all political programming looked like that on PBS, then the number of people watching political television would undoubtedly be much smaller. Only the political diehards, people who will watch political television in virtually any form, would be likely to watch such programs. In this sense, my findings can be viewed as a classic case of a market failure; the kind of presentation that attracts audiences and builds television revenues is not the one that best serves democratic citizens.

For most people, politics on its own merits is not sufficiently exciting to compete with *American Idol* or *ER* for television audiences, so it requires the drama and tension of uncivil human conflict to make it more interesting to watch. Although some defenders of public virtue argue that the American public is eager for serious, high-quality political television, the ratings that programs receive suggest that this is not the case.

Political television cannot inform the public unless they watch it. And unless they have no other choices, it seems unlikely that audiences who are only mildly interested in politics would be attracted to dull but civil programming. Instead, the public as a whole would probably watch even less political television and have lower levels of awareness and knowledge about political affairs. The gap between the political haves and have-nots would likely widen as only extreme partisans followed political affairs.[13]

A second common target of blame is political elites. Contemporary political observers have a widespread sense that things are different now with respect to how political elites talk to one another. However, empirical evidence of this change in discourse is thin to nonexistent. To be sure, the U.S. Congress is more polarized now than it has been in the recent past. And more extreme differences of opinion could lead to harsher rhetoric and rising frustration due to an inability to find acceptable compromises. But, as the contentious Zell Miller–Chris Matthews exchange reminds us, it has been a very long time since American politicians had a good duel to the death. It is worth remembering that there was an era when challenging someone to a duel over political differences, though illegal in some states, was not as bizarre as it would seem today. Thankfully, few domestic political advocates kill each other over differences of opinion. Indeed, one could deem this evidence of improvement over the harsh language and accusations of an earlier era.

As a practical matter, it would be difficult to systematically catalogue everything that political elites said over a substantial historical period or to find a population from which to sample candidate discourse. As a result of the growth of mass media, and the widespread availability of media technology, far more of what political elites say goes on some kind of public record today. Without evidence, I think it unfair to lay the blame at political elites' feet by comparing them to some romanticized version of their forefathers. Even if it were documented that they are less civil now than in some past period, one could argue that they are merely responding to the dictates of the contemporary media environment; in order to attract audiences in a market with extreme competition, politicians may have to be more provocative than in the past.

Among political elites, popular scapegoats include the candidates and their staffs. If only they did not insist upon prepackaged political pabulum, television would have something worth covering, and citizens would have something worth watching. I think there is some truth to this argument, yet it is pointless to tell a candidate that he or she should be doing something counter to his or her electoral self-interest.

Another common reaction to this state of affairs is to wag a finger disapprovingly at the American public. If only they were more civic-minded, we lament, they would be willing to sit though even the most soporific political debate as part of a sense of civic duty. From this perspective the problem is that large portions of the public will not, given a choice, watch calm, civil (read: boring) political exchanges. They want theater! They want lively in-your-face repartee!

And thus much of the blame has been directed toward the public for wanting to be entertained rather than edified. Some point to well-known examples such as the Lincoln-Douglas debates for evidence that the publics of the past were more virtuous than today's citizens: "Here was a time when people would stand outside for hours listening to detailed, erudite, complex arguments on the nation's most pressing political controversy."[14] But as Schudson has argued, the virtuousness of citizens during the era of high participation is highly dubious.[15] The audiences for Lincoln-Douglas debates were impressively large, to be sure, but this was "the best show in town," and people were there for grand entertainment rather than for their political edification. Douglas's opening speech was interrupted again and again by chants of "Hit him again." The speeches were infused with ad hominem attacks and personal rather than politically substantive debates. In a word, they were uncivil.

In the end, I find the argument of lost public piety largely irrelevant to our contemporary problem. A nation that is accustomed to sports and entertainment available around the clock is not going to voluntarily abandon more entertaining fare in order to listen to dry policy debates. Even if today's citizens are less admirable, wagging fingers to shame them for their own lack of serious interest in American politics is not likely to be effective. As long as incivility attracts viewers, promotes retransmission of content to still larger audiences, and is interesting, if uncomfortable, to watch, it will persist.

To summarize, all three of these targets of blame are unfair. The problem is neither the commercial nature of mass media, nor the laziness of citizens, nor the behavior of candidates for office. Instead, the problem is that politicians and the media have grown accustomed to a very limited repertoire for calling public attention to themselves. In an era when even the president is no longer guaranteed an audience,[16] there has been surprisingly little innovation in how to create arousing political programs.

To be fair, most politicians and the media are unaware of the potential consequences of using incivility as a means of attracting audiences. While there is a generalized concern that incivility is bad for political comity, this has been mostly speculation. The negative effects of incivility result from the characteristics of a political medium that we are only slowly beginning to understand. Although I refer to television as the source of effects throughout this book, and most consider television to be an "old" medium, my conclusions are intended to apply to audiovisual media no matter where or how it is viewed. Although television in the sense we have known it in the past may be on its way out, the audiovisual content to which we are exposed is likely to become even more similar in appearance to real life.

Incivility in political television may be widely renounced, but at the moment it is also extremely necessary. Despite the many efforts to liven up political television, the large amounts of money spent on campaigns, and the many talented political consultants, political television still "goes down like cod-liver oil." As a journalist wryly observed, the candidates "have already spent $150 million, and their campaigns get built-in coverage from the networks, yet not only have they failed to produce a spectacle as compelling as the World Wrestling Federation's 'SmackDown!' they can't even muster the ratings of the 'King of Queens' reruns. Politicians like to pretend campaigns are mano-a-mano death struggles, but in truth they are eerily devoid of direct conflict. . . . The candidates are staying above the fray, but as a result, there's no fray and little worth watching."[17] I found this journalist's observation interesting, first because I think he is correct, and second because he actually blamed the candidates for not producing a *more* compelling spectacle. This is not a particularly common perspective in the United States. Instead, candidates are frequently blamed for *creating* a spectacle, for emphasizing campaign hoopla over substance.

It is worth remembering that the decline of popular participation in American politics did not happen because Americans simply lost interest. The decline that began at the end of the nineteenth century resulted in part from purposeful efforts on the part of election reformers. It was a self-conscious effort to replace the extravagant campaigns of the Civil War era with more intellectual and educational political campaigns.[18] The goal was to discourage the parades, fireworks, marches, and big brass bands. The reformers wanted to make political discourse more solemn, more rational, with individuals gathering information from many sources, critically evaluating it, and then making up their minds individually.

As this reform took hold, participation rates dropped precipitously, further suggesting that people's motivations for political involvement may not have been entirely virtuous and civic-minded. As the pageantry and hoopla dwindled, an important dimension of political involvement was lost. It was not as much fun anymore. Political participation became more of an individualistic, solitary act than a grand social occasion. It was no longer something entertaining to do with your friends, or to talk about with people. By the 1920s the new emphasis on "perusing, not parading" had successfully transformed American political campaigns.[19] Unfortunately, the emphasis on campaign pageantry appears to be what attracted the uninvolved into politics in the previous era.[20]

According to historians, the campaign spectacle also served an important purpose beyond entertainment and filling people's leisure time with political theater. Spectacular electioneering—much like rock-and-roll concerts today—energized the public: "By taking up campaign pageantry, politicians and voters carried out a ritual struggle in which each side declared friendship and common origin in order to win the support of the other."[21]

Beyond serving as a ritual, the extravaganzas of political campaigns also served to convey what McGerr dubbed "the visible assent of the governed."[22] Because political theater was, and probably still is, a necessary part of the democratic process, now transpiring primarily on television, it is incumbent upon anyone calling for greater civility to explain how such programs can eliminate incivility, yet maintain their audiences. A less dramatic style of politics than we have now is unlikely to get very far.

WHAT CAN BE DONE?

So what can be done about in-your-face politics? Some suggest that at least in part, it is our polarized populace that drives the demand for incivility.[23] If so, incivility will probably wane with time if polarization does. But leaving aside the ongoing debate over whether the American public is truly more polarized or not, it seems unlikely that incivility will disappear on its own if public opinion becomes more moderate. I say this in part because I have shown that in-your-face tactics are not limited to partisan political programs; the intensity and incivility of conflict have increased on politically neutral political programs as well. Nonpartisan programs in particular need a means of attracting audiences because they do not have the advantage of feeding viewers strictly what they want to hear.

In order to improve political television in ways that are both palatable to viewers and beneficial for the larger political culture, I advocate the creation of a coalition parallel in goals to the alliance of television producers and academic researchers who created *Sesame Street*. The problem this group faced was not unlike the one I have described: what attracted children's attention was violent programming, and these programs turned out to have negative externalities, at least for some children. What was commercially successful and popular was not necessarily good for the collective as a whole.

The Children's Television Workshop (now the Sesame Workshop) was charged with the mission of creating appealing children's programming that did not promote violence or other antisocial behaviors. The question boiled down to what would produce viewer arousal and draw viewers' attention other than violence. As the success of many CTW-inspired programs such as *Sesame Street* attests, there are other means of attracting attention.

Likewise, a Political Television Workshop composed of scholars and television producers would seek ways to produce political television that holds citizens' attention and attracts viewer interest, without suggesting to the public that political advocates are antisocial ne'er-do-wells. After all, televised violence is not a far cry from televised incivility. Both are highly arousing and violate social norms, with violence constituting a more extreme form of incivility.

So what might be used in place of incivility to create arousal and encourage viewers to pay attention to political events? In order to consider alternatives, an important first step is to disabuse ourselves of the notion that good political television must be a solemn affair. There is a tendency to equate the style of political presentation with its quality. Serious, staid programming that appears self-consciously educational and dull is generally given higher marks than something entertaining and frivolous. And yet the most valuable contribution that political television could probably make in the contemporary political environment is to bring the political "middle" back. Television, much more than any print medium, is still the most widely accessible political medium. Virtually all American households have one or more televisions, and this low-effort medium has the kind of populist potential that is essential to bringing the public back in.

One possibility already being pursued is the use of humor. When a program is amusing, it gives people alternative motivations for watching it other than educating themselves. Thus shows like *The Daily Show* and *The Colbert Report* can attract young audiences who seldom watch standard political fare. Interestingly, when coders evaluated these two political comedy programs in the list of most watched programs, they judged them only slightly to the uncivil side of the mean. Instead, they scored high on a totally separate dimension, which was sarcasm.

The humor on these programs is sufficiently sophisticated that many news items are not funny unless one already knows something about politics.[24] For this reason, some have questioned how much new knowledge people really get from watching such programs. Because most of the studies claiming political learning from *The Daily Show* have been observational, it is difficult to know if these associations represent a causal impact.[25] The politically substantive content of *The Daily Show* is roughly on par with that presented on network news programs, although it sacrifices substance for humor.[26] Others have cautioned that the sarcasm on such programs decreases support for political institutions and leaders.[27] Although the jury is out as to whether and how much people learn through their viewership, there is a great deal of optimism that comedy shows and other "soft news" outlets may help to elevate awareness and knowledge among less politically involved segments of the population.[28] If people elect to watch a program for reasons other than political interest, incidental political exposure may occur.

Another approach used for many years in other countries has been to place news programs immediately after highly arousing and popular entertainment programs. To the extent that people are engaged in real-time viewing, this strategy can be quite effective. People would be more likely to watch the political program, and their residual arousal from the previous program could increase their recall of the political content and make them more likely to talk to others about what they have seen. However, as American viewers increasingly turn to time-delayed viewing, this strategy may not be effective.

A potentially arousing factor that politics already has going for it is the allure of competition. Competition can be very engrossing when the outcome is unknown. Uncertainty breeds excitement. One need only observe the popularity of sports in America, and it becomes clear that Americans love a good competition and the excitement and tension that come with it. Reality shows incorporate competitions for the very same reason. As one journalist pondered, "A population that won't miss a weekly election on 'Survivor' can't be bothered to notice the world's most important political contest."[29] Consider *America's Got Talent*, *The Biggest Loser*, *Who Wants to Be a Millionaire?*, *Worst Cooks in America*, *America's Next Top Model*, *Top Chef*, *The Amazing Race*, and *Bad Girls All Star Battle*, to name just a few. The uncertainty of the outcome and the concomitant desire to learn the winner compel people to watch incredibly low-quality television.

Elections already have this form of excitement and arousal built into their basic structure. But interestingly, when the so-called horse race is emphasized in news coverage, journalists are scorned for paying attention to the game rather than the substance of policy debates. I think this is unfortunate. To be clear, a focus on who is ahead and by how much is not the same as an emphasis on the strategy and tactics behind a campaign. I do not see much merit in the latter, as there is no evidence that it leads to better political decision making, and there is evidence linking it to increased public cynicism. But the benefits of emphasizing the competitive and suspenseful aspects of elections far outweigh the potential harm. There is excitement in following a competition, and it would be the height of foolishness to say that it is detrimental to have citizens care who wins or loses. Caring about who wins or loses is what political involvement is all about.

One highly entertaining example of how horse race coverage might be used toward attracting viewers comes from the 2012 South Korean presidential election. There, as in the United States, election night television consists of hours and hours of updates of poll results and election returns. But the Seoul Broadcasting System (SBS) went well beyond presenting tables and graphics on a large screen. Instead, it ran animations based on popular movies and sporting events to show who was surging ahead or falling behind.

Inspired by South Korea's Olympic performance, one animation showed the candidates in a fencing match, and when one of the candidates would win the vote in some part of the country, he or she would then land a successful blow. Another animation was based on a chase scene from a popular movie, and showed the candidates in school uniforms running through the streets. In yet another animation, the candidates were dressed in the style of Indiana Jones in *Raiders of the Lost Ark*, and faced a series of life-threatening situations. A road race through various parts of the country illustrated who was ahead or behind within each geographic area. A cartoon character of successful candidate Park Geun-hye danced and "gyrated ecstatically" as votes went her way, while her opponent's dancing was subdued. The most widely talked about animation came at the end of the evening and featured a massive eyeless teddy bear roaming the nation.[30] As one viewer remarked,

> I watched SBS's coverage, simply because that was the first TV station I found while I was looking. I was not interested in watching the whole programme . . . [but] it was not long before I was drawn into the programme. This was because of the way that SBS was showing the results. Instead of showing the results in complex, text-based charts and graphics, SBS used animations of the two

leading candidates to show them running races or tackling obstacle courses. It was compelling and made what could quite easily be a boring factual TV show into something I could not take my eyes off.[31]

Mark MacKinnon, a senior international correspondent for the *Globe and Mail*, likewise tweeted, "After watching how South Korean TV covers an election, I'll never watch CNN election coverage again!" One can easily imagine how younger generations raised on animation and video games would be particularly drawn to this kind of content. SBS further encouraged voters through an outreach campaign that asked people to take a selfie in front of the polling station after they voted and send it to the broadcasting station. The pictures were then circulated through the lower right-hand side of the television screen for all viewers to see.[32]

Entertaining political television need not be limited to election night coverage. One can imagine ongoing horse race coverage during the campaign set to similarly entertaining animation. Would such silliness undermine the respect and dignity of electoral office? I seriously doubt it. To laugh with others is not to laugh at them, and whatever dignity our elected leaders have left is not going to be taken away by creative efforts to visualize the campaign struggle.

Of course, another time-tested source of arousal is sex. In addition to the well-known sex scandals of U.S. political candidates and elected officials, in 2000 a Canadian firm seized on this idea to launch the first unclothed news program, suitably billed, "Naked News, the program with nothing to hide." This web-based news service features twenty-five-minute newscasts six days a week. Their North American Report is indistinguishable from any other mainstream news report as a nonpartisan, straightforward account of newsworthy events of the day. The only difference is that the anchors either read the news of the day fully nude or strip as they present successive news segments.

When *Naked News* was free on the web, it did not advertise its existence, but its popularity nonetheless spread informally, until it eventually had as many as six million viewers. It currently exists only as a pay-per-view subscription service. However, a free-to-view channel in Britain still broadcasts the show each evening, and it has spinoffs in other countries.

Although such an approach has potential among some viewing groups, I would be remiss here not to raise the issue of the curvilinear relationship between arousal and recall. In general, arousal increases attention and recall of content. But when arousal levels become extremely high, memory declines as people's systems are overwhelmed to the point where attention can no longer be focused on the content at hand. This scenario seems all too likely in the case of *Naked News*, although one can imagine tamer versions of this program that might approximate ideal levels of attention and arousal.

Yet another possibility might be to capitalize on Americans' insatiable appetite for celebrity news. Although it is common to decry the culture of celebrity surrounding public officials, rather than simply lament this preference, it makes more sense to play into it. In order to broaden the base of those who view political television, we should allow politicians to communicate directly with voters outside the context of highly structured, sanitized debates and thirty-second ads. Why not treat them like celebrities, feature them regularly in *People* magazine, and capitalize on the attention garnered by this approach? Many who prefer a more puritanical approach to politics may find this idea demeaning and distasteful, but it is worth considering that these are not the audiences that need to be reached. When Bill Clinton played the saxophone on the *Arsenio Hall Show* and Obama played basketball in front of the television cameras, each endeared himself to the apolitical American public by appearing to be "one of us." Of course, there was nothing politically educational about either event; nonetheless, by allowing politicians to appear in contexts that are entertaining, we would encourage mass public interest in them.

When the long sequential presidential primary season rolls around every four years, I often envision it as another season of *American Idol* in which a full complement of candidates starts the season, but only one ultimately finishes. Ideally the one who finishes has the broadest base of appeal, but because of the structure of the primaries, only hard-core party regulars tend to participate; moreover, the sequential system privileges certain states over others in the process of winnowing candidates, thus leaving the two parties doubtful about whether they have selected the best candidate for purposes of winning in the fall.

But what if all candidates in a given party were invited to appear on a nationally televised program that provides free airtime on a weekly basis? Instead of a weekly musical theme such as Queen or Michael Jackson, the program—I'll call it *Our Next American President*—would have a policy theme each week: health care one week and perhaps immigration policy the next. Viewers would tune in to see what each candidate chose to do with his or her airtime.

The candidates would be free to use the airtime however they wish so long as they address the topic at hand. They could be as formal, serious, or lighthearted as they wished. When the field of candidates is large, the time per candidate would be short, just as the songs are in the early weeks of *American Idol*. But the person with the fewest call-in votes each week would no longer receive free airtime in subsequent weeks.

It may sound frivolous at first, but the problem with debate audiences as well as political television audiences more generally is that they draw people who are already highly politically involved. Moreover, these programs tend to be quite boring. Drawing large, broad-based audiences of people who are not already strong partisans requires more than dry political exchanges to excite and entertain people.

Why would the relevant parties agree to such an undertaking? For candidates early in the primary season, often with limited budgets, visibility is of the utmost importance, and free airtime is an extremely valuable commodity. It is difficult to imagine candidates turning down free airtime to do with as they please, especially time that does not require them to debate an adversarial journalist or political opponent. This would be their opportunity to communicate directly with the American public. It could also serve as a proving ground for candidates to convince their parties that they are viable and electable candidates to the American public at large.

But why would a television network offer free airtime to candidates when they have not done so in the past? Usually political programs produce revenue losses relative to what might be aired instead.

Thus, the key to making this work would be both its entertainment value and the suspense regarding who continues to the next week's program. People watch *American Idol* because they want to see who gets eliminated each week. *Our Next American President* would have a similar tension that would make it exciting and unpredictable. Voting each week would make viewers feel directly involved in the process, and the audience would be more than the political hard core, so it might help parties select more broadly electable candidates as well. Although the votes would not be binding, the prize—still more free airtime—would be something of real value to candidates.

Because political primaries are controlled by individual states, and there is constant jockeying for position and supposed influence, the television-based elimination process would be completely independent of the legally binding process. But I would bet it would have a huge influence on how states voted. If a candidate demonstrates a great deal of popular appeal, actual primary voters will take note. A call-in process would probably be subject to vote manipulation, just as it is with *American Idol*, but so long as the competition's outcome has no legal status and simply awards additional free airtime, this would not be highly problematic. The winner would already have demonstrated broad appeal, thus answering one of the most important questions for primary voters.

And the judges? They should not be journalists or political experts, but a politically balanced group could provide lively commentary after each performance, though just as in *American Idol*, the judges' opinions would not define the winner. Is it hoopla? Clearly. But many Americans need to be convinced that politics is exciting and interesting if it is to become more than a spectator sport. Moreover, having the candidates talk about a single issue the same week will make it far easier for people to make comparisons than the fragmented pieces of information they get through debate questions and political advertisements. A whole program devoted to sustained information and opinions on health care, unemployment, or virtually any issue would be far more in-depth than what we have in current media coverage or in debates.

I should note that similar programs already exist in other countries. For example, in Canada Alex Trebek (host of the well-known game show *Jeopardy!*) hosts a reality show called *The Next Great Prime Minister*, in which young Canadians aged eighteen to twenty-five debate questions posed to them by politicians. In 2007 the politicians included four former Canadian prime ministers: Brian Mulroney, Kim Campbell, Joe Clark, and Paul Martin. In this case, an in-studio audience representing the Canadian population votes for an ultimate winner of the competition. Apparently Bulgaria and Germany have also aired variations on this kind of program.

My own preference would be to structure *Our Next American President* so that mass participation was facilitated as much as possible, in addition to a raucous studio audience. What is missing from today's campaigns that was present in the era of mass participation is the ability to see other people expressing their enthusiasm for their candidate of choice. After catching my own kids with their cell phones under the blankets trying to vote (perhaps twice) for their favorite *Idol* contestants, I am convinced that the ability to participate actively and in an ongoing way makes it more fun and gives people an investment in the process that they would not otherwise have.

Journalists would probably argue that such a program amounts to giving candidates free advertising time; why not just allow them to run half-hour ads or to show their slick introductory films from the party conventions? Candidates would undoubtedly use such opportunities to promote themselves, but so what? To create drama and attract viewers, the candidates need enough airtime to establish a storyline, and thirty seconds does not cut it in that regard.

Perhaps this is giving candidates carte blanche to get away with all kinds of false claims that could go unchallenged by the judges or their opponents. But this already occurs in debates as well as in advertisements. The controversial claims tend to be discussed and debated after the event itself rather than in real time, and I assume the same would happen after each episode including on television, in the blogosphere, and in print.

Yet another possibility for increasing ongoing political involvement occurred to me during a sabbatical year when I was riding a commuter train regularly. The major topic of conversation on the train virtually every day was fantasy football. Although I am an NFL fan, I had never realized just how popular fantasy football was, or just how involved people could become in something that was "just a game." To be clear, I realize that real football is also just a game, but fantasy football is a game within a game, basically an extremely clever way to increase the viewership and ratings of real football games.

For those who have not previously participated in a fantasy league, individuals compete against each other by acting as general managers for fantasy teams that are composed of real-life football players. Those playing this interactive game can draft players, trade them, and so forth, just as real teams do. How well a person's team does depends on the performance of those real players in their weekly games. Statistics are tracked online by the NFL, and are fed directly into people's fantasy league standings.

The genius of fantasy leagues is that they give participants an incentive to pay attention to more than just their favorite team's game. Because one's fantasy team includes players from multiple teams, it now matters how those players perform in their games, even if one does not really care who wins or loses that game. According to the Fantasy Sports Trade Association, fantasy sports players watch more football games on television and attend more games. Moreover, a fantasy team owner will watch a game differently if someone on his or her fantasy team is playing. He or she will root for specific things to happen that will improve the fantasy team's score.

Interestingly, the players themselves fear that fantasy leagues may have overshadowed the real ones. Star quarterback Peyton Manning reported that only requests for autographs exceeded requests for "more fantasy touchdowns." He recounts a typical conversation with a fantasy fan as follows:

Fan: Hey, great game last week.
Manning: Yeah, but we lost.
Fan: But you threw five touchdowns, and that's all I need from you.

I have indulged in this tangent only because I think that this same general idea could be used to give citizens a vested interest in paying more attention to national politics as well. Instead of weekly sports scores, people's political Dream Teams could be evaluated on a regular basis by the latest summary of poll results (such as what was reported on the blog FiveThirtyEight), based on their success as of public fund-raising filing dates, the number of individual donors contributing to their campaigns, and so forth. Just as with *Our Next American President* and with fantasy football, the real campaigns and the fantasy ones would continuously interact in real time. Demonstrations of support via strong primary results could be incorporated into candidate standings as well as their later general election progress. Natural language programs could track both the amount and the relative positivity and negativity of media coverage that the candidates receive in order to update their prospects on a weekly basis. As in fantasy football, there would be different kinds of leagues with different rule structures and various criteria for performance as well.

There are obviously many technical details that would need to be worked out for such a system to work smoothly, but fantasy politics would be affected by real-world politics, and thus would give citizens an additional incentive to track the progress of various campaigns over time. Moreover, as with fantasy football, citizens could boast about having selected the best performing political leadership team long before the campaign began. Moreover, they would be competing with one another in selecting those they feel to be the most promising political leaders, and talking with one another about the political events that were unfolding.

MAKING POLITICS PALATABLE

In the contemporary United States we experience political figures very differently from how they were encountered in a pretelevision era. Watching political advocates vehemently disagree from an up-close and personal perspective rather than from a great distance intensifies citizens' negativity toward those people and ideas that they dislike. In the days when such intimate perspectives were not technologically possible, as when exposure to politicians was limited to newspapers, or when extreme close-ups of candidates were technologically difficult, the intensity of our disgust for those with whom we disagreed remained more muted. Likewise, we might have remained more trusting of government if we were not directly exposed to its conflict on a day-to-day basis. I have not been convinced that politicians are any less civil than they were in the past, or that the public is any less virtuous than publics of an earlier era. But the mass public now witnesses a great deal more of the political process than in the past.

The ideas that I have suggested for potentially replacing incivility in political television are obviously very preliminary. They are offered in the spirit of stimulating additional creative ideas about what people find naturally exciting about the political process. They are premised on the idea that unless there is something besides voting for ordinary citizens to do during elections, something fun and more akin to parades and rallies, fireworks, and other public demonstrations of their allegiances, it will not be possible to draw large numbers of people into the process.

To clarify, increasing participation per se is not the ultimate goal of these activities. Instead, the goal is to make it possible for people to see "the visible assent of the governed."[33] Today most mass politics takes place behind closed doors, in the privacy of our email queues, among Facebook friends, through online donations, or behind the curtain of the voting booth. We might see comments in support of a candidate online, but we seldom if ever see crowds of people gathering in support of a candidate except at conventions and victory celebrations. As a result we hear a constant refrain from people who cannot imagine how the other candidate was elected. Political television is still overwhelmingly the most popular way people obtain political information. In order to continue to reach mass audiences, politics needs to be a really big show, a performance extraordinaire.

These days, in-your-face politics makes visible *dissent* all too obvious. As entertaining as that dissent may be to watch, it tarnishes the kind of aspirations the public has for politics and politicians. How can they hope to work together when they can't even sit next to one another during the president's speech? Why would one want to run for office if it means being treated that way? We need the arousal that incivility provides to make politics exciting, but that does not mean we should be unconcerned about its negative effects. I am confident that with time we will develop alternative ways to accomplish that same end.

APPENDIX A

SUMMARY OF EXPERIMENTAL DESIGNS

	Design	Issues discussed	Sample	Venue
Experiment I	Within-subject, Latin square; crossing civility (low/high) with close-up versus medium camera angle	Tobacco restrictions, Internet taxes, Glass-Steagall repeal, public service experience	Adults, convenience sample, $N = 16$	Stanford, CA, laboratory, 2000
Experiment II	Between-subjects, 2 (civility) by 2 (camera angle) plus control group design	Tobacco restrictions, free trade, Internet taxes, public service experience	Adults, convenience sample, $N = 155$	Columbus, OH, laboratory, 2002
Experiment III	Between-subjects, civil versus uncivil, (both close-up versions)	NASA funding, mental health coverage in insurance plans, Internet taxes, free trade	Adults, convenience sample, $N = 67$	Columbus, OH, laboratory, 2003
Experiment IV	Between-subjects, 2 by 2 design, liked versus disliked person's face by photo size (small/large)	Photos of famous people chosen from pretest for each R as most liked or disliked by R	Representative sample of adults, $N = 1,440$	Online national survey experiment, 2004

(continued)

	Design	Issues discussed	Sample	Venue
Experiment V	Between-subjects, civil versus uncivil, (both close-up versions), with party ID assigned to candidates	Internet taxes, NASA funding, Tobacco restrictions, public service experience	Adults, convenience sample, $N = 34$	Philadelphia, PA, laboratory, 2004–5
Experiment VI	Between-subjects, civil versus uncivil, using real-world media clips	Civil: abortion, judicial appointments, Middle East (from *Hardball* and *This Week*); uncivil: Republican convention, Young Democrats (from *Hardball*)	Adults, convenience sample, $N = 43$	Philadelphia, PA, laboratory, 2007
Experiment VII	Between-subjects, 2 by 3 design crossing civil versus uncivil with medium (print/radio/television)	NASA funding, tobacco restrictions, Internet taxes, public service experience	Adults, convenience sample, $N = 98$	Philadelphia, PA, laboratory, 2007
Experiment VIII	Between-subjects, 2 by 2 design crossing civility (low/high) and medium (print/television)	NASA funding, tobacco restrictions, Internet taxes, public service experience	Adults, convenience sample, $N = 109$	Philadelphia, PA, laboratory, 2007

APPENDIX B

SUMMARY OF EXPERIMENTAL DEPENDENT VARIABLES

	Dependent variable	Items	Alpha
Experiment I	Skin conductance level	Physiological test	N/A
Experiment II	Trust in politicians	1. Politicians generally have good intentions. 2. Politicians in the U.S. do not deserve much respect. 3. When politicians make statements to the American people on television or in the newspapers, they are usually telling the truth. 4. Most politicians can be trusted to do what is right. 5. Despite what some people say, most politicians try to keep their campaign promises. 6. Most politicians do a lot of talking but they do little to solve the really important issues facing the country. 7. Most politicians are dedicated people and we should be grateful to them for the work they do.	.53
	Trust in Congress	1. As far as the people running Congress are concerned, would you say you have a great deal of confidence, only some confidence or hardly any confidence at all in them? 2. How much of the time do you think you can trust members of the U.S. Congress to do what is right? Just about always, most of them or only some of the time? 3. Again using this same feeling thermometer, how do you feel about the U.S. Congress?	.29

(continued)

Dependent variable	Items	Alpha
Trust in the political system	1. At present I feel very critical of our political system. 2. Whatever its faults may be, the American form of government is still the best for us. 3. There is not much about our form of government to be proud of. 4. It may be necessary to make some major changes in our form of government in order to solve the problems facing our country. 5. I would rather live under our form of government than any other I can think of.	.63
Political trust index	1. Trust in politicians index. 2. Trust in Congress index. 3. Trust in the political system index.	.75
Popularity of political program	1. In general, I found the program to be entertaining for a political talk show. 2. This program was sometimes very lively. 3. This program was dull and boring even by the standards of political talk shows. 4. The pace of the show was too slow. 5. Compared to other political talk shows, this one was better as keeping my attention.	.88
Perceived informativeness of political program	1. In general, I found the program to be informative. 2. I learned new things about public issues from this program. 3. This program gave me food for thought. 4. If I needed information about an upcoming election, I would watch this program. 5. I felt like I got to know the candidates by watching this program. 6. As a result of watching this program, I'd be more comfortable talking to friends about this race or about these issues.	.83

	Dependent variable	Items	Alpha
	Awareness of rationales for op-positional positions	"What are some of the reasons [Candidate Name] gave in support of his opinion on the talk show? Please write as many as you can think of in the box below." Coded for total number of arguments correctly recalled.	N/A
	Attitudes toward the opposition	"Using our 'Feeling Thermometer,' where 0 means you feel extremely cold toward the candidate and 100 means you feel extremely warm toward him, how do you feel about [Candidate Name] based on viewing the talk show?" "Using the same feeling thermometer, how do you feel about [Candidate Name] based on viewing the talk show?"	N/A
	Perceived legitimacy of opposing arguments	"Regardless of your own view on this issue, we would like you to tell us how strong or weak an argument you think each of the following reasons is." All arguments listed were drawn directly from the statements made by the candidates. A 4-point scale ranged from *very strong argument* (3) to *very weak argument* (0). Six separate reasons were listed for each issue, three in support of one side, and three in support of the other side. The average strength ratings for items on one's own side of the issue were combined across the four issues, and the same was done for arguments supporting the side opposite the respondent's own view. Thus perceived legitimacy was based on 12 items for own side and another 12 items for the other side.	Computed separately for each issue; all >.75

(*continued*)

	Dependent variable	Items	Alpha
Experiment III	Trust in politicians	1. Politicians generally have good intentions. 2. Politicians in the U.S. do not deserve much respect. 3. When politicians make statements to the American people on television or in the newspapers, they are usually telling the truth. 4. Most politicians can be trusted to do what is right. 5. Despite what some people say, most politicians try to keep their campaign promises. 6. Most politicians do a lot of talking but they do little to solve the really important issues facing the country. 7. Most politicians are dedicated people and we should be grateful to them for the work they do.	.79
	Trust in Congress	1. As far as the people running Congress are concerned, would you say you have a great deal of confidence, only some confidence or hardly any confidence at all in them? 2. How much of the time do you think you can trust members of the U.S. Congress to do what is right? Just about always, most of them or only some of the time? 3. Again using this same feeling thermometer, how do you feel about the U.S. Congress?	.74
	Trust in the political system	1. At present I feel very critical of our political system. 2. Whatever its faults may be, the American form of government is still the best for us. 3. There is not much about our form of government to be proud of. 4. It may be necessary to make some major changes in our form of government in order to solve the problems facing our country. 5. I would rather live under our form of government than any other I can think of.	.66

Dependent variable	Items	Alpha
Political trust	1. Trust in politicians. 2. Trust in Congress. 3. Trust in the political system.	.84
Awareness of rationales for oppositional positions	"What are some of the reasons [Candidate Name] gave in support of his opinion on the talk show? Please write as many as you can think of in the box below." Coded for total number of arguments correctly recalled.	N/A
Attitudes toward the opposition	"Using our 'Feeling Thermometer,' where 0 means you feel extremely cold toward the candidate and 100 means you feel extremely warm toward him, how do you feel about [Candidate Name] based on viewing the talk show?" "Using the same feeling thermometer, how do you feel about [Candidate Name] based on viewing the talk show?"	N/A
Perceived legitimacy of opposing arguments	"Regardless of your own view on this issue, we would like you to tell us how strong or weak an argument you think each of the following reasons is." All arguments listed were drawn directly from the statements made by the candidates. A 4-point scale ranged from *very strong argument* (3) to *very weak argument* (0). Six separate reasons were listed for each issue, three in support of one side, and three in support of the other side. The average strength ratings for items on one's own side of the issue were combined across the four issues, and the same was done for arguments supporting the side opposite the respondent's own view. Thus perceived legitimacy was based on 12 items for own side and another 12 items for the other side.	Computed separately for each issue; all >.75

APPENDIX C

NATIONAL SURVEY QUESTIONS FOR ORIENTATION TOWARD CONFLICT COMMUNICATION SCALES

Please tell us how much you agree or disagree with each of these statements. All items coded on 7-point scales from *strongly agree* to *strongly disagree*.

Confrontation Subscale

I feel more comfortable having an argument in person than over the phone.
I dislike when others have eye contact with me during an argument.
If I were upset with a friend, I would discuss it with someone else rather than the friend who upset me.
When I have a conflict with someone, I try to resolve it by being extra nice to him or her.
I always prefer to solve disputes through face-to-face discussion.
After a dispute with a neighbor, I would feel uncomfortable seeing him or her again, even if the conflict had been resolved.

Public/Private Subscale

I feel uncomfortable seeing others argue in public.
I don't mind strangers arguing in my presence.
It doesn't bother me to be in a situation where others are arguing.
I feel uncomfortable when others argue in my presence.

Emotional Expression Subscale

Getting emotional only makes conflicts worse.
Everything should be out in the open in an argument, including emotions.
It makes me uncomfortable watching other people express their emotions in front of me.
I feel like running away when other people start showing their emotions during an argument.
It shows strength to express emotions openly.
Showing your feelings in a dispute is a sign of weakness.

Conflict Approach/Avoidance Subscale

I hate arguments.
I find conflicts exciting.
I enjoy challenging the opinions of others.
Arguments don't bother me.
I feel upset after being involved in an argument.

APPENDIX D
CODING FORM FOR POLITICAL TELEVISION PROGRAMS

Program_____   Date Aired_____   Coder _____

CIVILITY:

1. Overall, how would you describe the discussion and disagreement on this program?

	1	2	3	4	5	6	7	8	9	
emotional	•	•	•	•	•	•	•	•	•	unemotional
quarrelsome	•	•	•	•	•	•	•	•	•	cooperative
hostile	•	•	•	•	•	•	•	•	•	friendly
rude	•	•	•	•	•	•	•	•	•	polite
agitated	•	•	•	•	•	•	•	•	•	calm
sarcastic	•	•	•	•	•	•	•	•	•	earnest

2. Overall, the tone of this program was: (circle one)

   Extremely friendly and warm (1)
   Mostly calm, polite and civil (2)
   A mix of polite disagreement and some heated interactions (3)
   Mostly heated interactions (4)

SENSE OF VISUAL CLOSENESS TO HUMANS ON SCREEN:

1. During the time when people are shown on the screen, how much of each individual person is generally visible? (Choose most common kind of shot used in the program)

Whole body	2	3	4	Head & shoulders	6	7	8	Face only
↓								↓
•	•	•	•	•	•	•	•	•

2. In the tightest shot you saw of 1 or more people talking, what proportion of the TV frame was taken up by the faces? (circle one)

Less than ¼ of screen area (1)
About ¼ of screen area (2)
About 1/3 of screen area (3)
About ½ of screen area (4)
More than ½ of screen area, but not 100% (5)
All or almost all of screen area (6)

OVERALL FORMAT OF PROGRAM:

1. Mark the main format used in this show with a 1, the second most common with a 2, and the third with a 3:

☐ Face to face interaction between 2 people in same physical space

☐ Face to face interaction among 3+ people in same physical space

☐ Interview by one or more people of person/people in another physical location (no split screen)

☐ Monologue by host directed at viewers

☐ Out of studio video clip with no interviewer visible

☐ Out of studio video clip with interviewer visible on site

☐ Split screen interview involving 2 or more people

APPENDIX E
CODING INSTRUCTIONS FOR TELEVISED CONFLICTS

Coding Instructions/Clarifications

The unit of analysis is the *news program*, so fill out one *packet* of questions per program. List all conflicts, but only code characteristics of *visual* content of program, not audio.

Date aired: Here enter the date of the news program that you are coding.
Length of broadcast without ads: Although we have a stopwatch which you may opt to use, it is easiest to simply pay attention to the running timer at the top of the screen during the news program. Keep track of which minutes are news, and which minutes are commercials.
Number of distinct news stories/items: This refers to the number of unique topics addressed in the broadcast. If a broadcaster mentions that there is a flood in California, a student protest at UC Berkeley about affirmative action, and a continuing war, these are 3 distinct news items. Note that still pictures that give information about the stock market or the weather *are* considered a story.
Number of unique conflicts: Here we ask about the subset of stories that involve a conflict of some sort—either current or resolved.

FAQ: What qualifies as a "conflict"?

A "conflict" in this case can be between two people, two groups, two organizations or institutions or any combination thereof. For example, there was Bücher versus the Navy; Adam Clayton Powell versus the House of Representatives, the priests versus their superiors. Any two or more parties who disagree about something qualifies as a conflict.
Note that a president simply stating their new policies about something (a war, Medicare, etc.) is not a conflict unless it is explicitly the opposition is explicitly discussed or shown. However, the opposition could be as simple as a reporter asking a leading question, that implies a different opinion.
Furthermore, we are limiting this to internal conflict within the U.S. If the president is discuss his policies on the war in Iraq, the simple fact of there being a war does not make it a conflict. It is only if different views on the war in Iraq (between people in the U.S.) are presented, that it counts as a conflict.

Coder: If you are the coder, please write your name here.
Notes: If there is anything unique that you believe we should know about this broadcast that is not otherwise covered, please indicate that here.

For the following pages of the Coding Sheets, we are only coding **VISUAL CONFLICTS**.
This means that in addition to meeting the above criteria for being a conflict, there

must be a visual image besides the broadcaster speaking to accompany the story. The visual image could be pictures of the conflict, or interviews with people expressing their opinion about the conflict. Each visual conflict has one coding page, front and back. If there are more than 4 conflicts in a given news broadcast, please use the "Additional Conflict Sheets" and attach them at the end of the packet.

Conflict 1: Please briefly describe the conflict that you will be coding.
Are individually identifiable (though not necessarily identified by name) faces shown? When I ask about "individually identifiable people," I mean people whom you could recognize after having seen the broadcast. Blurry distant crowd shots or backs of heads do not count. If you can only see half of their face, it does not count. Imagine if it were a friend of yours—the shot must be close enough that you could recognize the person's face if you knew them. If a broadcaster describes rioting on a college campus between students and administration over affirmative action, and the only visual that accompanies the story is a distant shot of the riot, there would *not* be any individually identifiable faces shown.
Are individually identifiable people shown from multiple sides of the conflict, only one side, or neither? Here, if the broadcaster cuts from the riot to an interview with one of the rioting students, but does not have any visuals of anyone representing the school administration (perhaps only speaks about it), only one side of the conflict are visually depicted.
Person 1: _____ The blanks after Person 1, Person 2, etc. are just for you to jot down any notes that might help you keep the people straight. Do not worry about spelling or correctly identifying public figures. This is just for you. If there are more than 7 people visually depicted in one conflict, feel free to use the "Additional People in a Conflict" coding sheets, and attach them at the end of the conflict.
Shot 1 to 5: Each time that you see this person on-screen, you are going to record some information about how they are visually displayed. A shot is defined as ending when the camera cuts to a new screen. If the camera was showing the President at a press conference, and then *cut* to a close up shot of the President, this would be two distinct shots.
Body Perspective (Body perspt): Please indicate the body perspective (1 to 9) of the person you are coding.
Proportion of Screen taken up by body (Prop of screen): Please indicate the proportion (A to F) of the person you are coding.
Angle: Please indicate the camera's perspective (1 to 4) on the body of the person you are coding.

Coding for the Actions of the Person on the Video

For Spk? Enter 1 if the person speaks in the story while on-screen, 0 if they do not, and -1 if the person speaks but partly as a voice-over. A partial voice-over is when a person is talking on camera, then they cut to a new shot (perhaps of the conflict), but the person continues talking (Note: If you *never* see the person's face (i.e., strictly a voice-over), you will not be coding them in this form. Only code individually identifiable people.)
For WI? This codes for a walk-in, that is when the camera is stationary and the person being filmed walks towards or away from the camera. Enter 1 for yes, a walk in; enter -1 for a walk away; and 0 if the person being filmed is not moving towards or away from the camera.

FAQ: What body perspectives and proportions should I code when there is a walk in or a camera zoom?

In these cases, code the last perspective you see. Meaning, if someone is walking towards the camera, in a "walk-in," code the *closest* camera perspective and proportion. If they are walking away from the camera, code the *furthest* camera perspective and proportion. The same holds for a zoom. If there is a zoom-in, code the *closest* camera perspective and proportion. Similarly, if the camera zooms out, code the *furthest* camera perspective. This holds true even if a person is talking at a distance for a couple minutes, and in the last second the camera zooms in.

For number? Indicate the number of people, relevant to the story, on the screen during the shot. Enter 1 if there is only one person, 2 if there are two people and 3 if there are three or more people. Note that if there is a shot of 2 relevant people (ex. President and First Lady), that zooms in on one person (the President), you still need only code the *closest* perspective of the President; but you would describe the shot as having *two* people. And, of course, you would indicate that there was a zoom.

Coding the Camera Techniques

For DZ? This refers to whether the person filming is using the technique of zooming or dollying. Enter 1 for yes, a zoom-in; enter–1 for a zoom-out; and 0 for no zooming or dollying.
For Med? This analyzes what medium is used in the shot.
This ranges from least realistic to most realistic:
1 = drawing
2 = still shot or photograph
3 = standard video
4 = video pan (video moving from one person to another person without cutting the film)
5 = handheld video (the person filming is carrying the video recorder on his/her shoulder)

FAQ: How do I code shots where panning is used instead of cuts?

To code a video pan shot, where the shot is a continuous back and forth between 2 or more people, code only the *closest* perspective that we see each person in, and indicate that it is a video pan by putting "4" in the Medium category. If a zoom is ever used, make sure to indicate that as well.

To determine the length of time for the shot, look at the length of time that the camera is a person before panning to another person. If the time varies, average it.

For example, imagine a 90 seconds clip, where the camera is panning back and forth between two political candidates that looked like this:

Candidate A	Candidate B
20 seconds	20 seconds
10 seconds	11 seconds
8 seconds	12 seconds
4 seconds	8 seconds

To determine whether candidate A is a long, medium or short clip, look at on *average* how long candidate A spent talking before the camera panned to candidate B. Here is looks like about 10 seconds, so it would be medium shot.

For Time? Circle short if the visual clip of the person in only a couple seconds long. Circle medium if the visual clip is under 15 seconds, but longer than only a couple seconds. Circle long if the visual clip is over 15 seconds.

Final Questions about Each Conflict

Would you classify the intensity of conflict **viewed** *as:*
Low *(1)* = opponents in controversy are calm and civil, do not raise voices or act angry
Medium *(2)* = anything in between low and high
High *(3)* = opponents in controversy yell, chant, demonstrate, or otherwise raise their voices to indicate a certain intensity of conflict; direct threats also count, even if issued calmly or in writing
Physical *(4)* = Fighting with weapons—e.g., guns, bombs, etc. or threatening physical violence
*Note that in the above we are interested in conflict *viewed*, not just conflict. For example, even though a broadcaster might be describing a violent war, if what we see is simply a general sitting there telling us about it, the *viewed* conflict is low intensity.
Would you classify the pace of this story as slow, medium or fast? Please indicate your perception of the pace of the story. Bear in mind that your frame of reference should be all news stories, not just the one you are watching. Make sure that if you describe a story from 1969 as "fast paced," it has an equal pace as one you code as "fast paced" from 1999.
Were crowd shots used? If so, describe: Use this space to describe any crowd shots that were not coded, because there were no individually identifiable people.

Coding Sheet (One Set per Program) for Perspectives on Conflict

1. Date aired: MONTH ____ ____, DAY ____ ____ , YEAR ___ ___ ___ ___

2. Length of broadcast without ads: ___ ___ Minutes [*Round to nearest minute*]

3. Number of distinct news stories/items: ____ ____

4. Number of unique CONFLICTS featured in broadcast: ____ _____ [*Fill in specifics below*]

Coder: _____
Notes: _____

For Each Conflict, Answer the Following about the *Visual Content*:

Conflict 1: Topic/Opponents: _____

Are individually identifiable (though not necessarily identified by name) faces shown? *Yes (1)*, *No (2)*
Are individually identifiable people shown from: *Multiple sides of the conflict (3)*, *Only one side (2)*, or *Neither (1)*?
Would you classify the intensity of conflict viewed as: *Low (1)*, *Medium (2)*, *High (3)*, *Physical violence (4)*
Would you classify the pace of this story as: *Slow (1)*, *Medium (2)*, or *Fast (3)*?
Were crowd shots used? If so, describe: _____

Broadcaster
Shot 1: Body perspt:___ Prop of screen: ___ Angle:___ Spk?___ #?___ WI?___
DZ?___ Med?___Time? *Srt (1) Med (2) Lng (3)*

Shot 2: Body perspt:___ Prop of screen: ___ Angle:___ Spk?___ #?___ WI?___
DZ?___ Med?___Time? *Srt (1) Med (2) Lng (3)*

Shot 3: Body perspt:___ Prop of screen: ___ Angle:___ Spk?___ #?___ WI?___
DZ?___ Med?___Time? *Srt (1) Med (2) Lng (3)*

Shot 4: Body perspt:___ Prop of screen: ___ Angle:___ Spk?___ #?___ WI?___
DZ?___ Med?___Time? *Srt (1) Med (2) Lng (3)*

Shot 5: Body perspt:___ Prop of screen: ___ Angle:___ Spk?___ #?___ WI?___
DZ?___ Med?___Time? *Srt (1) Med (2) Lng (3)*

Person 1: _____
Shot 1: Body perspt:___ Prop of screen: ___ Angle:___ Spk?___ #?___ WI?___
DZ?___ Med?___Time? *Srt (1) Med (2) Lng (3)*

Shot 2: Body perspt:___ Prop of screen: ___ Angle:___ Spk?___ #?___ WI?___
DZ?___ Med?___Time? *Srt (1) Med (2) Lng (3)*

Shot 3: Body perspt:___ Prop of screen: ___ Angle:___ Spk?___ #?___ WI?___
DZ?___ Med?___Time? *Srt (1) Med (2) Lng (3)*

Shot 4: Body perspt:___ Prop of screen: ___ Angle:___ Spk?___ #?___WI?___
DZ?___ Med?___Time? *Srt (1) Med (2) Lng (3)*

Shot 5: Body perspt:___ Prop of screen: ___ Angle:___ Spk?___ #?___WI?___
DZ?___ Med?___Time? *Srt (1) Med (2) Lng (3)*

Repeat Person blocks for up to 7 people per conflict.
Repeat Conflict coding sequence for each identified conflict.

NOTES

CHAPTER 1: WHAT IS "IN-YOUR-FACE" POLITICS?

1. See Altschuler and Blumin (2000) and Shea and Fiorina (2013).
2. See also Herbst (2010).
3. E.g., Barker (2002).
4. Based on personal interview with Lawrence Laurent, Washington, DC, 2007.
5. Most of these examples may still be found on YouTube. For some prominent examples, search Robert Novak and James Carville, Zell Miller and Chris Matthews, Joe Wilson and President Obama, and Jon Stewart and Tucker Carlson. *Time* magazine even maintains a list of the "Top Ten TV Feuds" (see http://content.time.com/time/specials/packages/completelist /0,29569,1884499,00.html).
6. See John Boehner and Harry Reid on YouTube.
7. The question asked was "Do you think civility in politics is important for a healthy democracy?" See Allegheny College (2010).
8. Papacharissi (2004, 260), for example, defines it as "respect for the collective traditions of democracy" and as "a manner of offensive discussion that impedes the ideal of delibera-tion" (see also Anderson et al. 2013). For purposes of empirical research, these kinds of definitions are problematic because incivility is being defined by its effects, thus making it impossible to assess whether incivility has any particular effects.
9. Likewise, although some authors have argued that "outrage" is a subset of what I call incivility, I do not use the same criteria that these authors do. Their criteria include "mal-feasant inaccuracy and intent to diminish" (Sobieraj and Berry 2011, 20). Because what is accurate is often contested in politics, and one seldom knows for certain a speaker's intent, these definitions differ from my own.
10. E.g., Durr, Gilmour, and Wolbrecht (1997); Hibbing and Theiss-Morse (2002).
11. E.g., Sapiro (1999); Carter (1999); Brooks and Geer (2007).
12. E.g., Brown and Levinson (1987); Grice (1989).
13. Mills (2003, 6).
14. Grice (1975); Lakoff (1973).
15. See Brooks and Geer (2007).
16. Brooks and Geer (2007) define "negative" political messages as claims suggesting something bad about the opponent, whereas "positive" claims say something good about the self. One can make a positive or negative claim with or without incivility because incivility involves style rather than substance. For example, a politician who claims "I care more about helping people keep their homes and jobs than preserving the tax advantages of the wealthy" could do so in a civil or an uncivil fashion.
17. Brown and Levinson (1987, 1); Leech (1983, 82).
18. See Kingwell (1995); Grice (1989).
19. For some purposes, scholars have found it useful to make distinctions among particu-lar kinds of emotion based on cognitive appraisals as reported by individuals (see Brader and

Marcus 2013 for a review). Because there is no consensus on the number of different appraisals and emotions, most studies focus on a small number relevant to the study at hand. The fact that emotional arousal affects political attitudes formed in response to televised incivility does not offer support for any one particular theoretical conceptualization over another; all conceptualizations of emotion acknowledge the role of physiological arousal.

20. E.g., Frijda (1988).
21. See Hall (1963).
22. See Aiello (1987).
23. Clark (1973); Mandler (1992).
24. Mandler (1992).
25. Mobbs et al. (2007).
26. Williams and Bargh (2008).
27. Mandler (1992, 596).
28. Williams and Bargh (2008).
29. Eisenstein (1940/1974).
30. See Storms and Thomas (1977).
31. Nass, Moon, and Green (1997).
32. See Fogg and Nass (1997).
33. All results are identified according to which experiment generated them; however, sometimes a single experiment comes up in more than one chapter because it was designed with multiple purposes in mind.
34. See Dilliplane, Goldman, and Mutz (2013).

CHAPTER 2: THE CONSEQUENCES OF IN-YOUR-FACE POLITICS FOR AROUSAL AND MEMORY

1. Heilman (1997).
2. Lombard (1995).
3. Clark and Uetz (1990); Van (1991).
4. Flavell et al. (1990).
5. See, e.g., Reeves et al. (1985).
6. Lombard et al. (1995).
7. Reeves and Nass (1996).
8. Lombard (1995, 290).
9. Middlemist, Knowles, and Matter (1976).
10. The research generated immediate controversy once published (see Koocher 1977).
11. Gilligan and Bower (1984).
12. E.g., Christianson et al. (1986); Eysenck (1976).
13. E.g., Keeter (1987).
14. Messaris (1994, 91).
15. Kraft (1987).
16. Mottahedeh (2008).
17. Reeves and Nass (1996).
18. Lombard (1995).
19. Reeves and Nass (1996).
20. Reeves and Nass (1996, 46).
21. See Carnagey, Anderson, and Bushman (2007); Geen (1975).
22. Anderson et al. (2004).

23. Straus (2007).
24. Wilson (2006, 18).
25. Mutz (2006).
26. Hibbing and Theiss-Morse (2002).
27. See, e.g., Christianson (1986); Bradley et al. (1992); Christianson et al. (1986).
28. O'Reilly (2001, 52).
29. Uslaner (1993); Tannen (1998).
30. See also McGraw, Willey, and Anderson (1999).
31. See also Elving (1994); Cappella and Jamieson (1997); Funk (2001).
32. Comparisons to Hitler are rampant in mass media. For example, singer Linda Ronstadt labeled Republicans "a bunch of Hitlers," and Hank Williams, Jr. lost his job singing *Monday Night Football*'s theme song for comparing President Obama to Hitler.
33. The questions used for these scales can be found in Mutz and Reeves (2005).
34. Hopkins and Fletcher (1994).
35. For examples, see Lang (2000) and Reeves and Nass (1996).
36. See Lodge, McGraw, and Stroh (1989).
37. Funk (2001).
38. See, e.g., Christianson (1986); Bradley et al. (1992); Christianson et al. (1986).
39. See J. Berger (2011).
40. Stelter (2009).
41. Berger and Milkman (2012).
42. Chen and Berger (2013).

CHAPTER 3: EFFECTS ON PUBLIC PERCEPTIONS OF THE LEGITIMACY OF THE OPPOSITION

1. Mutz (2006).
2. Calhoun (1988); Page (1996); Mutz and Martin (2001).
3. Benhabib (1992); Arendt (1968).
4. Manin (1987).
5. Fearon (1998, 62).
6. Anderson et al. (2005).
7. E.g., Fiorina and Abrams (2009); Abramowitz (2010); Fleisher and Bond (2004); Levendusky (2009).
8. Iyengar, Sood, and Lelkes (2012).
9. Jacobson (2007).
10. Fiorina (1999); Jacobson (2000).
11. Hetherington (2001).
12. Hibbing and Theiss-Morse (2002).
13. E.g., Anderson et al. (2005).
14. Meyrowitz (1986).
15. Meyrowitz (1986).
16. Wright et al. (1997); Mazziotta, Mummendey, and Wright (2011).
17. See Gilbert (1991).
18. Storms and Thomas (1977).
19. See also Schiffenbauer and Schiavo (1976).
20. Smith and Knowles (1979).
21. E.g., Smith and Knowles (1979); Middlemist, Knowles, and Matter (1976).

22. See Reeves, Lombard, and Melwani (1992); see also Detenber and Reeves (1996) and Reeves, Detenber, and Steuer (1993).

23. See Bowler and Donovan (2003).

24. These responses were coded by two independent coders, producing a reliability of .90 for the number of unique arguments generated.

25. E.g., Baum (2003).

26. See also Levendusky (2013).

27. Although many understandings of the concept of legitimacy are possible, the term "legitimacy" is used here to suggest that a person has heard the other side and granted it some degree of reasonableness as an oppositional viewpoint, despite continued disagreement. If one attributes evil, undesirable motives as the basis of explanation for another's views, or has no comprehension of the opponent's basis for differing views, then one does not perceive the opposition as legitimate.

28. Wilson (2006, 15).

29. Barry (2004).

30. See, e.g., Schudson (1995).

31. Persson (1998).

32. Sullivan and Masters (1987). Although their studies focused specifically on the effects of politicians' nonverbal facial displays on public attitudes, they likewise suggest that expressive displays have a direct emotional impact on viewers (see Sullivan and Masters 1987; McHugo et al. 1985).

CHAPTER 4: THE COSTS OF IN-YOUR-FACE POLITICS FOR POLITICAL TRUST

1. See Forgette and Morris (2006).

2. Elving (1994); Cappella and Jamieson (1997).

3. Robinson (1975).

4. Robinson and Appel (1979).

5. Ranney (1983, 86).

6. E.g., Cappella and Jamieson (1997).

7. Patterson (1993).

8. Citrin and Muste (1999, 465).

9. Barber (1983).

10. Brown and Levinson (1987).

11. Reeves and Nass (1996).

12. Fenno (1975).

13. See Mutz and Flemming (1999) for a review.

14. Citrin and Muste (1999, 467).

15. E.g., Hibbing and Theiss-Morse (2002).

16. See Goldstein (1999).

17. Arguably, this null result could be due to the substantially lower reliability of the indexes in Experiment II. However, given that the combined index was suitably reliable, and it was nonetheless still not significantly different from the control, the pattern of results remained consistent with this interpretation.

18. Interviewers began attempting contact roughly three weeks after the experiment, but the interviews were completed, on average, one month after participation occurred. Although attrition in sample size between the laboratory results and the follow-up interview reduced the strength of the original laboratory findings, the posttest means for the subsample that was observable a month later maintained the same initial pattern of results.

19. To analyze these data, we used a two-factor mixed-model analysis of variance with one repeated measure, within-subjects factor (levels of political trust immediately after the experiment and one month later), and one between-subjects factor (experimental condition), plus the interaction between the two. Although the interaction between experimental condition and time approached statistical significance, this finding occurred because of differential change over time by experimental condition.

20. Allegheny College (2010). The actual question asked was "Many people in this country—politicians included—hold strong views on certain issues. Given the difficulty and often personal nature of these issues, do you believe it is possible for people to disagree respectfully, or are nasty exchanges unavoidable?"

21. Hibbing and Theiss-Morse (1995, 147).

22. Durr, Gilmour, and Wolbrecht (1997).

23. See Miller (1974a); Citrin (1974); Miller (1974b).

24. Dahl (1971).

25. Barber (1983).

26. Tyler (1990); Tyler and Degoey (1995).

27. Scholz and Lubbell (1998).

28. Hetherington (1999).

29. Hetherington (2005, 4).

30. Bianco (1994).

31. Chanley, Rudolph, and Rahn (2000); Hetherington (2005).

32. Rudolph and Evans (2005).

CHAPTER 5: REAL-WORLD CONTEXTS

1. This was accomplished by offering participation in the experiments as a fund-raising opportunity to civic groups that we expected to be composed of mostly conservatives or Republicans. For any given study, the compensation per subject was the same, but it varied across experiments depending upon the difficulty of recruitment.

2. Amodio et al. (2007).

3. Hatemi et al. (2011).

4. E.g., Jost and Amodio (2012); Hibbing, Smith, and Alford (2014).

5. Oxley et al. (2008).

6. See Lang et al. (1993).

7. For the results of these analyses, see Ben-Porath (2008).

8. These data were collected by what was then known as Knowledge Networks (currently GfK Custom Research NA).

9. Sato and Yoshikawa (2007); cf. Reeves and Nass (1996).

CHAPTER 6: WHO WATCHES THIS STUFF ANYWAY?

1. Some have suggested that those who dislike such content would not choose to watch it anyway (Arceneaux and Johnson 2007); however, this study simultaneously altered many aspects of the program being chosen, making it difficult to know how much choice was due to incivility as opposed to other factors.

2. Due to technical constraints and the need to use first-run episodes of programs from within the same time period, not all programs were judged on the basis of ten episodes.

3. See Dilliplane (2011).

4. Blonsky (1988).

5. From 2012 onward, the American National Election Studies adopted a similar approach in order to more comprehensively capture exposure to political media.

6. Dilliplane, Goldman, and Mutz (2013).

7. Dilliplane, Goldman, and Mutz (2013).

8. Sobieraj and Berry (2014, 144).

9. See Prior (2007).

10. The actual wording used in 2008 was "Below is a list of different types of television programs that some people like to watch. Which of these types of programs do you like the best? Put a 1 next to it. Then select your second best liked type of television program, and put a 2 next to it, and put a 3 and 4 next to your 3rd and 4th most liked type of program. [RANDOMIZE ORDER OF PRESENTATION] Science Fiction shows like Heroes or Star Trek Voyager, Comedies/sitcoms like Two and a Half Men or The Simpsons, Drama Shows like Grey's Anatomy or Law and Order, Soap Operas like General Hospital or One Life to Live, Reality TV shows like Survivor or Cops, Sports programs, Game shows like Jeopardy or Family Feud, News programs, Documentary programs on channels like the History Channel or the Discovery Channel, Music videos."

11. Mutz and Ben-Porath (2006). Perhaps not surprisingly, this was also the name of a popular British sitcom, and then later a U.S. sitcom. Men behaving badly apparently has obvious audience potential.

12. See Eckel and Grossman (2008).

13. Goldstein (1999).

14. See Appendix C for all items included in each index.

15. See Eckel and Grossman (2008).

16. Goldstein (1999).

17. Goldstein (1999).

CHAPTER 7: DOES THE MEDIUM MATTER?

1. Patterson and McClure (1976).

2. Patterson (1993); see also Miller, Goldenberg, and Erbring (1979).

3. Cf. Sigelman and Bullock (1991).

4. Gould (1952/1972, 21).

5. Hart (1994); Sennett (1977).

6. Hofstetter (1976); Meadow (1973); Patterson (1980).

7. Patterson and McClure (1976); Miller and Jackson (1973).

8. Lenz and Lawson (2011).

9. Amit, Algom, and Trope (2009, 400).

10. Amit, Wakslak, and Trope (2012).

11. E.g., Williams and Bargh (2008).

12. Amit, Algom, and Trope (2009, 400); see also Henderson et al. (2006).

13. Trope and Liberman (2010).

14. Williams and Bargh (2008).

15. Williams and Bargh (2008).

16. Stephan, Liberman, and Trope (2010).

17. Keeter (1987).

18. Druckman (2003).

19. Lippmann (1925).
20. Reeves and Nass (1996).
21. Reeves and Nass (1996, 49).
22. Funk (2001).
23. See Matheson (2000).
24. Lang (1990).
25. Johnson et al. (2004).
26. Altschuler and Blumin (2000).
27. Cooke (2005).
28. Appiah (2006).
29. See, e.g., Pew Research Center (2010); Mutz and Young (2011).
30. E.g., Borah (2013); Thorson, Vraga, and Ekdale (2010).
31. Anderson et al. (2013); Borah (2013).
32. See, e.g., Borah (2013).
33. Goode, McCullough, and O'Hare (2011).
34. Santana (2013).
35. Blom et al. (2014).
36. Edgerly et al. (2013).
37. See Goffman (1959).
38. Berger and Milkman (2012).
39. Eckler and Bolls (2011).
40. Guadagno et al. (2013); Berger and Milkman (2012); J. Berger (2011).
41. Reeves, Lombard, and Melwani (1992).
42. Lombard et al. (2000).
43. Lombard (1995).
44. Bracken and Botta (2010, 39).
45. See Grobart (2012).
46. Ivory and Magee (2009).
47. Steuer (1992).
48. Lombard and Ditton (1997).
49. Bracken et al. (2010).
50. Ivory and Magee (2009).

CHAPTER 8: HOW POLITICS ON TELEVISION HAS CHANGED

1. Ben-Porath (2010, 323).
2. See Trope and Liberman (2010).
3. E.g., Stephan, Liberman, and Trope (2010).
4. Dates randomly selected for viewing in each decade included (1) the fourth Monday in January, (2) the second Tuesday in February, (3) the first Wednesday in May, (4) the third Thursday in May, (5) the fourth Friday in May, (6) the fifth Monday in June, (7) the second Tuesday in July, (8) the third Wednesday in July, (9) the second Thursday in September, and (10) the third Friday in October.
5. Lang et al. (1993).
6. Reeves and Nass (1996).
7. See, e.g., Altschuler and Blumin (2000); Sapiro (1999).
8. E.g., Bradley et al. (1992); Lang, Dhillon, and Dong (1995).

CHAPTER 9: MAKING POLITICS PALATABLE

1. B. Berger (2011).
2. E.g., Nyhan (2010); Hofstetter et al. (1999).
3. See Dilliplane, Goldman, and Mutz (2013).
4. See, e.g., Marcus (2000).
5. Plotz (2000).
6. Sandel (2005, 54).
7. Maynor (2009).
8. E.g., Gitlin (2013); Strachan and Wolf (2013).
9. DeMott (1996, 14).
10. Kennedy (1998, 84); see also DeMott (1996, 16).
11. See Shea and Fiorina (2013).
12. Stewart (2004).
13. E.g., Prior (2007).
14. Schudson (1998, 133).
15. Schudson (1998, chap. 3).
16. Baum and Kernell (1999).
17. Plotz (2000).
18. McGerr (1986).
19. Schudson (1992, 158).
20. McGerr (1986).
21. McGerr (1986, 31).
22. McGerr (1986, 6).
23. Sobieraj and Berry (2011, 36).
24. See Young (2004).
25. See Xenos and Becker (2009) for a review.
26. Fox, Koloen, and Sahin (2007).
27. Baumgartner and Morris (2006).
28. Baum (2002, 2003).
29. Plotz (2000).
30. For examples, see *Wall Street Journal Asia*, http://blogs.wsj.com/korearealtime /2012/12/20/the-other-election-winner-sbs-animations/.
31. http://presentinenglish.com/page/4.
32. http://asiafoundation.org/in-asia/2013/03/13/sbs-shakes-up-voter-malaise-in-korea/.
33. McGerr (1986).

REFERENCES

Abramowitz, Alan I. 2010. *The Disappearing Center*. New Haven, CT: Yale University Press.

Aiello, John R. 1987. "Human Spatial Behavior." In *Handbook of Environmental Psychology*, vol. 1, ed. Irwin Altman and Daniel Stokols, 389–504. New York: John Wiley.

Allegheny College. 2010. "Nastiness, Name-Calling and Negativity: The Allegheny College Survey of Civility and Compromise in American Politics." April 20.

Altschuler, Glenn C., and Stuart M. Blumin. 2000. *Rude Republic: Americans and Their Politics in the Nineteenth Century*. Princeton, NJ: Princeton University Press.

Amit, Elinor, Daniel Algom, and Yaacov Trope. 2009. "Distance-Dependent Processing of Pictures and Words." *Journal of Experimental Psychology: General* 138 (3): 400–415.

Amit, Elinor, Cheryl Wakslak, and Yaacov Trope. 2012. "The Use of Visual and Verbal Means of Communication across Psychological Distance." *Personality and Social Psychology Bulletin* 39:43–56.

Amodio, D. M., J. T. Jost, S. L. Master, and C. M. Yee. 2007. "Neurocognitive Correlates of Liberalism and Conservatism." *Nature Neuroscience* 10 (10): 1246–47.

Anderson, Ashley A., Dominique Brossard, Dietram A. Scheufele, Michael A. Xenos, and Peter Ladwig. 2013. "The 'Nasty Effect': Online Incivility and Risk Perceptions of Emerging Technologies." *Journal of Computer-Mediated Communication* 19:373–87.

Anderson, C. A., N. L. Carnagey, M. Flanagan, A. J. Benjamin, J. Eubanks, and J. C. Valentine. 2004. "Violent Video Games: Specific Effects of Violent Content on Aggressive Thoughts and Behavior." *Advances in Experimental Social Psychology* 36:199–249.

Anderson, Christopher J., Andre Blais, Shaun Bowler, Todd Donovan, and Ola Listhaug. 2005. *Losers' Consent: Elections and Democratic Legitimacy*. New York: Oxford University Press.

Appiah, Osei. 2006. "Rich Media, Poor Media: The Impact of Audio/Video vs. Text/Picture Testimonial Ads on Browsers' Evaluations of Commercial Web Sites and Online Products." *Journal of Current Issues and Research in Advertising* 28 (1): 73–86.

Arceneaux, Kevin, and Martin Johnson. 2007. "Channel Surfing: Does Choice Reduce Videomalaise?" Paper presented at the meeting of the Midwest Political Science Association, Chicago.

Arendt, Hannah. 1968. *Between Past and Future: Eight Exercises in Political Thought*. New York: Viking.

Barber, Benjamin. 1983. *The Logic and Limits of Trust*. New Brunswick, NJ: Rutgers University Press.

Barker, David C. 2002. *Rushed to Judgment: Talk Radio, Persuasion, and American Political Behavior*. New York: Columbia University Press.

Barry, Dave. 2004. "An Off-Color Rift." *Washington Post Magazine*, December 19, W32.

Baum, Matthew A. 2002. "Sex, Lies and War: How Soft News Brings Foreign Policy to the Inattentive Public." *American Political Science Review* 96 (March): 91–109.

———. 2003. *Soft News Goes to War: Public Opinion and American Foreign Policy in the New Media Age*. Princeton, NJ: Princeton University Press.

Baum, Matthew A., and Samuel Kernell. 1999. "Has Cable Ended the Golden Age of Presidential Television?" *American Political Science Review* 93 (1): 99–114.

Baumgartner, Jody, and Jonathan S. Morris. 2006. "The Daily Show Effect: Candidate Evaluations, Efficacy, and American Youth." *American Politics Research* 34 (3): 341–67.

Benhabib, Seyla. 1992. *Situating the Self.* New York: Routledge.

Ben-Porath, Eran N. 2008. "Codes of Professionalism; Norms of Conversation: How Political Interviews Shape Public Attitudes toward Journalists." Doctoral dissertation, University of Pennsylvania. Available from ProQuest. Paper AAI3309396.

——. 2010. "Interview Effects: Theory and Evidence for the Impact of Televised Political Interviews on Viewer Attitudes." *Communication Theory* 20 (3): 323–47.

Berger, Ben. 2011. *Attention Deficit Democracy: The Paradox of Civic Engagement.* Princeton, NJ: Princeton University Press.

Berger, Jonah. 2011. "Arousal Increases Social Transmission of Information." *Psychological Science* 22 (7): 891–93.

Berger, Jonah, and Katherine L. Milkman. 2012. "What Makes Online Content Viral?" *Journal of Marketing Research* 49 (2): 192–205.

Bianco, William T. 1994. *Trust: Representatives and Constituents.* Ann Arbor: University of Michigan Press.

Blom, R., S. Carpenter, B. J. Bowe, and R. Lange. 2014. "Frequent Contributors within U.S. Newspaper Comment Forums: An Examination of Their Civility and Information Value." *American Behavioral Scientist.* Published online March 28, 2014. Retrieved from http://abs.sagepub.com/content/early/2014/03/28/0002764214527094.

Blonsky, Marshal. 1988. "Ted Koppel's Edge." *New York Times Magazine,* August 14.

Borah, Porismita. 2013. "Interactions of News Frames and Incivility in the Political Blogosphere: Examining Perceptual Outcomes." *Political Communication* 30 (3): 456–73.

Bowler, Shaun, and Todd Donovan. 2003. "The Effects of Winning and Losing on Attitudes about Political Institutions and Democracy in the United States." Paper presented at the Midwest Political Science Association meeting, Chicago.

Bracken, C. C., and R. Botta. 2010. "Telepresence and Television." In *Immersed in Media: Telepresence and Everyday Life,* ed. C. C. Bracken and P. D. Skalski, 39–62. New York: Routledge.

Bracken, C. C., G. Pettey, T. Guha, and B. E. Rubenking. 2010. "Sounding Out Small Screens and Telepresence: The Impact of Audio, Screen Size, and Pace." *Journal of Media Psychology: Theories, Methods, and Applications* 22 (3):, 125–37.

Brader, Ted, and George E. Marcus. 2013. "Emotion and Political Psychology." In *The Oxford Handbook of Political Psychology,* 2nd ed., ed. Leonie Huddy, Jack S. Levy, and David O. Sears, 165–204. New York: Oxford University Press.

Bradley, Margaret M., Mark K. Greenwald, Margaret C. Petry, and Peter J. Lang. 1992. "Remembering Pictures: Pleasure and Arousal in Memory." *Journal of Experimental Psychology: Learning, Memory and Cognition* 18 (2): 379–90.

Bradley, Margaret M., and Peter J. Lang. 1994. "Measuring Emotion: The Self-Assessment Manikin and the Semantic Differential." *Journal of Behavioral Therapy and Experimental Psychiatry* 25 (1): 49–59.

Brooks, Deborah J., and John G. Geer. 2007. "Beyond Negativity: The Effects of Incivility on the Electorate." *American Journal of Political Science* 51 (1): 1–16.

Brown, Penelope, and Stephen C. Levinson. 1987. *Politeness: Some Universals in Language Usage.* New York: Cambridge University Press.

Calhoun, Craig. 1988. "Populist Politics, Communications Media and Large Scale Societal Integration." *Sociological Theory* 6:219–41.

Cappella, Joseph N., and Kathleen Hall Jamieson. 1997. *Spiral of Cynicism.* New York: Oxford University Press.

Carnagey, Nicholas L., Craig A. Anderson, and Brad J. Bushman. 2007. "The Effect of Video Game Violence on Physiological Desensitization to Real-Life Violence." *Journal of Experimental Social Psychology* 43:489–96.

Carter, Stephen L. 1999. *Civility: Manners, Morals, and the Etiquette of Democracy.* New York: Harper Perennial.

Chanley, Virginia A., Thomas J. Rudolph, and Wendy M. Rahn. 2000. "The Origins and Consequences of Public Trust in Government: A Time Series Analysis." *Public Opinion Quarterly* 64 (3): 239–56.

Chen, Zoey, and Jonah Berger. 2013. "When, Why and How Controversy Causes Conversation." *Journal of Consumer Research* 40 (3): 580–93.

Christianson, Sven-Åke. 1986. "Effects of Positive Emotional Events on Memory." *Scandinavian Journal of Psychology* 27:287–99.

Christianson, Sven-Åke, Lars-Göran Nilsson, Tom Mjörndal, Carlo Perris, and Gunnar Tjellden. 1986. "Psychological versus Physiological Determinants of Emotional Arousal and Its Relationship to Laboratory-Induced Amnesia." *Scandinavian Journal of Psychology* 27:300–310.

Citrin, Jack. 1974. "Comment: The Political Relevance of Trust in Government." *American Political Science Review* 68:973–88.

Citrin, Jack, and Christopher Muste. 1999. "Trust in Government." In *Measures of Political Attitudes*, ed. John P. Robinson, Phillip R. Shaver, and Lawrence S. Wrightsman, 465–532. New York: Academic Press.

Clark, Daniel L., and G. W. Uetz. 1990. "Video Image Recognition by the Jumping Spider, Maevia inclemens (Araneae: Salticidae)." *Animal Behavior* 40:884–90.

Clark, H. H. 1973. "Space, Time, Semantics, and the Child." In *Cognitive Development and the Acquisition of Language*, ed. T. E. Moore, 27–63. New York: Academic Press.

Cooke, L. 2005. "A Visual Convergence of Print, Television, and the Internet: Charting 40 Years of Design Change in News Presentation." *New Media & Society* 7 (1): 22–46.

Dahl, Robert A. 1971. *Polyarchy.* New Haven, CT: Yale University Press.

DeMott, Benjamin. 1996. "Seduced by Civility: Political Manners and the Crisis of Democratic Values." *Nation* 263 (19): 11–19.

Detenber, Benjamin H., and Byron Reeves. 1996. "A Bio-Informational Theory of Emotion: Motion and Image Size Effects on Viewers." *Journal of Communication* 46 (3): 66–84.

Dilliplane, Susanna. 2011. "All the News You Want to Hear: The Impact of Partisan News Exposure on Political Participation." *Public Opinion Quarterly* 75 (2): 287—316.

Dilliplane, Susanna, Seth K. Goldman, and Diana C. Mutz. 2013. "Televised Exposure to Politics: New Measures for a Fragmented Media Environment." *American Journal of Political Science* 57 (1): 236–48.

Druckman, James. 2003. "The Power of Television Images: The First Kennedy-Nixon Debate Revisited." *Journal of Politics* 65:559–71.

Durr, Robert H., John B. Gilmour, and Christina Wolbrecht. 1997. "Explaining Congressional Approval." *American Journal of Political Science* 41:175–207.

Eckel, Catherine C., and Philip J. Grossman. 2008. "Men, Women and Risk Aversion: Experimental Evidence." In *Handbook of Experimental Economics Results*, vol. 1, ed. Charles R. Plott and Vernon L. Smith, 1061–73. Amsterdam: Elsevier.

Eckler, P., and P. Bolls. 2011. "Spreading the Virus: Emotional Tone of Viral Advertising and Its Effect on Forwarding Intentions and Attitudes." *Journal of Interactive Advertising* 11 (2): 1–11.

Edgerly, S., E. K. Vraga, K. E. Dalrymple, T. Macafee, and T. K. F. Fung. 2013. "Directing the Dialogue: The Relationship between YouTube Videos and the Comments They Spur." *Journal of Information Technology & Politics* 10 (3): 276–92.

Eisenstein, S. M. [1940] 1974. "En Gros Plan." In *Au-delà des étoiles*, ed. Jacques Aumont, 111–13. Paris: Union Générale d'Éditions.

Elving, Ronald D. 1994. "Brighter Lights, Wider Windows: Presenting Congress in the 1990s." In *Congress, the Press, and the Public*, ed. Thomas E. Mann and Norman J. Ornstein, 171–204. Washington, DC: American Enterprise Institute and Brookings Institution.

Eysenck, Michael W. 1976. "Arousal, Learning, and Memory." *Psychological Bulletin* 83 (3): 389–404.

Fearon, James. 1998. "Deliberation as Discussion." In *Deliberative Democracy*, ed. Jon Elster, 44–68. New York: Cambridge University Press.

Fenno, Richard F. 1975. "If, as Ralph Nader Says, Congress Is 'The Broken Branch,' How Come We Love Our Congressmen So Much?" In *Congress in Change: Evolution and Reform*, ed. Norman J. Ornstein, 277–87. New York: Praeger.

Fiorina, Morris P. 1999. "Whatever Happened to the Median Voter?" Paper presented at the MIT Conference on Parties and Congress, Cambridge, MA.

Fiorina, Morris P., with Samuel J. Abrams. 2009. *Disconnect: The Breakdown of Representation in American Politics*. Vol. 11 of the Julian J. Rothbaum Distinguished Lecture Series. Norman: University of Oklahoma Press.

Flavell, J. H., E. R. Flavell, F. L. Green, and J. E. Korfmacher. 1990. "Do Young Children Think of Television Images as Pictures or Real Objects?" *Journal of Broadcasting & Electronic Media* 34:399–419.

Fleisher, Richard, and Jon R. Bond. 2004. "The Shrinking Middle in the U.S. Congress." *British Journal of Political Science* 34:429–51.

Fogg, B. J., and Clifford Nass. 1997. "Silicon Sycophants: The Effects of Computers That Flatter." *International Journal of Human-Computer Studies* 46 (5): 551–61.

Forgette, Richard, and Jonathan S. Morris. 2006. "High-Conflict Television and Public Opinion." *Political Research Quarterly* 59 (3): 447–56.

Fox, Julia R., Glory Koloen, and Volkan Sahin. 2007. "No Joke: A Comparison of Substance in The Daily Show with Jon Stewart and Broadcast Network Television Coverage of the 2004 Presidential Election Campaign." *Journal of Broadcasting & Electronic Media* 51 (2): 213–27.

Frijda, Nico H. 1988. "The Laws of Emotion." *American Psychologist* 43 (5): 349–58.

Funk, Carolyn L. 2001. "Process Performance: Public Reaction to Legislative Policy Debate." In *What Is It about Government That Americans Dislike?*, ed. John R. Hibbing and Elizabeth Theiss-Morse, 193–204. New York: Cambridge University Press.

Geen, Russell G. 1975. "The Meaning of Observed Violence: Real vs. Fictional Violence and Consequent Effects on Aggression and Emotional Arousal." *Journal of Research in Personality* 9 (4): 270–81.

Gilbert, Daniel T. 1991. "How Mental Systems Believe." *American Psychologist* 46 (2): 107–19.

Gilligan, Stephen G., and Gordon H. Bower. 1984. "Cognitive Consequences of Emotional Arousal." In *Emotion, Cognition and Behavior*, ed. Carroll E. Izard, Jerome Kagan, and Robert B. Zajonc, 547–88. New York: Cambridge University Press.

Gitlin, Todd. 2013. "The Uncivil and the Incendiary." In *Can We Talk? The Rise of Rude, Nasty, Stubborn Politics*, ed. Daniel M. Shea and Morris P. Fiorina, 53–66. New York: Pearson.

Goffman, Erving. 1959. *The Presentation of Self in Everyday Life*. New York: Doubleday.

Goldstein, Susan. 1999. "Construction and Validation of a Conflict Communication Scale." *Journal of Applied Social Psychology* 29 (9): 1803–32.

Goode, L., A. McCullough, and G. O'Hare. 2011. "Unruly Publics and the Fourth Estate on YouTube." *Participations: Journal of Audience and Reception Studies* 8 (2): 594–615.

Gould, Jack. 1952. "The X of the Campaign: TV 'Personality.'" *New York Times Magazine*, June 22. Reprinted in *The Mass Media and Politics*, ed. James F. Fixx, 20–22. New York: Arno Press, 1972.

Grice, H. Paul. 1975. "Logic and conversation." In *Speech Acts*, ed. P. Cole and J. L. Morgan, 41–58. New York: Academic Press.

———. 1989. *Studies in the Way of Words*. Cambridge, MA: Harvard University Press.

Grobart, Sam. 2012. "Is This Living Room Big Enough for My TV?" *New York Times*, February 8.

Guadagno, R. E., D. M. Rempala, S. Murphy, and B. M. Okdie. 2013. "What Makes a Video Go Viral? An Analysis of Emotional Contagion and Internet Memes." *Computers in Human Behavior* 29 (6): 2312–19.

Hall, Edward T. 1963. "A System for the Notation of Proxemic Behaviour." *American Anthropologist* 65 (5): 1003–26.

Hart, Roderick P. 1994. *Seducing America: How Television Charms the Modern Voter*. New York: Oxford University Press.

Hatemi, Peter K., et al. 2011. "A Genome-Wide Analysis of Liberal and Conservative Political Attitudes." *Journal of Politics* 73:271–85.

Heilman, K. M. 1997. "The Neurobiology of Emotional Experience." *Journal of Neuropsychiatry* 9:439–48.

Henderson, Marlone D., Kentaro Fujita, Yaacov Trope, and Nira Liberman. 2006. "Transcending the 'Here': The Effect of Spatial Distance on Social Judgment." *Journal of Personality and Social Psychology* 91:845–56.

Herbst, Susan. 2010. *Rude Democracy: Civility and Incivility in American Politics*. Philadelphia: Temple University Press.

Hetherington, Marc J. 1998. "The Political Relevance of Political Trust." *American Political Science Review* 92 (4): 791–808.

———. 1999. "The Effect of Political Trust on the Presidential Vote, 1968–96." *American Political Science Review* 93 (2): 311–26.

———. 2001. "Resurgent Mass Partisanship: The Role of Elite Polarization." *American Political Science Review* 95:619–31.

———. 2005. *Why Trust Matters*. Princeton, NJ: Princeton University Press.

Hibbing, John R., Kevin B. Smith, and John A. Alford. 2014. *Predisposed: Liberals, Conservatives and the Biology of Political Differences*. New York: Routledge.

Hibbing, John R., and Elizabeth Theiss-Morse. 1995. *Congress as Public Enemy*. Cambridge: Cambridge University Press.

———. 2002. *Stealth Democracy*. New York: Cambridge University Press.

Hofstetter, C. Richard. 1976. *Bias in the News*. Columbus: Ohio State University Press.

Hofstetter, C. Richard, David Barker, James T. Smith, Gina M. Zari, and Thomas A. Ingrassia. 1999. "Information, Misinformation and Political Talk Radio." *Political Research Quarterly* 52 (2): 353–69.

Hopkins, Robert, and James E. Fletcher. 1994. "Electrodermal Measurement: Particularly Effective for Forecasting Message Influence on Sales Appeal. In *Measuring Psychological Responses to Media Messages*, ed. Annie Lang, 113–32. Hillsdale, NJ: Lawrence Erlbaum.

Ivory, J. D., and R. G. Magee. 2009. "You Can't Take It with You? Effects of Handheld Portable Media Consoles on Physiological and Psychological Responses to Video Game and Movie Content." *CyberPsychology & Behavior* 12 (3): 291–97.

Iyengar, Shanto, Gaurav Sood, and Yphtach Lelkes. 2012. "Affect, Not Ideology: A Social Identity Perspective on Polarization." *Public Opinion Quarterly* 76 (3): 405–31.

Jacobson, Gary. 2000. "The Electoral Basis of Partisan Polarization in Congress." Paper presented at the annual meeting of the American Political Science Association, Washington, DC.

———. 2007. *A Divider, Not a Uniter: George W. Bush and the American People*. New York: Pearson Longman.

Johnson, Jeffrey G., Patricia Cohen, Stephanie Kasen, Michael B. First, and Judith S. Brook. 2004. "Association between Television Viewing and Sleep Problems during Adolescence and Early Adulthood." *Archives of Pediatric and Adolescent Medicine* 158 (6): 562–68.

Jost, J. T., and D. M. Amodio. 2012. "Political Ideology as Motivated Social Cognition: Behavioral and Neuroscientific Evidence." *Motivation and Emotion* 36:55–64.

Keeter, Scott. 1987. "The Illusion of Intimacy: Television and the Role of Candidate Personal Qualities in Voter Choice." *Public Opinion Quarterly* 51:344–58.

Kennedy, Randall. 1998. "The Case Against Civility." *American Prospect* 9 (November): 84.

Keynes, John Maynard. 1933. "National Self-sufficiency." *New Statesman and Nation*, July 15, 5.

Kingwell, M. 1995. *A Civil Tongue: Justice, Dialogue and the Politics of Pluralism*. University Park: Pennsylvania State University Press.

Koocher, Gerald P. 1977. "Bathroom Behavior and Human Dignity." *Journal of Personality and Social Psychology* 35 (2): 120–21.

Kraft, R. N. 1987. "The Influence of Camera Angle on Comprehension and Retention of Pictorial Events." *Memory and Cognition* 15:291–307.

Lakoff, Robin T. 1973. "The Logic of Politeness; or, Minding Your p's and q's." Paper presented at the ninth regional meeting of the Chicago Linguistic Society, Chicago.

Lang, Annie. 1990. "Involuntary Attention and Physiological Arousal Evoked by Structural Features and Emotional Content in TV Commercials." *Communication Research* 77 (3): 275–99.

———. 2000. "The Limited Capacity Model of Mediated Message Processing." *Journal of Communication* 50 (1): 46–70.

Lang, Annie, Kuljinder Dhillon, and Qingwen Dong. 1995. "The Effects of Emotional Arousal and Valence on Television Viewers' Cognitive Capacity and Memory." *Journal of Broadcasting & Electronic Media* 39 (3): 313–27.

Lang, P. J., M. K. Greenwald, M. M. Bradley, and A. O. Hamm. 1993. "Looking at Pictures: Affective, Facial, Visceral, and Behavioral Reactions." *Psychophysiology* 30 (3): 261–73.

Leech, G. 1983. *Principles of Pragmatics*. New York: Longman.

Lenz, Gabriel S., and Chappell Lawson. 2011. "Looking the Part: Television Leads Less Informed Citizens to Vote Based on Candidates' Appearance." *American Journal of Political Science* 55 (3): 574–89.

Leslie, Jack. *Civility in America 2011*. New York: Weber Shandwick.

Levendusky, Matthew. 2009. *The Partisan Sort: How Liberals Became Democrats and Conservatives Became Republicans*. Chicago: University of Chicago Press.

———. 2013. "Partisan Media Exposure and Attitudes toward the Opposition." *Political Communication* 30 (4): 565–81.

Lippmann, Walter. 1925. *The Phantom Public*. New York: Harcourt, Brace.

Lodge, Milton, Kathleen M. McGraw, and Patrick Stroh. 1989. "An Impression-Driven Model of Candidate Evaluation." *American Political Science Review* 83 (2): 399–419.

Loftus, Elizabeth F., and Terrence E. Burns. 1982. "Mental Shock Can Produce Retrograde Amnesia." *Memory and Cognition* 10 (4): 318–23.

Lombard, Matthew. 1995. "Direct Responses to People on the Screen: Television and Personal Space." *Communication Research* 22 (3): 288–324.

Lombard, Matthew, and Theresa Ditton. 1997. "At the Heart of It All: The Concept of Presence." *Journal of Computer-Mediated Communication* 3 (2). Retrieved from http://onlinelibrary.wiley.com/doi/10.1111/j.1083–6101.1997.tb00072.x/full.

Lombard, Matthew, Robert D. Reich, Maria E. Grabe, Cheryl C. Bracken, and Theresa B. Ditton. 2000. "Presence and Television: The Role of Screen Size." *Human Communication Research* 26 (1): 75–98.

Lombard, Matthew, Robert D. Reich, Maria E. Grabe, Cheryl M. Campanella, and Theresa B. Ditton. 1995. "Big TVs, Little TVs: The Role of Screen Size in Viewer Responses to Point of View Movement." Paper presented at the meeting of the Mass Communication Division of the International Communication Association, Albuquerque.

Mandler, J. M. 1992. "How to Build a Baby: II. Conceptual Primitives." *Psychological Review* 99:587–604.

Manin, Bernard. 1987. "On Legitimacy and Political Deliberation." *Political Theory* 15 (3): 338–68.

Marcus, George E. 2000. "Emotions in Politics." *Annual Review of Political Science* 3:221–50.

Matheson, Donald. 2000. "The Birth of News Discourse: Changes in News Language in British Newspapers, 1880–1930." *Media, Culture & Society* 22 (5): 557–73.

Maynor, John. 2009. "Why Be Civil?" Paper presented at the meeting of the Midwest Political Science Association, Chicago.

Mazziotta, A., A. Mummendey, and S. C. Wright. 2011. "Vicarious Contact Can Improve Intergroup Attitudes and Prepare for Direct Contact." *Group Processes and Intergroup Relations* 14:255–74.

McGerr, Michael E. 1986. *The Decline of Popular Politics: The American North, 1865–1928*. New York: Oxford University Press.

McGraw, Kathleen, Elaine Willey, and William Anderson. 1999. "It's the Process Stupid!? Procedural Considerations in Evaluations of Congress." Paper presented at the annual meeting of the Midwest Political Science Association, Chicago.

McHugo, Gregory J., John T. Lanzetta, Denis G. Sullivan, Roger D. Masters, and Basil G. Englis. 1985. "Emotional Reactions to a Political Leader's Expressive Displays." *Journal of Personality and Social Psychology* 49 (6): 1512–23.

Meadow, Robert G. 1973. "Cross Media Comparisons of Coverage of the 1972 Presidential Campaign." *Journalism Quarterly* 50:482–88.

Messaris, Paul. 1994. *Visual Literacy: Image, Mind and Reality*. Boulder, CO: Westview.

Meyrowitz, Joshua. 1986. *No Sense of Place: The Impact of Electronic Media on Social Behavior*. New York: Oxford University Press.

Middlemist, R. Dennis, Eric S. Knowles, and Charles F. Matter. 1976. "Personal Space Invasions in the Lavatory: Suggestive Evidence for Arousal." *Journal of Personality and Social Psychology* 33:541–46.

Miller, Arthur H. 1974a. "Political Issues and Trust in Government, 1964–70." *American Political Science Review* 68:951–72.

———. 1974b. "Rejoinder to Comment by Jack Citrin: Political Discontent or Ritualism?" *American Political Science Review* 68:989–1001.

Miller, Arthur H., Edie N. Goldenberg, and Lutz Erbring. 1979. "Typeset Politics: Impact of Newspapers on Public Confidence." *American Political Science Review* 73:67–84.

Miller, Roy E., and John S. Jackson III. 1973. "Mass Media, Candidate Image, and Voting Behavior in the 1972 Presidential Election." Paper presented at the annual meeting of the American Political Science Association, New Orleans, LA.

Mills, S. 2003. *Gender and Politeness*. Cambridge: Cambridge University Press.

Mobbs, D., P. Petrovic, J. L. Marchant, D. Hassabis, N. Weiskopf, B. Seymour, et al. 2007. "When Fear Is Near: Threat Imminence Elicits Prefrontal-Periaqueductal Gray Shifts in Humans." *Science* 317:1079–83.

Mottahedeh, Negar. 2008. *Displaced Allegories: Post-revolutionary Iranian Cinema*. Durham, NC: Duke University Press.

Mutz, Diana C. 2006. *Hearing the Other Side: Deliberative versus Participatory Democracy*. New York: Cambridge University Press.

———. 2007. "Effects of 'In-Your-Face' Television Discourse on Perceptions of a Legitimate Opposition." *American Political Science Review* 101 (4): 621–35.

Mutz, Diana C., and Eran N. Ben-Porath. 2006. "Men Behaving Badly: Gender Differences in Reactions to Uncivil Political Discourse." Paper presented at the annual meeting of the American Political Science Association, Philadelphia.

Mutz, Diana C., and Gregory Flemming. 1999. "How Good People Make Bad Collectives: A Social-Psychological Perspective on Public Attitudes toward Congress." In *Congress and the Decline of Public Trust*, ed. Joseph Cooper, 79–100. Boulder, CO: Westview.

Mutz, Diana C., and Paul Martin. 2001. "Facilitating Communication across Lines of Political Difference: The Role of Mass Media." *American Political Science Review* 95 (March): 97–114.

Mutz, Diana C., and Byron Reeves. 2005. "The New Videomalaise: Effects of Televised Incivility on Political Trust." *American Political Science Review* 99 (1): 1–15.

Mutz, Diana C., and Lori Young. 2011. "Communication and Public Opinion: Plus Ça Change?" *Public Opinion Quarterly* 75 (5): 1018–44.

Nass, Clifford, Youngme Moon, and Nancy Green. 1997. "Are Machines Gender Neutral? Gender-Stereotypic Responses to Computers with Voices." *Journal of Applied Social Psychology* 27 (10): 864–76.

Nivola, Pietro S., and David W. Brady, eds. 2006. *Red and Blue Nation? Characteristics and Causes of America's Polarized Politics.* Vol. 1. Washington, DC: Brookings Institution.

Nyhan, Brendan. 2010. "Why the 'Death Panel' Myth Wouldn't Die: Misinformation in the Health Care Reform Debate." *Forum* 8 (1). http://www.dartmouth.edu/~nyhan/health-care-misinformation.pdf.

O'Reilly, Bill. 2001. *The No-Spin Zone: Confrontations with the Powerful and Famous in America.* New York: Broadway.

Oxley, Douglas R., Kevin B. Smith, John R. Alford, Matthew V. Hibbing, Jennifer L. Miller, Mario Scalora, Peter K. Hatemi, and John R. Hibbing. 2008. "Political Attitudes Vary with Physiological Traits." *Science* 321:1667.

Page, Benjamin I. 1996. *Who Deliberates? Mass Media in Modern Democracy.* Chicago: University of Chicago Press.

Papacharissi, Zizi. 2004. "Democracy On-line: Civility, Politeness, and the Democratic Potential of On-line Political Discussion Groups." *New Media & Society* 6 (2): 259–84.

Patterson, Thomas E. 1980. *The Mass Media Election: How Americans Choose Their President.* New York: Praeger.

———. 1993. *Out of Order.* New York: Knopf.

Patterson, Thomas E., and Robert D. McClure. 1976. *The Unseeing Eye: The Myth of Television Power in National Politics.* New York: Putnam.

Persson, Per. 1998. "Towards a Psychological Theory of Close-ups: Experiencing Intimacy and Threat." *KINEMA: A Journal for Film and Audiovisual Media* 9 (Spring): 24–42.

Pew Research Center's Project for Excellence in Journalism. 2010. "The State of the News Media 2010: An Annual Report on American Journalism." Retrieved from http://www.stateofthemedia.org/2010

Plotz, David. 2000. "Dead Air." *New York Times Magazine*, August 13.

Prior, Markus. 2007. *Post-Broadcast Democracy: How Media Choice Increases Inequality in Political Involvement and Polarizes Elections.* New York: Cambridge University Press.

Ranney, Austin. 1983. *Channels of Power: The Impact of Television on American Politics.* New York: Basic Books.

Reeves, Byron, Benjamin Detenber, and J. S. Steuer. 1993. "New Televisions: The Effects of Big Pictures and Big Sound on Viewer Responses to the Screen." Paper presented at the meeting of the International Communication Association, Washington, DC.

Reeves, Byron, Matthew Lombard, and Geetu Melwani. 1992. "Faces on the Screen: Pictures or Natural Experience." Paper presented at the meeting of the International Communication Association, Miami.

Reeves, Byron, and Clifford Ivar Nass. 1996. *The Media Equation: How People Treat Computers, Television and New Media Like Real People and Places.* New York: Cambridge.

Reeves, Byron, Esther Thorson, Michael L. Rothschild, Daniel McDonald, Judith Hirsch, and Robert Goldstein. 1985. "Attention to Television: Intrastimulus Effects of Movement and Scene Changes on Alpha Variation over Time." *International Journal of Neuroscience* 27:241–55.

Robinson, Michael J. 1975. "American Political Legitimacy in an Era of Electronic Journalism: Reflections on the Nightly News." In *Television as a Social Force*, ed. Richard Adler, 97–140. New York: Praeger.

Robinson, Michael J., and Kevin R. Appel. 1979. "Network News Coverage of Congress." *Political Science Quarterly* 94 (3): 407–18.

Rodin, Judith. 1996. "An Urgent Task." Keynote address to the Penn National Commission on Society, Culture and Community. Retrieved from http://www.upenn.edu/pnc/pubkeynote.html

Rudolph, Thomas J., and Jillian Evans. 2005. "Political Trust, Ideology, and Public Support for Government Spending." *American Journal of Political Science* 49 (3): 660–71.

Sandel, Michael. 2005. *Public Philosophy: Essays on Morality in Politics*. Cambridge, MA: Harvard University Press.

Santana, A. D. 2013. "Virtuous or Vitriolic." *Journalism Practice* 8 (1): 18–33.

Sapiro, Virginia. 1999. "Considering Political Civility Historically: A Case Study of the United States." Paper presented at the meeting of the International Society for Political Psychology, Amsterdam.

Sato, Wataru, and Sakiko Yoshikawa. 2007. "Enhanced Experience of Emotional Arousal in Response to Dynamic Facial Expressions." *Journal of Nonverbal Behavior* 31 (2): 119–35.

Schiffenbauer, Allen, and R. Steven K. Schiavo. 1976. "Physical Distance and Attraction: An Intensification Effect." *Journal of Experimental Social Psychology* 12:274–82.

Scholz, John T., and Mark Lubbell. 1998. "Trust and Taxpaying: Testing the Heuristic Approach to Collective Action." *American Journal of Political Science* 42:398–417.

Schudson, Michael. 1992. "Was There Ever a Public Sphere? If So, When? Reflections on the American Case." In *Habermas and the Public Sphere*, ed. C. Calhoun, 143–63. Cambridge, MA: MIT Press.

———. 1995. *The Power of News*. Cambridge, MA: Harvard University Press.

———. 1998. *The Good Citizen: A History of American Civic Life*. New York: Free Press.

Sennett, Richard. 1977. *The Fall of Public Man*. New York: Knopf.

Shea, Daniel M., and Morris P. Fiorina, eds. 2013. *Can We Talk? The Rise of Rude, Nasty, Stubborn Politics*. New York: Pearson.

Sigelman, Lee, and David Bullock. 1991. "Candidates, Issue, Horse Races and Hoopla: Presidential Campaign Coverage, 1888–1988." *American Politics Quarterly* 19:5–32.

Smith, Robert J., and Eric S. Knowles. 1979. "Affective and Cognitive Mediators of Reactions to Spatial Invasions." *Journal of Experimental Social Psychology* 15:437–52.

Sobieraj, Sarah, and Jeffrey M. Berry. 2011. "From Incivility to Outrage: Political Discourse in Blogs, Talk Radio, and Cable News." *Political Communication* 28 (1): 19–41.

———. 2014. *The Outrage Industry: Political Opinion Media and the New Incivility*. New York: Oxford University Press.

Stelter, Brian. 2009. "CNBC Proudly Replays Its Reporter's Tirade." *Business/Media and Advertising*, February 23.

Stephan, Elena, Nira Liberman, and Yaacov Trope. 2010. "Politeness and Psychological Distance: A Construal Level Perspective." *Journal of Personality and Social Psychology* 98 (2): 268–80.

Steuer, Jonathan. 1992. "Defining Virtual Reality: Dimensions Determining Telepresence." *Journal of Communication* 42 (4): 73–93.

Stewart, Jon. 2004. "Appearance on CNN Crossfire with Paul Begala and Tucker Carlson." October 15. Retrieved from http://transcripts.cnn.com/TRANSCRIPTS/0410/15/cf.01.html

Storms, Michael D., and George C. Thomas. 1977. "Reactions to Physical Closeness." *Journal of Personality and Social Psychology* 35:412–28.

Strachan, J. Cherie, and Michael R. Wolf. 2013. "Calls for Civility: An Invitation to Deliberate or a Means of Political Control?" In *Can We Talk? The Rise of Rude, Nasty, Stubborn Politics*, ed. Daniel M. Shea and Morris P. Fiorina, 41–52. New York: Pearson.

Straus, Scott. 2007. "What Is the Relationship between Hate Radio and Violence? Rethinking Rwanda's 'Radio Machete.'" *Politics and Society* 35 (4): 609–37.

Sullivan, Denis G., and Roger D. Masters. 1987. "'Gut Reactions' and the Political Effects of the Media." *PS: Political Science & Politics* 20 (4): 880–89.

Tannen, Deborah. 1998. *The Argument Culture: Stopping America's War of Words*. New York: Random House.

Thorson, Kjerstin, Emily Vraga, and Brian Ekdale. 2010. "Credibility in Context: How Uncivil Online Commentary Affects News Credibility." *Mass Communication and Society* 13 (3): 289–313.

Trope, Y., and N. Liberman. 2010. "Construal Level Theory of Psychological Distance." *Psychological Review* 117:440–63.

Tyler, Tom R. 1990. *Why People Obey the Law*. New Haven, CT: Yale University Press.

Tyler, Tom R., and Peter Degoey. 1995. "Collective Restraint in Social Dilemmas: Procedural Justice and Social Identification Effects on Support for Authorities." *Journal of Personality and Social Psychology* 69:482–97.

Uslaner, Eric M. 1993. *The Decline of Comity in Congress*. Ann Arbor: University of Michigan Press.

Van, Jon. 1991. "Their Favorite Video? 'Charlotte's Web.' Spider Watchers Find Their Subjects Are No Couch Potatoes When It Comes to TV." *Chicago Tribune*, February 13.

Williams, Lawrence E., and John A. Bargh. 2008. "Keeping One's Distance: The Influence of Spatial Distance Cues on Affect and Evaluation." *Psychological Science* 19 (3): 302–8.

Wilson, James Q. 2006. "How Divided Are We?" *Commentary* (February): 15–21.

Wright, Stephen C., A. Aron, T. McLaughlin, and S. A. Ropp. 1997. "The Extended Contact Effect: Knowledge of Cross-Group Friendships and Prejudice." *Journal of Personality and Social Psychology* 73:73–90.

Xenos, M. A., and A. B. Becker. 2009. "Moments of Zen: Effects of The Daily Show on Information Seeking and Political Learning." *Political Communication* 26 (3): 317–32.

Young, D. G. 2004. "Late-Night Comedy in Election 2000: Its Influence on Candidate Trait Ratings and the Moderating Effects of Political Knowledge and Partisanship." *Journal of Broadcasting & Electronic Media* 48:1–22.

INDEX

Page numbers in *italics* refer to figures and tables